Guardians of the Buddha's Home

Contemporary Buddhism
MARK M. ROWE, SERIES EDITOR

Guardians of the Buddha's Home

*Domestic Religion in
the Contemporary Jōdo Shinshū*

Jessica Starling

UNIVERSITY OF HAWAI'I PRESS
HONOLULU

© 2019 University of Hawai'i Press
All rights reserved
Paperback edition 2020

Printed in the United States of America

25 24 23 22 21 20   6 5 4 3 2 1

Library of Congress Cataloging-in-Publication Data

Names: Starling, Jessica, author.
Title: Guardians of the Buddha's home : domestic religion in the contemporary
    Jeodo Shinshu / Jessica Starling.
Other titles: Contemporary Buddhism.
Description: Honolulu : University of Hawai'i Press, [2019] | Series:
    Contemporary Buddhism | Includes bilbliographical references and index.
Identifiers: LCCN 2018027848 | ISBN 9780824866921 (cloth alk. paper)
Subjects: LCSH: Shin (Sect)—Japan—Customs and practices—Case studies. |
    Women in Buddhism—Japan—Case studies. | Buddhist women—Religious
    life—Japan—Case studies.
Classification: LCC BQ8736.7.W66 S73 2019 | DDC 294.3/926—dc23
LC record available at https://lccn.loc.gov/2018027848

ISBN 978-0-8248-8839-8 (pbk.)

All uncredited photographs are by the author.

Cover art: A *bōmori* watches as her son (the *jūshoku*) performs the morning service.

Contents

Series Editor's Preface

EVERY STUDY OF CONTEMPORARY JAPANESE BUDDHISM WILL need to engage with the concepts and approach put forth in this book. In her pioneering study of temple wives (*bōmori*), Jessica Starling offers a comprehensive investigation of contemporary temple Buddhism that moves beyond male priests and takes in the marvelous totality of the temple's domestic sphere. Starling's exhaustive fieldwork focuses on the domestic labor of temples, allowing her to demonstrate how polishing ritual implements, preparing boxed lunches, and serving tea all constitute vital aspects of both temple life and Buddhist propagation.

Here is an intimate portrait of Japanese Buddhism that locates temple wives at the center of the action. By viewing *bōmori* as religious professionals and their activities as vital to the larger mission of Shin temples, Starling invites us "back stage" and thus opens up a previously neglected but foundational arena of temple activity. This refocused perspective on temple wives encourages us to extend ideas of Buddhist teachings and propagation to include the material objects, economic activities, family obligations, biological imperatives, and institutional constraints that shape temple Buddhism in Japan today.

Acknowledgments

Such is the benevolence of Amida's great compassion,
That we must strive to return it, even to the breaking of our bodies;
Such is the benevolence of the masters and true teachers,
That we must endeavor to repay it, even to our bones becoming dust.

—*"Ondokusan"*

IT SHOULD BE CLEAR FROM THE CENTRAL thesis of this book that I am well aware my work is the product of a large number of serendipitous connections, dear friendships, and unseen support. Although I cannot hope to exhaust the list of people to whom I owe a debt of gratitude, I will try to name at least a few of the most prominent contributors to this work. All shortcomings are, of course, my own.

I would like first of all to thank my graduate adviser, Paul Groner, for taking a chance on me as a clueless graduate student and giving me the academic training, intellectual freedom, and unconditional support that allowed me to grow into a scholar.

Paul was also kind enough to send me to the gifted teachers at the Inter-University Center for Japanese Studies, who gave me the competence in Japanese to be able to speak and listen to my informants, and to translate what they told me into the pages of this book. Special thanks must go to Tanaka-sensei, my patient and generous Japanese tutor in Kyoto.

My fieldwork in Japan was made possible by financial support from the Japan Foundation, the Fulbright-Hays Doctoral Dissertation Research Abroad program, and the Ōtani-ha Pure Land Studies Fellowship. Officials from both Nishi Honganji and Higashi Honganji were extremely generous in their cooperation and support for my research. Two individuals in Kyoto, Henry Adams and Michael Conway, provided immeasurable help as well as treasured friendship. Ōtani University generously hosted me for my initial dissertation research, providing me with library access and a glorious desk at which countless words were read, transcribed, and written.

Stephen Covell's 2005 book, and in particular his formulation of the category of "Temple Buddhism," opened up for me a host of new questions and a world of research possibilities. I know I am not alone. Mark Rowe has been like my own personal battery charger—every conversation leaves me more excited, more able, and more confident to do this work. Other important mentors and interlocutors during my graduate study and later research include Heather Blair, Mark Blum, James Dobbins, Daniel Friedrich, Richard Jaffe, Noriko Kawahashi, Jessica Main, Levi McLaughlin, Matt McMullen, Matt Mitchell, Hillary Pederson, and Jolyon Thomas. These scholars know well the highs and lows of this work and how important colleagues are in sustaining one in it, so they will know how much their support has meant to me.

I must also acknowledge every provider of childcare for my children between 2008 to 2018, including but not limited to the two Nakamura-senseis at Funaoka Hoikuen, Sarah Riggs Stapleton, my parents, Miss Shonda and Miss Kennedy at UCF Creative School for Children, Malinda Bass, Mustard Seed Preschool, Eva Sharf, Honganji Yōchien, and Richmond Elementary School.

My time at the University of California, Berkeley, as a Shinjō Itō postdoctoral fellow in Japanese Buddhism provided me with a number of things that made this book better: a year to reflect on my dissertation material while benefiting from a stimulating intellectual atmosphere; a well-stocked library; and an occasion to present my ideas as they were developing, post-dissertation, to an engaged and thoughtful audience. I would like to thank Robert Sharf in particular for his support that year.

Lewis & Clark College, where I have taught since 2013, has provided various forms of support for the completion of this book, including research funds, a pre-tenure sabbatical, and a culture of protecting junior faculty from doing too much committee work. My colleagues in the Department of Religious Studies and the Asian Studies program especially have been a constant source of good advice, support, humor, and inspiration. The Scholarly Writing Retreat at Lewis & Clark, which I attended for three summers in a row, provided me with the structure, accountability, and community that I needed to complete the most difficult parts of the revision of this manuscript. Special thanks are due to two of my students from Lewis & Clark, Colette Willard and Carly Houk, for reading various drafts of the manuscript, giving me their honest feedback, and keeping me focused on this project.

Everyone at the University of Hawai'i Press, in particular Stephanie Chun and Barbara Folsom, have been wonderful to work with and have helped me to improve this manuscript immeasurably.

I would also like to thank my mother and my father and stepmother for their patient help with proofreading and formatting the book manuscript. I must also acknowledge all of my relatives for their tolerance of my tendency to take their grandchildren and great-grandchildren eight thousand miles away from them in order to complete my own selfish projects. Thank you, Mama Joyce.

My husband and our two children (one of whom was born just before this research began, and the other of whom joined us just before I turned in my dissertation), have been the most surprising, wonderful, undeserved blessings of my life these past ten years. Without Jason's loving support, intellectual engagement, and geographic flexibility, this project never would have begun. Without Claudia and Sam's delightful obliviousness to the importance of mommy's "work," I might never have found the focus necessary to complete this formidable project, nor the perspective to keep it from consuming me. Thank you, Claudia, for letting me miss your first lacrosse game so I could complete these final revisions.

Last on this list but first in gratitude are my informants, who, out of respect for their privacy, I will not name. I am grateful for their continued friendship, and I am in constant awe and inspiration of their unbounded patience and generosity.

Introduction

HALF AN HOUR BEFORE MURYŌJI TEMPLE'S SPRING equinox ritual began, the sliding paper door leading out of the main hall (*hondō*) slid open abruptly and two preschool-aged sisters darted out, scampering barefoot down the narrow hallway leading to the guest reception room. Shooed out of this room by their grandmother, they finally toppled, squealing, out into the entryway, where the shoes of parishioners were steadily accumulating below the bottom step. The older sister had won their game of tag and in the process managed to make her younger sister cry. The two girls retreated to the spacious temple kitchen, where an army of women was preparing the vegetarian feast (*otoki*) to be served to guests after the service. One of these women was the girls' pregnant mother, who was kneeling at a low table in the dining area, along with several female parishioners, arranging sweet beans, stewed vegetables, and other vegetarian fare in individual lunch boxes.

As the two girls elbowed each other in a struggle to climb into their mother's lap at the same time, she patiently placed her chopsticks on the table and began to dry her younger daughter's tears. The elder daughter, who had just turned five, soon lost interest in the tussle and turned her attention to the massive television set, whose screen was split four ways between three camera feeds of the temple grounds and a television broadcast of a popular cartoon. Her sister, who was just three, continued to sob, but then asked her mother if she could have another of the treats brought by one of the parishioner volunteers. After devouring their individually wrapped sponge cakes, the two girls bounded upstairs to their playroom. The family's residence was located on the second floor atop this sprawling industrial-sized kitchen and the adjoining carport.

The children's grandmother sat in the guest reception room, where notices for temple events and newsletters from Higashi Honganji, the headquarters of the Buddhist sect to which the temple belonged, were spread on the low table for visitors to pick up on their way to the temple's main hall. The grandmother and one of the temple's lay leaders were chatting with the recently arrived visiting priest who would deliver the sermon after the service; he was an old family friend and the resident priest of another temple. When he was finished with his tea and snack, she gathered his dishes onto a lacquered tray and carried them into the kitchen, where she rejoined the manual labor of preparing the communal meal. Shortly before the service was to begin, she slipped on her priestly robes and collar and went out into the hall to ring the bell that marked the start of the service. She entered the main hall and knelt by the sliding door, pointing out empty seats to a few late arrivals.

Her son, the temple's resident priest (*jūshoku*), emerged from behind the altar and the attendees grew quiet. He performed the liturgy alone, kneeling on the right side of the inner altar and intoning excerpts from Shinran's (1173–1263) written works before the main image of Amida (Skt. Amitābha) Buddha. Some thirty parishioners, an even mix of men and women averaging around sixty years old, looked on from their rows of low seats. One man, the lay leader of the congregation, had passed out copies of the reading that would follow the main ritual, one of Rennyo's (1415–1499) collected letters.[1] He now knelt by himself in front of the congregation but still outside of the inner altar. There was a liturgy book under each seat, and many parishioners read or recited the *Shōshinge* (The hymn of true faith, a section of Shinran's writings that is used frequently in liturgies) and Shinran's *Jōdo Wasan* (Verses on the pure land) along with the priest.

Just after the ritual started, the young mother and her two daughters entered the main hall as quietly as they could manage, the two girls wearing pink prayer beads around their wrists and squirming quietly in their mother's lap. They listened to their father's chanting for as long as they could bear to before darting out through the sliding doors as their mother let them go to play in the kitchen. Their younger sister, due to be born in a few weeks, was still just a large bulge under her mother's tunic.

This snapshot of the Nagai family's life in the temple is similar to what one would witness when attending any major event at a parish temple in Japan today.[2] The scene is more domestic than monastic: the obvious manifestations of Buddhist doctrine (for instance, the chanting of Shinran's *Shōshinge* and the melodic reading of Rennyo's letters), and even its more overtly religious material forms (the main image of Amida, the incense, the clerical robes), are surprisingly intermingled with more domestic activities like the serving of tea, the preparing of a midday meal, and the rearing of children. The boundary between the religious and the domestic spheres of the temple—represented in this scene by the constantly opening and closing paper door that separates the main hall from the communal dining room, the guest-receiving room, and the kitchen—is far more permeable than most scholarly studies of Buddhism would lead us to believe.

This book is a study of the position of the temple wife, whose life illustrates this permeability better than perhaps any other type of Buddhist practitioner.[3] It will address several important issues in the study of Buddhism and gender in contemporary Japan. First, it highlights the integral role of family as the connective tissue of Buddhist communities: family is instrumental in providing religious education and, in Shin Buddhist doctrinal formulations, in facilitating the fruition of a person's karmic seeds. As an intimate study of nonelite practitioners of Buddhism, it also sheds light on the way doctrinal ideas are embodied through rituals, human relationships, ethical decisions, and autobiographical narratives. In bringing the temple wife's activities into the purview of scholarly study, the book integrates discussions of gender, family, and the material-economic dimensions of religious life into the scholarly study of Buddhism.

Women in Buddhism

For roughly the first century of its existence, the field of Buddhist studies tended to define its object of study in relation to Buddhist doctrine and texts (Lopez 1995). It has long been a challenge for scholars to bring women fully into the picture of a Buddhist tradition so conceived, however, because of the dearth of texts written by Buddhist women prior to the modern period. Most male-authored Buddhist texts are relatively ambivalent toward women, if not overtly misogynistic. To cite but one example from the Pali canon of the Theravada Buddhist tradition, the *Anguttara Nikaya* has the Buddha saying, "Monks, if ever one could properly say that something is in all respects a snare of Māra [the Buddhist tempter and god of death], one can surely say of women that they are in all respects a snare of Māra" (Wilson 1996, p. 71). Liz Wilson's 1996 study, *Charming Cadavers: Horrific Figurations of the Feminine in Indian Hagiographic Literature,* catalogs many more instances of the demonization of women in Pali hagiographies, monastic codes, and meditation guides for monks. Passages such as these have been much discussed by scholars, with most surmising that they reflect a kind of "ascetic misogyny," an attempt to inculcate disgust in their male audience toward women's bodies the better to successfully overcome desire and adhere to a life of celibate renunciation (Sponberg 1992). It has been difficult for scholars who rely on textual sources to do more than speculate—if they even bother to do so—about possible female reception of these prescriptive texts.[4]

In some respects, the Mahayana tradition, with its newly conceived goal of becoming a perfectly enlightened buddha (Skt. *samyak-saṃbuddha*) and its doctrine that women were unable to reach this goal while still inhabiting a female form, provides even more fuel for the idea of Buddhism as a misogynistic tradition. For East Asian Buddhists, the two most widely referenced examples of androcentrism in Indian Mahayana scriptures are the Dragon Girl of the *Lotus Sutra* and the thirty-fifth vow of the Buddha Amitābha (J. Amida) of the *Sukhāvatīvyūha Sūtra*. In chapter 12 of the *Lotus Sutra,* a seven-year-old girl, princess of the underwater dragon kingdom, famously transforms herself into a man before attaining buddhahood. This highly suggestive scriptural episode gave rise to a rich interpretive tradition in Japan (see, e.g., Yoshida 2002, Moerman 2005, and Abe 2015).[5] The *Sukhāvatīvyūha Sūtra* is one of three canonical scriptures of the Pure Land Buddhist tradition, of which the Jōdo Shinshū is a part. In this text, the Buddha Amitābha, when he was a young bodhisattva embarking on the long and arduous journey to attain enlightenment, promised that, when he became a buddha, if female devotees "upon hearing my name have serene thoughts of faith, generate in their mind the aspiration to attain awakening, [and] feel disgust at their female nature," they would no longer suffer the fate of being reborn as women (Gomez 1996, p. 74). Luis Gomez, who produced the translation just cited, explains in a footnote that the vow "is a classical example of early Indian misogyny" (p. 232). Gomez's fellow philologist Paul Harrison hesitates to conclude that the vow is precisely misogynistic, noting that the matter of whether and in what sense sexual differences exist at all in the Pure Land is actually quite ambiguous in the Indian textual tradition. He admits in a footnote, however, that "getting women themselves to loathe the fact that they are women and thus become, as it were, self-hating is a classic misogynist move" (1998, p. 568). Harrison adds that "the vow is an explicit illustration of the principle that hegemonic discourses work in part by inducing the oppressed to appropriate the instruments of their own subordination" (p. 568). For my purposes, what is important to emphasize here is that, from a bibliocentric perspective, Mahayana Buddhism's prospects for women are fairly grim. In Bernard Faure's influential 2003 study, *The Power of Denial: Buddhism, Purity and Gender,* he writes that "given that Buddhism is essentially a discourse on salvation and holiness," it "is indeed relentlessly misogynistic, but as far as misogynist discourses go, it is one of the most flexible and open to multiplicity and contradiction" (pp. 8–9). In other words, if Buddhism is understood to be a set of texts or a coherent discourse or ideology, it is difficult to escape the conclusion that the tradition itself is misogynistic; it is harder still to determine how women before the twentieth century understood the misogynistic discourses that are so glaring in the tradition's texts.

In Japan, prominent male monks' deployment of doctrinal concepts like *henjō nanshi* (a woman's transformation into a man in order to attain buddhahood) and *goshō sanshō* (the five karmic obstructions and three objects of obedience for women—father, husband, and son) in sermons and commentaries has often been the starting point for thinking about women's place in the Buddhist tradition. A substantial body of work by Japanese scholars exists surrounding the subject of women's salvation (*nyonin jōbutsu* or *nyonin ōjō* in the case of rebirth in the Pure Land); it is almost all centered on doctrinal or popular texts composed by male priests (for example, Kasahara 1975, Oguri 1987, and Taira 1992).[6] Perhaps understandably, scholars who take a textual approach to the tradition have been at a loss to explain women's participation in the religion as anything other than an internalization and reproduction of the terms of their own subjugation. There are a number of problems with this approach, however. Focusing on doctrinal or prescriptive elements of the tradition assumes not only that most women have learned and understood the doctrine propounded by scholar-monks but also that they have believed and internalized it. It also tends to cast Buddhist women into one of two opposing categories: either they are unconscious victims of a misogynistic discourse, or they are heroic resisters asserting their agency against a patriarchal structure.

Some historical studies of Buddhism in Japan have sought to think beyond the prescriptive literature that is available to us, augmenting it with nondoctrinal, female-authored sources and asking questions about how Buddhist women would have learned about doctrine and how they actually understood such teachings to relate to their own condition.[7] The scholarship of Nishiguchi Junko (1987), Katsuura Noriko (1989, 1995), and Barbara Ruch (2002) helped to shift the focus from the normative presentations of women in scriptural sources and male-authored exegesis to the various ways in which women have made use of Buddhist symbols and institutions to further their own agendas. James Dobbin's 2006 study of Shinran's wife Eshinni's (1182–1268) letters, for instance, revealed a surprisingly complicated relationship between prescriptive or "idealized" forms of Buddhism such as those found in the writings of the Japanese sectarian founders, and Buddhism-as-lived in the context of practitioners' everyday experiences and concerns. Lori Meeks has observed that nuns in the medieval Hokkeji convent employed such strategies as "talking past" the elements of doctrine that were disadvantageous to them, meanwhile marshaling the social and ritual resources available to them as nuns to secure salvation for themselves and their patrons and to ensure the viability of their monastic community (2010). Gina Cogan's fine-grained historical study revealed the complicated strategies and agendas of the early modern princess-nun Bunchi (2014), and Barbara Ambros' textbook on women in Japanese religions similarly attempted to capture the nuances and ambiguity involved in women's participation in androcentric institutions and their consumption of misogynistic religious literature (2015).

Ethnographic studies have a special advantage in this regard: it often turns out that the norms found in religious texts do not exhaustively account for what is normative for women in everyday life. Studies of Buddhist women by Arai (1999, 2011), Gutschow (2004), Falk (2007), and Salgado (2013) have addressed the lacuna in a body of scholarship once preoccupied by male-authored depictions of women and the female gender in Buddhist monastic codes, hagiography, and doctrinal texts. These authors focus instead on the complexities of women's active negotiation of the Buddhist tradition on the ground.

In the last decade or so, however, a critical divide has emerged in studies of Buddhist nuns, especially—but not only—those in Southeast Asia. Wei-Yi Cheng, in her book *Buddhist Nuns in Taiwan and Sri Lanka* (2007), exposed some of the orientalist assumptions of many feminist studies of Buddhism, especially those produced in the 1990s. She cites Donaldson and Kwok's observation that feminist studies of religion may have the effect of "replicating the colonial gaze in the name of serving a feminist agenda" (Donaldson and Kwok 2002; cited in Cheng 2007, p. 7). In other words, scholarship with a prescriptive feminist bent often casts non-Western women as an oppressed group in need of Enlightened Western intervention. Perhaps the most frequent recipient of charges of orientalism is Rita Gross' 1993 book *Buddhism after Patriarchy: A Feminist History, Analysis and Reconstruction.* Though the book itself is a critical-constructive study of the Buddhist tradition by Gross, an American Buddhist woman, Cheng reports feeling alienated by "the occasional East/West, Us/Other binary rhetoric in the book," and notes that Gross' "assumption that only Western Buddhists are capable or aware of the need for feminist transformation of Buddhism…echoes Orientalist rhetoric that subjugates Asian Buddhists" (p. 5). Although Cheng's stated aim in conducting sociological research was to critique Western feminists' one-sided accounts of Asian Buddhist women, she admits that she was unable to let go of her own feminist principles when interviewing women and writing about them in her book. Cheng laments: "the whole purpose of conducting this research through the method of interview is to listen to Asian Buddhist nuns' voices. [But] my research subjects [were] partially silenced because I forced them to speak about issues raised by Western feminists, rather than beginning with their own agenda" (p. 190).

Nirmala Salgado, in her 2013 book *Buddhist Nuns and Gendered Practice: In Search of the Female Renunciant,* tries to do better. Her chapter "Decolonizing Female Renunciation" exposes Western scholarship's tendency to "focus on an (ideal) consciousness that is not central to the subjects of study. That consciousness speaks, rather, to second- and third-wave feminists who seek meaning in seemingly universal categories" (p. 47). Though Salgado is fiercely critical of what she reads as Rita Gross' condescending view of Asian Buddhist women as being in need of Western feminist intervention in order to be truly "liberated," she also finds fault with historians and ethnographers who have a less explicitly feminist agenda. For instance, she critiques Tess Bartholomeusz' 1994 book *Women under the Bo Tree* about female renunciants in Sri Lanka for repeating Gross' mistake of relying too heavily on ancient texts to define the Buddhist tradition. Salgado feels that Bartholomeusz gives too little weight to the everyday practices and concerns of her informants and instead "relies on texts to speak for the contemporary realities of female renunciants" (p. 32).

The crux of this controversy is the uneven power dynamic inherent in the production of discourse by Western scholars about non-Western women. In the past, not only has scholarly discourse about Asian Buddhist women been based largely upon prescriptive texts, but it has also hinged upon notions of agency rooted in Western liberalism—notions that are often presumed to be universal and natural among human beings everywhere. Talal Asad cautions that scholars should not assume "that a proper understanding of agency requires us to place it within the framework of a secular history of freedom from all coercive control, a history in which everything can be made, and pleasure always innocently enjoyed.... Agency need not be conceptualized in terms of individual self-empowerment and resistance, or of utopian history" (2003, p. 73).[8] Such formulations of freedom and agency do not always align with the proclaimed goals and beliefs of religious subjects, nor is it always possible for them to attain Western liberal ideals within their actual lived conditions. As Salgado writes, "How easy it is to forget that one never lives one's life apart from the condition in which one finds oneself. Norms—if there are such things—exist as part of the conditions in which people live, not as superimposed ideals that one can 'choose' apart from these conditions" (p. 39).

A scholar's best hope of avoiding inauthentic representations of Buddhist women, such as the ones Salgado criticizes, is to try to enter into the everyday lives of her informants with an honest sense of humility in order to discover the categories and concepts that operate for them on a practical level. Specifically, scholars must take care not to import Western liberal notions of what freedom and agency should look like or to make assumptions about whether Buddhism will be an oppressive or a liberating force in a woman's life. Taking an ethnographic approach has allowed me to dig into those everyday conditions and observe what elements of the Buddhist tradition were most salient in women's construction of narratives, identities, and meanings. For example, most of my temple wife informants have been exposed to feminist ideas through their peer networks and Japanese and Western media; as a result, doctrinal concepts like women's transformation into men and the five obstacles and three obediences are the subject of many searching discussions at workshops for temple wives.

At the same time, in various venues and at various times, I observed the active and intentional cultivation of Buddhist subjectivity and the embrace of Buddhist frameworks for understanding human contingency. Many of my informants' narratives of their life journeys draw upon Shin Buddhist doctrinal concepts and values such as humility and gratitude. They see their encounters with hardship, blessings, mentors, and the like as signposts affirming that the Buddha's compassion is at work in their lives, and they strive to be responsive to it. Of course, Buddhism is not the only resource at their disposal in constructing meaning and identity, nor is it the only source of ideological or institutional inequality in their lives. Conducting fieldwork and getting to know women over the course of several years allowed me to observe more broadly what cultural resources—what strategies and tools for action (Swidler 1986)—temple wives must choose from, and how and why they choose Buddhist ones.

Finally, scholarship on women in Buddhism has overwhelmingly focused on those women who can be categorized as nuns or renunciants as opposed to laywomen. Salgado's recent work on Buddhist nuns has problematized the tidy dichotomy of "lay" versus "monastic" into which Buddhist practitioners are often swept. Instead, she points out that, even in Sri Lanka—a place where scholars often seek the "purest" form of Buddhism closest to that practiced at the time of the Buddha himself—renunciation does not always correlate precisely with becoming a monastic, "nor is it defined strictly in terms of precepts that practitioners observe" (2013, p. 55). Salgado suggests that, despite the narratives scholars tend to give of Buddhist renunciation, "transcending the lay realm" was not necessarily a goal of her informants, nor did the nuns she interviewed seek to completely sever ties with their natal families.

Temple wives conspicuously defy clear distinctions between lay and monastic; they also defy the etic dichotomy of public/private that is often used to assess the value of women's roles. As Salgado points out, feminist scholars working on Asian Buddhism have tended to assume that "freedom" in the liberal feminist sense is "ideally actualized outside the private sphere—for example, in the educational system and in the area of career, which are usually outside the home" (2013, p. 52). Thus, in a liberal feminist reading, unless Buddhist women can renounce their domestic obligations and enter the "public" world of men, economic value, and status, they cannot be freely exercising their will. Studying women who are enmeshed in, rather than removed from, familial relationships while carrying out their religious activities, as I do here, renders a richer, more nuanced picture of power and freedom as women negotiate them in the context of interpersonal relationships.

In addition to illuminating women's religious subjectivity, my focus on the experiences of the female half of the clerical partnership of Jōdo Shinshū temples reveals previously unseen dimensions of the broader tradition. As historians and social scientists have long noted, a focus on gender helps us to gain insight into phenomena we might never otherwise see, and this is certainly true of my study of temple wives. Asking a question such as "What are the women doing?" achieves a remarkable task, like pulling back the curtain on a large portion of the story of Shin Buddhism that had previously been concealed. This book focuses on the figure of temple wife in part because it is a hitherto uncategorized position in Buddhism, encompassing qualities of both nuns and laywomen. It is also a position that complicates the distinctions we might be inclined to draw between lay and cleric, priest and wife, domestic and religious, and sacred and mundane.

Buddhism and Family

For a long time, literature in the field of Buddhist studies treated Buddhism and family as if they should have little to do with each other. Referring to prescriptive texts such as the *vinaya* (monastic legal codes), many nineteenth- and twentieth-century studies concluded that Buddhism was essentially a virtuosic religion of renunciation.[9] Recent work, however, has begun to redress this mistaken appraisal. Though Indian Buddhist texts have often been conceived of as a preserve of the "true" or "pure" form of early Buddhism, Shayne Clarke's 2014 study of Sanskrit, Chinese, and Tibetan monastic disciplinary codes originating in India generates an alternative image of Indian Buddhist monasticism around the turn of the millennium. What Clarke calls a "family-friendly" monasticism is a stark contrast to the virtuosic ideal assumed by many scholars and exemplified by the free-roaming eremitic mendicant touted in the *Rhinoceros Horn Sutra*. Clarke's work merits a reconsideration of the conventional assumption that the Buddhist concept of renunciation must be taken literally—that "going forth" into monkhood requires the complete dissolution of familial ties. Clarke has shown, on the contrary, that families had a place—if a somewhat ambiguous one—in and around Buddhist monasteries at least as far back as the time of the compilation of these monastic codes. In addition, two recent volumes edited by Vanessa Sasson (2013) and Liz Wilson (2013), respectively, represent richly textured collections of studies drawing from a variety of sources spanning two dozen centuries. Together these volumes demonstrate rather compellingly that children and family have always been integral to the Buddhist tradition, even if they have not been at the center of its texts.

Nonetheless, prescriptive sources such as the *vinaya* have had such a strong influence on scholars' imaginations that contemporary Buddhism, particularly in Japan where most priests marry, has been largely ignored or written off as a degenerate form. As Robert Sharf observes, the tendency to presume that Buddhism's ideal form can be found in the ancient, prescriptive texts of Indian Buddhism (which may not ever have been descriptive of Indian Buddhism as it was truly practiced) has "served to discredit the testimony of living Buddhist communities" (2001, p. 5). Stephen Covell's 2005 book, *Japanese Temple Buddhism: Worldliness in a Religion of Renunciation,* enters into the complexity and contradiction that characterizes what Covell calls "Temple Buddhism"—a term for the common form of Buddhism practiced at parish temples across Japan, where priests marry and parishioner and clerical succession generally takes place along family lines. Covell highlights two competing ideals for Japanese priests today: one is the world-renouncing religious virtuoso; the other is that of the family man, ritual specialist, and administrator of the local parish temple. The wives of these would-be renunciants occupy a particularly ambiguous place institutionally: neither nuns nor laywomen, their existence is an uncomfortable reminder of the laic lifestyles that have been adopted by Japanese monks, but nevertheless their services are integral to the success of daily temple operations and the continuance of the temple inheritance system (Covell 2005). According to Noriko Kawahashi, the traditionally monastic sects' entanglement in the rhetoric of renunciation (*shukke shugi*) prevents them from adequately recognizing or supporting the position of temple wife (1995).[10]

I chose to focus my own research on the Japanese Buddhist tradition known as the Jōdo Shinshū (True Pure Land School) because in this tradition, the ideal of world renunciation—specifically, of leaving behind one's family in favor of a life of celibacy—had been deliberately and openly eschewed by the founder Shinran, an erstwhile Tendai monk. Shinran embraced the idea that Japan had entered the final, degenerate age of the dharma (*mappō*), in which practitioners were no longer able to engage in difficult practices like asceticism.[11] In such a time, Shinran reasoned, it was useless and even counterproductive to continue to draw distinctions between lay and monastic: those who continued to call themselves monks were rarely able to keep the vow of celibacy, and so the title of monk was mere pretense (Dobbins 2002, p. 37). While other Buddhist clerics in Japan did not join the Shinshū in openly marrying and bringing their families into the temple until the Meiji period (1868–1912), during the intervening seven centuries of defending their married lifestyle Shin Buddhist clerics developed a wealth of strategies for articulating positive roles for priests' families—especially their wives—in relation to temple operations.[12] Shin temple families have mobilized doctrinal resources to articulate the spiritual value of their decidedly non-monastic life. Even domestic activities like childrearing and hosting laypeople for tea, food, or sake at their temple home are sometimes included among religious practices. These doctrinal valuations of the everyday underpin the phenomenon of domestic religion that I take up in this book.

In particular, this study's revelation of the importance of interpersonal relationships in the practical theology of Jōdo Shinshū adherents urges the scholarly conversation about Buddhism to confront the importance of intimacy and intersubjectivity. As Constance Furey has noted, the turn in religious studies toward studying human subjectivity with a greater focus on the body and society has still left the important area of interpersonal relationships relatively unexamined. She writes: "[F]ew studies of religion track [the] subject as a participant in intimate relationships, defined by problems and pleasures of kinship, friendship, patronage, marriage and other relationships less easily named. In our quest to understand subjectivity, we have isolated the subject" (2012, p. 10). Giving greater attention to religious individuals as subjects who are embedded in families and other intimate relationships also promises to add nuance to our consideration of women's agency. In a recent article on "ladylike religion" among Heian-period (794–1185) Japanese aristocracy, Heather Blair emphasizes the notion of relational agency to show how individuals act in "webs of mutuality" to accomplish their goals (2016, p. 7). This book, then, adds to a current trend in scholarship that seeks to de-individualize notions of human agency and subjectivity.

In general, the experiences of temple wives challenge us to recognize

A temple son practices *gasshō* (clasping hands in prayer).

that the spiritual lives of Buddhist clerics are not lived in isolation from their familial, material, or economic lives. We as scholars must consider the possibility that this is not an especially scandalous or incriminating fact. Despite doctrinal and historical differences, all of the contemporary Buddhist schools (whether historically monastic or not) now have family-run temples at the parish level, so this study of female temple professionals in the Jōdo Shinshū has important implications for the broader phenomenon of the family-centric form of Buddhism that prevails in contemporary Japan. How do familial relationships and intimate connections with parishioners (who are often like family to young temple successors) inculcate Buddhist faith and doctrinal understanding among practitioners, whether lay or cleric? By focusing on domesticity, this study will begin to answer questions such as these.

Domestic Religious Professionals

Since the early 1990s, Robert Orsi, David Hall, and others have pushed for the study of what they termed "lived religion,"[13] arguing that the classic spirit/ matter divide had continued to inform academic views of religion, which were heavily shaped by a Protestant bias concerning what constitutes religion's authentic sphere of activity—namely, the disembodied, nonmaterial realm. In a 1997 essay, Orsi put it thus: "[S]omething called 'religion' cannot be neatly separated from the other practices of everyday life, from the way that human beings work on the landscape, for instance, or dispose of corpses, or arrange for the security of their offspring. Nor can 'religion' be separated from the material circumstances in which specific instances of religious imagination and behavior arise and to which they respond" (Orsi 1997, pp. 6–7).

In the field of Buddhist studies, scholarship began to take a material turn with the contributions of Gregory Schopen (1997) and Kevin Trainor (1997). Schopen suggested that Buddhist studies had been unreflectively guided by a "sixteenth-century Protestant polemical concept of where 'true' religion is located"—namely, in "the word" rather than in bodies, rituals, and material objects (1991, p. 22). Numerous critical genealogies of the academic study of religion by Talal Asad (1993, 2003), Russell McCutcheon (1997), Timothy Fitzgerald (1997, 2003), and others have affirmed Schopen's assertion and exposed the Protestant influences on the definition—implicit or explicit—of religion in the academy today, making an exclusive focus on the more ethereal, disembodied aspects of religion more difficult to justify.

Concerning the study of Japanese Buddhism, Jacqueline Stone wrote in 2006 that "the pendulum has now swung" from strictly textual and doctrinal research to a more historically, economically, and culturally grounded approach. Nonetheless, she notes the continuing shortage of "'on the ground' studies of what Buddhist institutions, ritual practices, and ideas meant in the lives of actual people, both monastics and laity" (p. 57). While most scholars now acknowledge in principle that religion encompasses more than the texts alone say, the prescriptive, philosophical, and textual forms of Buddhism still occupy the center of gravity of most studies, and many scholars struggle to engage the investigative tools of "practice" with those of "doctrine." As Ian Reader and George Tanabe (1998), Robert Sharf (1991), and others have lamented, academic labor is often divided into two camps, one concerned with anthropological studies of contemporary phenomena, and the other being more comfortable investigating the distant past with religious texts as their guide. In other words, the problem of how to examine both spirit and matter, doctrine and bodily practice, with the same scholarly lens remains.

It is at the intersection of these two religious planes that my subjects, temple wives or *bōmori* (literally, "temple guardians"), reside. As domestic religious professionals, temple wives' experiences directly challenge conceptual binaries such as public/private, outside/inside, professional/domestic, and sacred/profane. The local parish temple houses the priest and his family as well as the altar to the Buddha Amida—indeed, many Shin Buddhist sermons depict the temple as the Buddha's own home. As such, it is the site where all-important karmic connections (*en*) between the faithful and Amida are forged or come to fruition. It is therefore a place of utmost spiritual importance in the Jōdo Shinshū, which has no tradition of monasticism or cloistered religious practice, and in which religious efficacy is ascribed exclusively to the working of Amida's compassion rather than to individual efforts aimed at salvation.

While there is no way to encapsulate the rich doctrinal tradition of the Jōdo Shinshū in a few short paragraphs, at the very least the concept of *tariki,* or other-power, must be introduced. This doctrine represents a pivotal turn away from traditional Buddhist notions of practice and salvation. Shinran radically rejected the necessity for any kind of personal effort, or effort on behalf of others, in order to secure salvation, which in the Pure Land tradition is understood as the attainment of rebirth in Amida's paradise. One must instead rely solely on the power of the eighteenth vow of the *Larger Pure Land Sutra,* also known as the Primal Vow, which was "expansive enough to embrace even the most unworthy believer" (Dobbins 2002, p. 29). Only the attainment of faith, or true entrusting (*shinjin*), in Amida's saving power could assure one of rebirth in the Pure Land. No calculated effort was needed; in fact, such effort was counterproductive, leading to a lesser rebirth just outside of the Pure Land. The signature religious practice in the Jōdo Shinshū is simply the intonation of the *nembutsu* phrase *namu Amida Butsu,* (literally, "I take refuge in the Buddha Amida"). However, Shin piety may extend to any activity undertaken in a spirit of gratitude for Amida's compassion.[14] Primarily, this means propagation activities—letting others know about the salvific power of Amida's Primal Vow. As James Dobbins puts it, "The aspiration to awaken others to faith arises from one's own sense of indebtedness to Amida and from the desire to share the joys and rewards of with faith others" (2002, p. 30).

The notion of *tariki* underlies the distinctively Shin Buddhist interpretation of the role of religious professionals. Given the impossibility of attaining salvation through any calculated effort, the distinction of Shin clerics is not based on virtuosity in asceticism, privileged access to ritual technologies, or esoteric knowledge. Instead, their status as religious professionals is premised on their close relationship to Amida's saving power and their responsibility to let others know about it. This heightened responsibility is primarily a result of their residence in the temple itself and their material dependence on Amida. For instance, sermons and letters dating back at least to the fifteenth century entreated religious professionals in the Jōdo Shinshū not to think of gifts and donations that sustain the temple family as if they were goods obtained through ordinary labor in the general economy. They were, according to the prescriptive literature, the "goods of the Buddha."[15] Temple wives, in their stewardship of the communal, material, and intergenerational dimensions of temple life, have traditionally borne responsibility for overseeing the spiritual gift economy that circulates through the temple. As I detail in chapters 1 and 2, the attainment of faith is just as likely to occur in response to a show of hospitality, a sense of community, or an aesthetic affinity with the temple space as it is from hearing the words of one of the Pure Land sutras intoned by a professional priest. For temple wives, the spiritual practice of *button* or *butsu'on hōsha*—repayment of the debt owed to the Buddha for one's salvation—can mean showing gratitude through the conscientious stewardship of the Buddha's goods, caring for and opening the Buddha's home to lay followers, responsibly raising the temple's children, and propagating the teachings in the domestic sphere.

The phrase "domestic religion" as I employ it in this book refers to this unapologetic comingling of quotidian tasks and material objects with spiritual efficacy, often in the most domestic settings.[16] My informants are essentially professional housewives whose home is also the home of the Buddha. I find this intermingling of sacred and profane to be extremely useful in bridging the traditional scholarly divide between the study of doctrine and practice. It demands that we "comprehend religious practices as deeply embedded in the fabric of everyday life," as Mark Rowe urged us to do in his study of contemporary Japanese funerary practices (2011, p. 15). I also take up Robert Orsi's invitation to study religion as practiced, not in isolation from the profane, but rather as something that "comes into being in an ongoing, dynamic relationship with the realities of everyday life" (1997, p. 7). The temple wife's tendency to cross back and forth between the temple's formalized space of worship (the main hall) and the "back stage" of the temple kitchen and family residence highlights the way in which religious doctrine resists being confined to the zone designated for formal worship—or to canonical texts.

The demarcation and performance of domesticity in contemporary Japan is of course closely linked to the construction of modern gender norms. In Japan, "the home" (*katei*) as a theoretical and physical space is a modern phenomenon, whose invention was tied up with the creation of the Japanese nation-state in the second half of the nineteenth century. The physical division of private and public spaces in modern Japanese homes had as much to do with hygiene, class, and building a modern economy as it did with traditional cultural dichotomies like inside (*uchi*) and outside (*soto*). In modern newspapers, magazines, and architectural plans, home and society emerged as spatially and conceptually distinct realms, and women's and men's roles were divided accordingly. The feminized vocation of "housewife" (*shufu*) took shape during the Meiji period alongside other modern professions such as "psychology, medicine, hygiene, nutrition science, industrial management, and architecture" (Sand 2003, p. 55). Among the housewife's chief responsibilities were cleaning, educating the children, cooking, and managing household resources. More abstractly, she was responsible for the moral upbringing of the family. The feminine ideal of the "good wife, wise mother" (*ryōsai kenbo*), a commonplace in modern public discourse, referred to the Confucian-inspired model for married women as supportive wives who maintained the moral integrity of the home and saw to the education of their children. In theory, at least, men's and women's realms of activity were clearly divided into the public and the private, respectively.

Like other nineteenth-century adopters of an increasingly hegemonic "global domesticity" (Walsh 2004, p. 2), the architects of Meiji social and political reform were inspired by British notions of home and domesticity. The English word "home" (rendered *hōmu*) was even used as a gloss for the newly coined Japanese word *katei*. This does not mean, however, that Japanese modernizers understood domesticity and its significance in the same way that the Victorians did. Whereas the Victorian cult of domesticity idealized the home "as a sacred space, divorced from market relations," in Japan the economic, social and political import of women's work has always been explicit (Borovoy 2001, p. 93). The modern Japanese housewife was defined by, and mobilized in service to, the Meiji state's project of modernization.[17]

As used in this book, the term "domestic" does not refer to a specific domain of social action that is defined in opposition to the political or public, nor does it have a fixed spatial referent. Indeed, this study shows that the demarcation of religious spaces, roles, and relationships are much more fluid in practice than they appear to be in the prescriptive literature. Domestic religion, then, refers to religion as it is practiced in an intimate, quotidian key, outside of formal liturgical or canonical contexts. Crucially, attending to this domestic mode sheds light on the intimate relationships that exist among temple family members, parishioners, teachers, and even deities like the Buddha Amida.

The study of temple wives as domestic religious professionals, then, contributes to discussions of both Buddhism and gender in contemporary Japan—discussions that are by and large held in isolation from one another.[18] One example of this is the relationship between Japanese gender roles and clerical authority at family temples. It is widely noted that the gender ideology forged during the last decade of the nineteenth century, in particular the ideal image of the good wife and wise mother, continue to retain a tight grip on domestic relations in Japan. Olfra Goldstein-Gidoni, in her 2012 ethnography *Japanese Housewives,* reports that contemporary housewives describe their primary duty as being to "protect the home" by fulfilling their obligations as wives and mothers. Meanwhile, their husbands see themselves as protecting the home in their capacities as breadwinners. Successful embodiment of these complementary gender roles is usually based on the husband's identity as a salaryman, who must put in long hours of service to his employer, and the wife's handling of household finances, housework and food preparation, and childrearing.

At first glance, the *bōmori*'s position of "guardian of the temple" (the literal meaning of the characters for *bōmori*) would seem to be analogous to this: while temple husbands are moving about in the world, publicly conducting rituals and other propagation activities, the *bōmori* does her part to spread Buddhism from within the home. Inasmuch as the labor at the temple is ideally divided along gender lines, the activities and gendered strategies of temple wives tell us a good deal about how the modern Japanese gender contract works in a Buddhist temple. Close examination of the gender dynamics of the temple household, however, reveals an unexpected trend. When the resident priest leaves the temple to perform ceremonies, attend training, or work at a full-time job to supplement the temple's income, temple housewives become the sole adults in the temple when a parishioner calls. One of the surprising discoveries of my fieldwork was that the very gender ideology that divides labor along gender lines and "confines" women to staying at home in fact renders temple wives de facto religious professionals. This is but one of many insights that can be gained by decentering our study of Buddhism in contemporary Japan, previously focused on the activities of male clerics, and recentering it on the activities of women.

Ethnographic Research Methods

In the spring of 2009 I arrived in Japan along with my husband and infant daughter to embark on twenty-seven months of research based at Ōtani University in Kyoto. I began to make connections in the Shin Buddhist community in the spring of 2009 through my host university, which was affiliated with the Ōtani-ha, as well as through a friend who was attending the Kyoto seminary affiliated with the Honganji-ha. These two *ha* or denominations represent the major national organizations of the Jōdo Shinshū. In this way I gradually broadened my network of acquaintances in two major sects of the Jōdo Shinshū, which together represent roughly twenty thousand parish temples across Japan. Through my hosts at Ōtani University and the sect's administrative headquarters at Higashi Honganji, I was introduced to the leaders of the national and district temple-wife networks, and I was invited to their workshops and orientations for young temple wives, daughters, and daughters-in-law. Higashi Honganji's International Office generously provided me with the institutional information and statistics I requested; officials at Nishi Honganji did the same for the Honganji-ha. I was able to access back issues of the two sects' periodicals in the libraries of Ōtani and Ryūkoku Universities, and I learned more about institutional history from conversations with professors in the Shin Buddhist studies and sociology departments at the two schools. I was eventually introduced to the employees of the Office for Women's Affairs of Higashi Honganji, whose acquaintance unlocked the door to many invaluable introductions, documents, and invitations to women's conferences.

Using these connections, I was able to visit temples in Kyoto, Shiga, Ōsaka, Hyōgo, Mie and Niigata Prefectures, and various regions of Kyūshū. I also attended workshops and conferences for temple wives at the sects' main headquarters and district offices in Kyoto and Kobe, where I listened to group discussions and had casual conversations with numerous women between conference events. In addition, I studied the online conversations of a community of temple wives on Mixi, a popular Japanese social networking site on which participants generally use pseudonyms to preserve their anonymity.

Over the course of my fieldwork, I interviewed sixty women from temple families. I was able to follow up with a number of my informants in subsequent visits to Japan during the summers. The official titles of my informants varied: some were current temple wives (*bōmori*), others were temple daughters or daughters-in-law (*waka bōmori*). Some, known as *zen-bōmori*, had daughters-in-law who had taken over most of their duties. Some had even taken over the position of *jūshoku* of their family temple, but they were preparing to or had already passed the temple leadership on to their sons. In choosing which women's stories to highlight in this book, I tried to represent the diversity among temple wives, including differences between generations, rural and urban settings, family dynamics, and the size and financial prosperity of a temple. I should also note that I have included a mixture of examples of women from both the Ōtani and Honganji denominations, but the lived situation of temple residents depends much more upon the local conditions and size of their temple than on its sectarian affiliation. When discussing institutional developments, however, I am careful to specify which denomination I am referring to, as the two sects are institutionally distinct.

Most of my informants were reluctant to talk about themselves and were more comfortable serving me food and asking me about America than speaking about their own lives into my voice recorder. However, once I had convinced them that I was truly more interested in what they did in their everyday lives than in what a professor at the university could tell me about Buddhism, they began to open up. Accessing women's stories in intimate detail required a level of comfort and mutual fondness that sometimes crossed over into friendship. I often shared various personality traits, experiences, and even physical characteristics with those informants with whom I became closest. These women tended to be my own age, the age of my mother, or the age of my grandmother. We would share stories about motherhood, daughterhood, working and raising a family, and the practices and beliefs of Buddhism in contrast to the Quaker tradition to which I belong. Despite this closeness, though, I am aware that my relationship with informants was not without power imbalances. Ultimately, I was interviewing these women for the sake of my own professional projects, and the women I interviewed were unlikely to capitalize on our exchanges in the same way. Nonetheless, I do believe that my informants—particularly those who were most frank and disclosing, most instrumental in making introductions that multiplied my connections in the temple world—were collaborative partners in this research. Most of them expressed excitement that their position would attain more visibility and legitimacy as the result of being the subjects of a scholarly study.

Chapter Outline

Chapter 1 profiles the Nagai family, whose spring equinox ritual I described at the beginning of this introduction. This focus on a single temple family illuminates the significance of filial obligations and family relations in the formation of Buddhist professionals. It also introduces the gendering of religious labor, a topic I continue to explore in the subsequent chapters. Chapter 2 highlights the feminized form of Buddhist propagation (*kyōka*) performed by many temple wives. This inquiry into women's daily activities as housewives of the Buddhist temple reveals the ambiguity of the *bōmori*'s position as one that is both domestic and public. She is constantly pulled between the main hall, where more formal religious operations are performed, and the kitchen, where the less visible, reproductive labor of the religion takes place. I outline the resources within the Shin Buddhist tradition for valorizing the temple wife's constant presence at the temple. By staying at home and welcoming visitors, she is able to facilitate connections between laypeople and the temple by extending hospitality.

In chapter 3, I focus on the temple wife's oversight of the material dimensions of worship, receipt of gifts, preparation for events, and daily life at the temple. In her stewardship of the objects and money that are donated to the temple and her preparation of the rice that sustains both the temple family and the Buddhist image, the *bōmori* as housewife illuminates the flow of spiritual and material gifts through the temple. The notion of *button hōsha,* or repayment of one's debt to the Buddha, is often used to characterize the imperative to propagate that arises from the temple family's economic and spiritual dependence on both the laity and the Buddha.

Chapter 4 explores the world of young women who were born and raised in lay households, becoming connected to the Jōdo Shinshū primarily through marriage to a temple successor. I trace the ways in which the religious and the domestic are intertwined in the process of young temple daughters-in-law acquiring the practical expertise and doctrinal knowledge of a religious professional so that they can succeed their husband's mother as the temple's *bōmori*. In particular, the Buddhist notion of *en,* or karmic affinity, serves as an explanatory concept that links together marriage choice and religious vocation in some women's narratives. Further, in the identity formation of these young *bōmori* in training, the Shin Buddhist narrative of gratitude for hardship placed in one's path by Amida often subsumes their domestic identity as a filial, forbearing daughter-in-law.

Chapter 5 focuses on women who have become ordained as Shin priests. After surveying the process by which temple family women were first permitted to take ordination in the Jōdo Shinshū as guardians of their families' temples during the Pacific War, I describe contemporary *bōmori* who also have taken their priestly ordination before profiling one woman who currently acts as female *jūshoku* of her temple. The examples I introduce in this chapter reveal that, even in the cases of temple wives who venture into the putatively "public" sphere of the priesthood, their actions and motivations are inextricable from familial duty and a desire to protect their homes.

In chapter 6 I explore how *bōmori* negotiate the obligations of their position with the feminist ideals that many women educated in postwar Japan hold dear. In the Ōtani-ha, feminist pushback against a long tradition of androcentric institutions and doctrinal messages reached a fever pitch in organizations, publications, and petitions produced in the 1980s and early 1990s. Profiling one woman who had an uneasy path to reconciling herself to her position as a temple wife, I bring to the fore qualities such as resistance, ambivalence, contradiction, and evolution in the attitudes and actions of individual temple wives, particularly in those roles and activities that cut across personal and political realms.

Together, these chapters provide a comprehensive view of contemporary Jōdo Shinshū temple life with women at its center. The Buddhist temple wife's tendency to move back and forth between the temple's designated space for worship (the main hall) and the "back stage" of the temple kitchen and family residence highlights the ways in which religious meanings are not confined to the zone of the temple designated for formal worship or to canonical texts. The attainment of Buddhist faith (*shinjin*) is just as likely to occur in response to a show of hospitality, a sense of community, or an aesthetic affinity with the temple space as it is from hearing the words of one of the Pure Land sutras intoned by a professional priest. For temple wives, the spiritual practice of *button hōsha*—repayment of the debt owed to the Buddha for one's salvation—can mean showing gratitude through the conscientious stewardship of donations to the temple, caring for and opening the Buddha's home to lay followers, raising the temple's children, and propagating the teachings in the domestic sphere. This book follows the "turn to affect" taken by many scholars in recent years, by investigating in personal detail how religious dispositions are formed in individual practitioners. The answer, unsurprisingly, has as much to do with intimate relationships and daily practices as it does with formal liturgies or scripted sermons.

A Family of Clerics

The teachings are also important, of course—but first, the connection between people. From parent to child, the connection between one generation and the next, and "meeting people" (*deai to iu mono*). When you get married, you have to meet your partner first, right? If that doesn't happen, then you can't move forward to the next generation. The whole reason I'm here is because all of those people— my father, grandfather, and people even farther back—did what they did. When I thought about that, I thought that's really what's most worthy of respect.

—*Akira Nagai,* jūshoku

THE EARLIEST SHIN CONGREGATIONS THAT SPRUNG UP across Japan in the generation after Shinran transmitted clerical and lay membership along familial lines. Over the centuries, the definition of a cleric in the Jōdo Shinshū has solidified around the assumption that he (or she) should be a member of the temple family, whether through birth, marriage, or adoption. Other Buddhist schools in Japan since the Meiji period have followed suit, adopting, with varying degrees of formality and acceptance, a temple inheritance system for most parish temples.[1] While the parish temple's resident priest, or *jūshoku,* has received much attention in recent work on Japanese Temple Buddhism (Covell 2005; Borup 2008; Rowe 2011; Nelson 2013), most studies keep their eyes trained on the priest's official Buddhist activities—taking ordination, giving sermons, performing rituals, and interacting with the sectarian bureaucracy, for instance. Viewed from the perspective of the women in his life, however, he becomes a multidimensional figure: he is a father, a son, and a husband in addition to being a priest.

This chapter is dedicated to an intimate depiction of a single temple family, the Nagais. These brief portraits, extracted from my long-running friendship with this family, will introduce the reader to the seamless interweaving of family relationships, Buddhist doctrine, clerical work, and gender roles that will become even more evident throughout this book. The profiles given in this chapter dramatize the centrality of the family as the most significant social institution for the transmission of belief, practice, and authority at Shin Buddhist temples.

While no single profile can possibly represent the great diversity of practitioners in the Jōdo Shinshū, the three generations of Nagais are certainly within the realm of "typical." I begin with the *jūshoku*, who is the highest-profile member of the temple family, and the easiest to reach for interviews. It immediately becomes clear, however, that a full account of Temple Buddhism can be given only by including—and centering—other characters in our story.

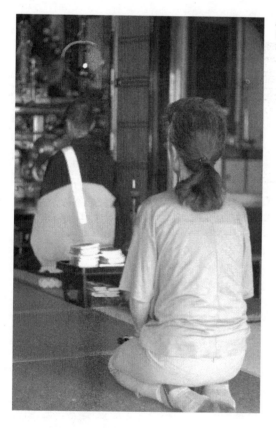

A *bōmori* watches as her son (the *jūshoku*) performs the morning service.

Akira

After exchanging a few e-mails with Nagai Akira, the forty-year-old *jūshoku* of a mid-sized temple (about two hundred parishioner households) in urban Kobe, I arranged to interview him in person. The day of our meeting it was raining heavily, and two small, yapping dogs greeted me as Akira's mother, who had short hair, wore glasses, and appeared to be about seventy, let me in through the front gate. Akira knelt at the top of the entry area while I shed my muddy shoes and poncho. He then led me into the temple's receiving room and waited patiently while I set up my voice recorder and opened my notebook. His mother brought us tea and sweets and then disappeared behind the sliding door to handle the temple calls while we talked.

I began by asking Akira how he felt about assuming the family "business" of running the temple. He explained that it had taken him a long time to come around to it, but after spending a few years in his early twenties trying out other jobs, he had finally, with a sense of inevitability, agreed. He had already received preliminary ordination as a matter of course as a young temple son, and while attending Ōtani University (which is affiliated with his temple's sect) he had received the religious instructor (*kyōshi*) degree by taking a special course. Having surrendered to his fate as a temple successor, Akira attended a training session for *jūshoku* at Higashi Honganji. It was only after that, however, that he began to feel a special duty to the temple and his family:

> Finally it was time for my inauguration ceremony. That's when I saw my temple's bylaws for the first time. The first article read: "At Muryōji, the first son of the *jūshoku* Nagai will be his successor."[2] That's the first thing that's written. Since it's the first thing that's written, I began to think that meant it's the most important thing. So I thought, what does that mean? If someone wants to run this temple, they must be a Nagai. Thus, it's saying that if you don't get married, and don't have children, there will be no "next one." This is required of me—well, there's no commandment that says that, but that's the implication of it.

It is important to note that, unlike in other Buddhist schools, where temple inheritance is merely a de facto practice (Covell 2005; Starling 2015), in the Jōdo Shinshū it is actually the normative model for priestly succession. In the boilerplate temple bylaws that Higashi Honganji provides to its affiliated parish temples, the family name is to be included in the definition of the successor priest. Reading these bylaws, which actually required that each generation of *jūshoku* have the same family name, prompted Akira to reflect on his interconnectedness to other people: "I thought more and more about what that meant. Isn't it saying that the Jōdo Shinshū, as a sect, holds that 'You should get married. You should have children.'? That's what Shinran did, he got married, and had children, and evangelized to people, spreading the teachings out in the world—within all of that, didn't our predecessors hold that to be most important?"

Akira explained that in the twenty-two generations of *jūshoku* and *bōzu* (as premodern Shin priests were called) named Nagai who preceded him surely there had been individuals who had wanted to do something else. But they had not, and for that he was filled with gratitude and a desire to repay his debt to those ancestors. Other informants, mainly *jūshoku,* had rehearsed for me the familiar story of how Shinran had descended from the monastic world of Mount Hiei (where he had trained as a Tendai monk) and lived among the laypeople, eschewing monastic celibacy as a mark of hypocrisy among monks in the latter age of the Buddhist teachings (*mappō*). This was the first time, however, that I had heard filial piety and temple succession linked so explicitly: Akira was basically articulating a definition of priestly vocation in the Jōdo Shinshū that was grounded in family obligation.

I then turned our conversation to the subject of temple wives. Akira, like many of my informants, assumed that I would want to talk about why things at the temple, and in the larger sectarian institution, were not more equal between men and women. The Ōtani-ha, the Jōdo Shinshū sect to which Akira's temple belonged, had in the past two decades seen a lively public debate on the subject of how best to define *bōmori*—a debate that is indicative of just how difficult it is to ascribe a normative framework for this highly individualized and family-based position at the temple. Some believed that the role was an intrinsically female one, and so the sect ought to codify the status of the position as "wife of the *jūshoku,*" which is how the title had been used in common practice for some seven centuries. A vocal contingent of equality-minded feminists within the Ōtani-ha temple wife network, however, pointed out that this threatened to relegate women to a secondary role at the temple as servants to their husbands, a blatant example of gender discrimination.

Akira revealed that he had attended several of the local temple-wife workshops where they had debated the definition of *bōmori* as it was to appear in the revised sectarian bylaws. Most of those who speak at those meetings are feminists, he explained, and he does not always agree with their points of view. But they were successful in lobbying the sect to amend the rules to allow women to become full-fledged *jūshoku.*[3] As a result of this, however, the definition of *bōmori* was thrown into question: Would the husband of a female *jūshoku* then become a male *bōmori*? This seemed terribly counterintuitive, although Akira said he had met one young man who had bravely become a pioneering male *bōmori* and had spoken at one of the workshops

Akira attended, but his experience sounded so difficult that Akira felt sorry for him. It must be very hard, Akira speculated, to be the only one of your gender doing what you're doing. The same is true for women who become *jūshoku* and have to attend meetings where they are the only woman. He then turned the question over to me: What did I think? Should there be female *jūshoku?*

I hesitated, as I knew that Akira had two daughters and no sons. I replied that it seemed to me a woman should be allowed to become *jūshoku* if she wanted to, but I imagined it must be very difficult for one to run a temple by herself, as she probably would not have a *bōmori* as an assistant (unless, perhaps, her mother could do it). Then he revealed his own opinion: the sect could do its best to change the bylaws and legislate gender equality at the temple, he said, but it would be hard to suddenly change such a thing. Reality doesn't change that quickly—even if they change the rules or the name of a particular position, he went on, the reality doesn't change.

I asked him then about his own wife. Because he claimed that family was so central to his Buddhist faith and connection to the temple, I assumed that his wife would be similarly enthusiastic. But Akira did not reveal much about his wife, only that she had come from a lay family in Mie Prefecture and was still just getting used to it all. She did plan to take *tokudo,* the initial ordination, a few years down the road. The plan was for her to do so along with her oldest daughter when the latter turned nine—but her daughter was still just three, and she also had a two-year-old to look after, so she was busy with childrearing most of the time. "So," I asked, "is your mother still the *bōmori* of this temple?"

Akira puzzled over that question for a moment before answering: "Well, actually I suppose her title is the *zen-bōmori* [previous *bōmori*], and my wife would be the *bōmori*. But in fact my mother handles most of the *bōmori*'s duties. She had also been the *jūshoku* of this temple for a while, so she still makes some of our monthly home visits to parishioners' home altars. She knows everyone so well as she has been at it for over forty years; they like to have her come."

I was surprised at this casual revelation that his mother had actually been the previous *jūshoku* and asked how that had come about. Akira explained that his father had died when he was very young, and his mother had managed the temple in the interim.

It suddenly occurred to Akira that I might want to speak to his mother as well. Eager to be helpful and exceedingly generous with his and his family members' time, he volunteered to set up an interview for me with her. I marveled at how easily and voluntarily his mother had withdrawn from view when I first visited the temple: she had been the one to bring us tea but had not wanted to intrude on my conversation with her son, who was, after all, the *jūshoku* of the temple.

It is worth noting that most scholars of Buddhism, if they take into consideration the activities of contemporary temples at all, would likely be content with obtaining the *jūshoku*'s account of things. Certainly, Akira's activities at Muryōji could be analyzed under the rubric of what John K. Nelson has termed "Experimental Buddhism" in his book of the same name (Nelson 2013). Akira is in some respects innovative, independent-minded, and open to new means of transmitting Buddhism to people who might not visit Buddhist temples for the usual reasons of family affiliation. By his own account, however, he is not an outlying modernizer who sees Buddhism in individualistic, commodified terms: as revealed in my interview with him, it is from the continuity of his family line and their long-running connection to the temple and the parishioner families affiliated with it that he derives purpose from his vocation as a Buddhist priest.

In this book, I wanted to go even further by asking what Buddhism looks like if we do not put male priests at the center of our story at all. While the women in the temple family may be less visible to scholars, they also have an important story to tell. I took Akira up on his offer to introduce me to his mother and was rewarded with another rich account of the meaning of life in a temple, the home of the Buddha.

Naoko

A month after I met Akira for the first time, I sat down with Naoko, sixty-eight years old, and her daughter-in-law, Hiroko, for an hour-long interview. Akira came in and out of the receiving room where we sat, occasionally tending to temple business, but also wanting to hear what his mother had to say. Naoko, who was diminutive in stature but formidable in spirit, with close-cropped hair and a strong dialect, was talkative, especially about her deceased husband and in-laws.

Naoko had grown up in a Jōdo Shinshū temple in Shimane Prefecture, several hours west of Kobe. She was a distant relative of her husband, and when she visited Kobe for an arranged meeting with another temple son, she happened to stop by his temple for a visit. They got along so well that his mother called her parents right away to ask if she might be willing to move in. During their five years of marriage she bore two sons before he suddenly fell ill; it was cancer. While her husband was in the hospital, he asked her to take care of the daily work of the temple. He said he would still perform the major events like funerals. But, in order for her to do the monthly home visits, he said, she would need to take *tokudo*. "So I would sit at his bedside," she explained, "and he would give me lessons to prepare me for ordination. Of course it wasn't my first time reading the *Amidakyō* or the *Shōshinge*[4]—I had known them since I was small—but my delivery was not perfect. He would tease me, 'The old parishioner ladies can recite them better than you!'" After receiving treatments for over a year, her husband succumbed to his disease. "That was the beginning of my real life," Naoko told me with a knowing smile.

After her husband died, Naoko was left in the temple with her mother-in-law, grandmother-in-law, and her two young sons, who were three and five years old at the time. She had promised her husband that she would make sure the temple continued, and she recalls telling her in-laws, "I am young and healthy, so I will handle the manual labor and outside work, like visiting parishioners' homes. You two can stay at home and do the housework." Their reply, she said, was "Don't be stupid." Customarily, the daughter-in-law in a Japanese family takes care of the housekeeping and food preparation. Having their young daughter-in-law go out of the temple dressed in masculine priests' robes would be an awkward embarrassment for the two older women.

Realizing that these two women could not be relied upon to help out, Naoko tried asking for help from neighboring priests. The most common practice in this kind of situation, she explained, was to impose upon another male relative, or perhaps the *jūshoku* of a nearby temple, to become the temple's proxy resident priest (*daimu jūshoku*). But all the surrounding temples in their area were too busy at that time, she said, and none of the other priests were willing or able to take on the work of another temple. So she decided to handle both the outside and the inside work all on her own. She picked up the robes and began performing monthly home visits and other services. "Technically you need a *kyōshi* (religious instructor) degree to run the temple," she said, "but in my own mind, I had made that promise to my husband." For these actions, she claims, the only ones to criticize her were her own in-laws: the two elderly women told anyone who would listen that she was running the temple without the proper credentials.

Word of her situation got around to her husband's good friend, a priest who occasionally lectured at Ōtani-ha's Kyoto seminary. He advised her that she needed to obtain full ordination: "The temple is an organization (*soshiki*); if you don't have credentials, you won't get anywhere," he told her. He brought her an application and made sure she was admitted on an emergency basis. Though Naoko had been thinking primarily of her duty to her husband, this friend chastened her to consider the larger picture, such as the parishioners and the Buddhist sect, to whom the temple also belonged.

When she began studying doctrine formally for the first time, Naoko's life, and her troubled relationship with her in-laws, began to make sense in light of Buddhism. "All the while I had thought of my in-laws as demons, but in the end, I put my hands together [in gratitude] and thought, 'That was the Buddha. That was the Tathāgata. Even though they broke their bones raising and educating me, I unfairly badmouthed them....' It was all because my husband fell ill that I had that opportunity to study the teachings," she noted.

Naoko's narrative strategy of spinning her difficult experiences into a single causal thread—Amida's compassionate action—is a common one in the Jōdo Shinshū, as we shall see in the ensuing chapters.

Other patterns common among temple families emerge from Naoko's story: for instance, her duty to her husband had compelled her to act outside of official parameters to continue running the temple. This is much less rare than we might think, and it demonstrates the practical fluidity of clerical labor within the temple family, as the absence of her husband had qualified her to act as priest, even though she lacked ordination at first. Also, the conservative, critical response to her transgression of gender roles came from the older women in her family rather than from men. This is our first glimpse of the strict hierarchy that exists among the multiple generations of women in temple households. With the intervention of male authorities—and out of obligation rather than individual desire—Naoko attended seminary, where she encountered a framework of meaning that turned her hardship into a learning experience (in Shin Buddhist terms, "a teacher"), which Amida had put in her path. After successfully obtaining her kyōshi degree, she registered herself as the temple's proxy resident priest (daimu jūshoku), and remained so for the next twenty years. At the same time she also acted as the bōmori, taking a turn as the leader of her neighborhood bōmori association and inviting teachers she had had at seminary to give lectures to the other temple wives.

I asked Naoko, as a bōmori born in 1940 who had played both the male and female clerical roles at the temple, what she thought of the Ōtani-ha debates about the definition of bōmori and the question of whether the role of bōmori should be opened up to men as well as women. She replied: "According to the sect, depending on the situation a man could be a bōmori and a woman could be a jūshoku.... But from the parishioners' perspective, these two [figures] are in the position of a mother and a father. We call them jūshoku and bōmori, but the jūshoku is the father, the older brother. The bōmori is the mother, the older sister. Because of that, my way of life is that of a bōmori."

In Naoko's view, because of the intimacy that exists between temple family members and their parishioners, while gender-specific wording might be deleted from the sect's bylaws, gender could never be removed from their personal relationships with the laity. Even though she had felt empowered to act as a jūshoku without credentials, this empowerment had taken place firmly in the context of her family relationship to the temple and her promise to her dying husband. Because she is a woman, her relationships with parishioners will always have the quality of how one relates to a woman. At the end of the day, regardless of whatever concrete duties she engages in at the temple—whether it is performing rituals, cleaning, or giving sermons—she categorizes herself as a bōmori, which she understands to be a female temple professional.

We should recall that Naoko was born before World War II and was "broken in" as a young daughter-in-law by two women who, she is always quick to point out, were "Meiji women"; in other words, they were born during the Meiji period and had more conservative views of social roles. What, then, I asked her, was the job of a *bōmori?* Naoko replied:

> It is to place your body in the temple and receive people, to the best of your ability. When we do things like cleaning or dusting, we think, "Oh, I'm dusty too" and we wipe it clean. "There, I got a bit of it." Like with polishing too, when we make something shine, we make ourselves shine too. The difference between a temple and a family business is, in the end, that we are allowed to live in the Buddha's temple. So it's important that we do things like protect the Buddha and always keep the Buddha's home clean.

Many *bōmori* of Naoko's generation whom I interviewed echoed her sense of religious vocation as something that that accompanied domestic life in the temple. They frequently mentioned that they were blessed to live in the Buddha's home, that their domestic labor related to their spiritual awareness, and they used similar gendered, familial analogies for the respective roles of *jūshoku* and *bōmori*. Naoko had given me so much to think about, and I had exhausted all of the questions I had prepared for this interview. So, somewhat abruptly—still turning over Naoko's rich responses in my mind—I turned to her daughter-in-law.

Hiroko

"What is your role at the temple?" I asked, and even as I heard the words leave my mouth I realized that they might inadvertently have the effect of exposing young Hiroko's inexperience and her naïve relationship to the temple, in stark contrast to her mother-in-law's decades of difficult service.

"Well, I really don't do anything at the temple," she started, and then began to cry. Her mother and I waited in silence for a full minute while she composed herself. "My mother here has done so much for the temple, her whole life. And I really don't know the first thing. She has been really kind to me, just showing me how to do the simple things, like arranging the flowers for the altar. But it's so superficial. I really don't know the first thing."

Akira's wife Hiroko was modest. With a kind smile and a quiet manner, she was adept at making one feel at home and yet deflecting all attention from herself. This made it a challenge for me to discover her role at the temple and how she felt about it. Eventually I gathered that she had grown up in a lay household in Mie Prefecture outside the industrial city of Nagoya. After graduating from college and living abroad in the United States for a year, she had originally come to Kobe to begin work as a physical therapist, for which she had obtained her degree. Before long, she met Akira through some mutual friends. She thought his living in a temple was very exotic, the temple having a flavor of "traditional" Japan, and she was drawn to that kind of atmosphere. Still, she was reluctant to speak directly about her relationship to Buddhism. After my initial clumsy attempt to inquire about her activities head-on, I realized I would have to be subtler in observing her role going forward.

In November 2010, over a year after I first met the Nagai family, I brought my one-year-old daughter with me to attend their temple's *hō-onkō* service, an annual ritual of gratitude for the Jōdo Shinshū's founder, Shinran. Muryōji's service was a one-day event beginning with a puppet show for children to attend in the morning (Akira had invited the local boy scout troop, of which he had been a member when he was young). The ritual itself would last about forty-five minutes, and would be followed by a sermon, lasting another thirty. Finally the attendees would file into the multipurpose room for the afternoon vegetarian meal known as *otoki*.

Akira performed the liturgy by himself in colorful robes and then exited the *hondō* through the back of the altar. For a few moments, the crowd of about thirty laypeople sat still, waiting patiently for the dharma lecturer to enter. Instead, Akira reemerged dressed in the simple black robes and clerical collar (*origesa*) that he would wear for the rest of the day. He explained to the attendees that the *hō-onkō* ceremony was now over and his wife Hiroko would lead them in stretching, just as she had done after the fall equinox ceremony. He asked the elderly audience members if they would like to do the stretching before or after the dharma talk. The old ladies smiled, looked downward, and demurred, but then finally volunteered that they would like to do the stretching now.

Then Hiroko entered the *hondō*, bringing a chair for herself up front and looking more confident this time than she had at the *ohigan* service I had attended the month before, where she had premiered her stretching routine. She announced that she had heard from a few people that they had specific ailments, so she was going to concentrate on those parts of the body. Also, she would do fewer stretches this time, as per requests. She gave lucid, simple explanations of what causes certain aches and pains and guided the audience through four different stretches of legs, shoulders, and neck. When she had finished, the atmosphere in the *hondō* was palpably relaxed and refreshed.

After the dharma talk by the visiting lecturer, the attendees filed into the multipurpose room, where box lunches were laid out on tables awaiting them. The members of the temple family sat down and, once the laypeople were settled, Akira led everyone in the pre-meal prayer (*shokuzen no kotoba*), the words of which were posted on the wall behind him.

Akira was seated next to a father of one of the boy scouts. The man was not a regular attendee of the temple, and as everyone began to eat he asked the *jūshoku* some questions about how one becomes a priest. Akira began by explaining the process of ordination, from *tokudo* to *kyōshi*, followed by *jūshoku* training. The conversation then turned to inheriting the family business, which the man said he had done too. The man remarked that, basically, all the kids had gotten together and decided who would take over. "I lost," he laughed. Akira agreed with a smile, "I lost too!" He confided to the man that he had not wanted to become a priest, and in fact the salary had been better at his old job. The man looked surprised at this and unsure of how to respond. Akira pointed out that his wife, who was sitting across the table, had had a different path to her profession. She had only wanted to do one thing since she was young, and that was to become a physical therapist. The man asked Hiroko, "but surely your parents urged you toward that career?" She shook her head: she had just seen a book when she was younger, and had done everything since she was in middle school to pursue that path. On the other hand, Akira had worked at several different jobs in his youth before entering the priesthood as his family had wanted him to.

Although no one at the table commented on it, the irony was clear: Akira had landed in a job that he never wanted, while his wife Hiroko, who had always been sure of what she wanted to do, had now had to give up her career. At this point, her hiatus from work was attributed to the need for her to stay at home with the young children, but as I continued to talk to the Nagais about their activities at the temple, it eventually became clear that the temple would keep Hiroko busy enough that she would never be at her leisure to work in an outside job again.[5]

Back at the *otoki* table, I sat finishing my meal with my daughter on my lap, hoping she would not get too tired before I was able to collect a few more observations. Hiroko's daughters, now two and four years old, sat next to us, with Hiroko on the other side. She leaned over her daughters and delivered the news to me in a low voice that she was expecting another child. "Wonderful!" I congratulated her. "When?"

She patted her stomach, beaming. "In the spring." Her due date was five months away. I looked at her two spirited and even rambunctious girls, stuffing rice balls wrapped in seaweed into their mouths and picking up large pieces of boiled eggs and tofu with their chopsticks, and then I glanced across the table at their father, thinking of his conversation about the family business. In a Japanese family having three children is unusual. They did not say so, but I assumed that on some level they were hoping for a boy.

Hiroko's experience reminds us that, along with other roles such as housewife, event coordinator, hostess, accountant, scheduler, home economist, listener-counselor, and sometimes priest, *bōmori* are also the mothers of the temple successor. Their actions as mothers—both in giving birth to the successor and in raising him to take over the temple—have important implications for the continuity of the temple community. The Shin sects themselves are keenly aware that temple succession is key to the survival of the institution. The records of a roundtable discussion among temple children who were attending Ryukoku University (affiliated with Nishi Honganji) were published in a 1977 issue of the Honganji-ha's *Shūhō* magazine under the title "Born in a Temple" (Otera ni umarete). The moderator of the panel writes: "At each of the more than 10,000 temples [in the Honganji-ha], the temple successor must be dealing with sorrows and difficulties, and becoming resolved. It is the job of both the temple family and the sect to help him with this" (p. 17). The sects' guidance to temple families in this regard is geared less toward the biological dimension of women's reproductive labor (for example, by urging women to give birth to sons) and more toward the social dimension, that of childrearing. In workshops and published literature, the institution works to give temple wives the tools to persuade their children of their obligation toward the temple and the Buddha. Lecturers and leaders of training sessions provide temple mothers with a childrearing narrative that envisages children as the beneficiaries of the gifts of the Buddha. Once the debt is recognized, the son (or daughter) will want to repay it by protecting the temple for another generation. This had been Naoko's strategy with Akira when she had allowed him to pursue various secular jobs in his early twenties before taking over the temple. In his case it had certainly worked.

The following spring, Chie-chan was born: a third girl. When I visited the Nagai family two years later, in the summer before I was to begin a new academic post back in the United States, the girls were growing bigger and the roles in their household were beginning to shift. Akiko was now eight, Saya was six, and little Chie had grown into a vivacious two-year-old who bore a strong resemblance to both of her sisters, though she had to struggle to keep up with their unending antics.

Hiroko continued to keep a low profile at the temple, providing support to her husband, mother-in-law, and lively daughters. However, Akira's mother Naoko had lost some mobility due to a hip injury, which had required Hiroko to take over more and more of the temple work over the course of the two years that I had been back in the United States. She was having a much busier time of it than when I had seen her last: she was now handling all the daily deliveries, cleaning, and scheduling during weekdays at the temple, and of course taking the lead in preparing for the five major ritual events the temple hosted throughout the year. Nonetheless, she was unable to get her youngest daughter, now a trouble-seeking toddler, admitted into the public nursery school because, when filling out the city's application forms, she was told she had to check the box for *shufu* (housewife) as she was not truly employed.

Privately, Hiroko begged to disagree, telling me with some annoyance, "But I do have a job!"

She also finally admitted to being an appropriate interview subject for my research. In a Facebook message I received from her recently, Hiroko wrote excitedly, "Jessie, I am finally doing the temple work. It is so hard!"

From these brief snapshots of encounters that took place over the course of five years during Hiroko's early career as a *bōmori*, we can observe some of her transformation from a young wife who claimed complete ignorance and inauthenticity as a temple professional, into a quiet assistant at the temple who made use of her credentials as a physical therapist by leading therapeutic exercises for the elderly parishioners, and finally into a "working mother" who struggled to balance the demands of parenting three children with the work of hosting visitors, cleaning the sprawling temple complex, and helping her husband and lay volunteers to prepare for major events.

Akiko

In the summer of 2016, I returned to Japan with my family for the first time in three years. As soon as we were settled, we headed to the Nagai family's temple for a barbecue. Their oldest daughter, Akiko, now a confident and energetic ten-year-old, had been too impatient to wait idly inside for our arrival and was standing on the street corner, peering down the road for us. As soon she spotted us, she ran to meet us and skipped beside us back to the temple, fawning over my blonde four-year-old son and greeting my daughter warmly in Japanese, then more tentatively trying the English she had begun studying with her after-school tutor. Later that evening, over beer and grilled vegetables in the temple courtyard, her mother Hiroko told me about Akiko's ordination the previous summer. At the age of nine (the same age Shinran was when he ordained) Akiko had attended the one-day study retreat and taken the chanting exam before undergoing the *tokudo* ordination ceremony at Higashi Honganji. She had been resistant, Hiroko confided, because she did not have any friends attending the ceremony or the one-day training before it: nearly all the participants were temple sons rather than daughters. Hiroko and Akira had coaxed her to participate by promising her that she could have her own room once she was an ordained priest. Because Akiko does not like to fail, her mother explained, she had worked hard and successfully completed the chanting exam.

A few weeks after the barbecue, I attended Muryōji's *obon* ritual in mid-August. Saya and Chie, now eight and five years old, sat in the front row of the audience and were eagerly showing my daughter how to hold her prayer beads and find the correct page of her children's liturgy book. Akiko, for the second time since her ordination, donned her black robes and priestly collar and joined her father in the ritual performance. After the brief introduction by the lay leader regarding the contents of the liturgy and the page numbers in the liturgy books, Akiko followed her father as he emerged from behind the inner altar and took her place on the opposite side of the altar from him. Sitting *seiza* (on her knees), she quietly and falteringly intoned the sutra and passage from Shinran's *Shōshinge,* hiding her voice well below her father's more confident chanting. Akiko is now poised to become the future face of her family's temple, the twenty-third *jūshoku* of Muryōji temple with the last name "Nagai."

This glimpse into the life and family dynamics of the Nagai family should give the reader a sense of the approach I take in this book. My study begins by asking questions not of Buddhist texts but of Buddhist actors. Adopting an ethnographic perspective reveals other centers of gravity at Buddhist temples beyond the Buddhist altar where liturgy and sermons are performed. The receiving room where visiting preachers are hosted, the temple kitchen where the vegetarian meal is served, and of course the family's adjoining residence are all important sites for the making of religious professionals and the transmitting of Buddhist tradition in the contemporary Jōdo Shinshū. Each of the themes introduced in this profile of the Nagai family—the gendered religious labor performed by *bōmori* as the stay-at-home mother or wife (chapter 2), the stewardship of the temple precincts and material possessions as expressions of Shin Buddhist piety (chapter 3), the possibility of wives or widows stepping in to perform priestly duties in their husband's absence (chapter 4), the acculturation of a lay-born daughter-in-law to the life and work of running a temple (chapter 5), and the question of updating roles at the temple to align with modern ideals of gender equality (chapter 6)—will be explored in more depth in the chapters that follow.

But there is also analytic value in recounting all of the family members' stories in one place: we can view the various temple professionals at different stages of their Buddhist careers, careers that take shape largely in the matrix of domestic life. This collective profile of the Nagai family's clerical life reveals that family relationships, as the connective tissue of community and clerical continuity from one generation to the next, are never far from the picture of Buddhism in contemporary Japan. It also demonstrates that beginning and ending our understanding of temple Buddhism with the male priest leaves much out of the picture. The subsequent chapters focus on more feminized modes of religiosity in order to address this glaring lacuna in our understanding of temple life in Japan.

Staying at Home as Buddhist Propagation

The Domestic Life of the Temple

WHEN I ASKED SACHIKO, A SIXTY-ONE-YEAR-OLD TEMPLE wife in western Japan, to help me create an outline of a typical *bōmori*'s day, she deferred. "There really is no typical *bōmori,* and I'm definitely not one." To prove her point she invited two of her peers, one in her forties and one in her fifties, from her urban neighborhood to help answer my questions. As we gathered around her kitchen table, over frequent protests that they were really just like housewives in any other family, the three women helped me to construct an outline of an "average" *bōmori*'s day. Despite some individual variations due to family structure, the age of their children, and the nature of their husband's employment (one woman's husband worked outside the home at an administrative office [*betsuin*] of the sect), they were able to agree on the following rough outline:

6:00 a.m.	Wake up
	Cook the Buddha's rice (*buppan*) and place on altar
6:45 a.m.	Open the temple gate
7:00 a.m.	Assist with morning service
	Prepare family's breakfast and school lunches
8:00 a.m.	Clean the main hall and altar, replacing flowers as necessary
9:00 a.m.	Household cleaning (e.g., dishes, laundry)
	Priest leaves for home visits (*omairi*) or for his outside job
9 a.m.–4 p.m.	Answer the phone, receive deliveries and pay invoices
	General temple upkeep (e.g., maintaining garden, preparing facilities for hosted community events)

Receive parishioner visitors

Office work (e.g., keeping the priest's schedule, temple accounting)

Care for elderly in-laws

Involvements outside the temple (PTA, volunteer groups, *bōmori* association activities)

Early evening   Care for children after school, prepare dinner for family

Looking over this daily schedule, one realizes how difficult it would be to divide the *bōmori*'s domestic activities from her duties related to temple operations. In other words, the *bōmori*'s daily routine, like other aspects of her life, resists easy categorization according to binaries like "sacred" and "profane."

This chapter focuses on the mundane activities of *bōmori* in order to bring attention to the permeability of the boundary between home and temple. By examining the construction of home and domesticity in Japanese society and in Shin Buddhism with an eye to the gendered division of labor at the temple, I identify a form of Buddhist propagation (*kyōka*) that has not garnered much scholarly attention but has been performed by women at temples all over Japan for centuries—that of Buddhist hospitality. Many of my informants feel, and are told, that the imperative of maintaining an open and inviting temple requires the temple wife's constant physical presence at home, so that she may provide hospitality when a guest appears.

A growing body of scholarship has shown how gender ideology may be materialized and negotiated in spatial terms (Massey 1994; Munro and Madigan 1999; Sand 2003; and Ronald 2011). As geographer Doreen Massey writes, "spaces and places are not only themselves gendered but, in their being so, they both reflect and affect the ways in which gender is constructed and understood" (1994, p. 179). The dual nature of the *bōmori*'s position—as both a religious and a domestic professional—plays out in the gendered spaces she inhabits. Pulled at once between the main hall (*hondō*), where more formal religious operations are undertaken, and the kitchen (*kuri*), where the family of the priest is raised and the parishioners' food is prepared, the *bōmori* sometimes finds herself in a double bind.

Constant Presence

The name for a temple wife in the Jōdo Shinshū, *bōmori,* is a term whose characters literally mean "temple guardian." One of the first appearances of this word is in an early folk biography of Shinran. Hōnen (1133–1212), Shinran's teacher, allegedly used the phrase "peerless bōmori" (*ruinaku bōmori*) to describe Shinran's mythical wife, Tamahi (Endō 2000, p. 25). At around the same time as this legend was circulating, it was also used as a term for the female half of the married couple who led early Shin congregations: the male was the *bōzu* (literally, "temple master," still a common term for monk) and the female was the *bōmori*. Today the sense of the *bōmori*'s underlying duty to "guard" or "protect" the temple is quite strong among temple wives, their husbands, their parishioners, and the administrators of the sect. The literal meaning of the characters "guardian of the temple" are often used to justify this.

But what does it mean, concretely, to "guard the temple"? I found from my fieldwork that primarily the temple must be protected from being empty. The notion that the Shinshū temple, whose historical antecedent is the lay-based congregation (*dōjō*) rather than the monasteries found in the non-Shin Buddhist sects, should be an open place where parishioners are always welcome is a strongly held ideal among temple families and laity alike. The consequence of this ideal is that a human presence is required at all times, most basically to protect the unlocked temple from material loss, but also to provide an opportunity for human connections to be made. No matter how insignificant they may seem, such interpersonal connections or simply an affinity with the temple space could translate into *en,* or the karmic conditions for the attainment of faith. In this sense, without a constant human presence the temple would not be fulfilling its function as a religious space.

The fact that *bōmori,* of all the temple family members, are seen as the most appropriate candidates for the "stay-at-home" (*rusuban*) role is the result of the gender norms forged over the past few centuries in Japan. As I have outlined elsewhere, early modern sermonizers had already interpreted the *bōmori*'s sphere as being inside the home (Starling 2012), and prescriptive accounts of the *bōmori*'s position from the Meiji period onward have portrayed her as an embodiment of the "good wife, wise mother" feminine ideal (Starling 2013). This paradigm, which was part of the state's strategy for dividing the labor of Japan's modernizing society along gender lines, assigned women the task of running the household and raising the children—in other words, performing the reproductive labor of society.[1] Kathleen Uno and others have cautioned that, while the linking of masculinity to laboring outside the home and femininity to managing the domestic sphere may seem clearcut in the prescriptive literature, the actual division of labor has surely varied widely by class and household structure (Uno 1991). Nonetheless, the normative definitions of femininity and masculinity are stitched into the social and economic structures of modern Japan, and gender ideals established in the Meiji period continue to hold sway even in the postwar period (see, for instance, Hidaka 2011 and Goldstein-Gidoni 2012). As a result, many older or rural *bōmori* especially feel that staying at home for a majority of the time is their overriding duty as temple guardians. This is certainly the case for Michiko Higashi, a *bōmori* in her late seventies whom I interviewed in her small rural temple in western Japan.

In her youth, Michiko was a track star, winning all the local and regional races. (I learned this from some of her neighbors in town, as she does not boast of it herself.) But in recent years her legs have given out, making it painful for her even to sit on the floor, and she suffers from high blood pressure. Her life is primarily lived within a radius of a few hundred yards from the temple; the grocery store where she does her shopping is just a few blocks away, and she does not have much business anywhere else. Some fifty years ago when she was in her twenties, she attended the ten-day training retreat at Nishi Honganji to receive her initial ordination (*tokudo*), but she has little memory of it now. There is no active temple wife association (*bōmori kai*) in this region as there are in some areas, and hers is the only Jōdo Shinshū temple in her town, so she has no community of *bōmori* peers to speak of. She primarily interacts with her own neighbors, who are also her parishioners. Once a year or so she joins her husband and a group of her parishioners on a pilgrimage to Nishi Honganji temple in Kyoto, three hours away by chartered bus.

On my first visit to her temple, Michiko was the last to enter the room where I sat in a low chair, chatting with her husband. She had been in the kitchen preparing black tea for us, and finally labored in with a visibly impaired gait, placing the tray on the table next to me and arranging cups of tea in front of me, her husband, and herself (although hers would remain untouched). As we talked, she answered my questions plainly, and usually self-effacingly, patiently explaining everyday temple concepts to this foreign researcher. Any time I would ask about what a *bōmori* does, she would insist that she was just like any other housewife, with the exception that her lifestyle and movements were somewhat restricted by the ubiquitous eyes and expectations of her parishioners.

Her temple, well known locally for the gorgeous blossoms of its massive plum tree, is lodged against a hill roughly a hundred yards from the harbor in a sleepy fishing town. Although tourists occasionally come through the area and stay in one of the seaside pensions in the surrounding inlets, here in the old downtown the aging and dwindling local population maintains a quiet and familiar atmosphere. In such a small town, Michiko explained to me, you have to know and greet and respond to the parishioners all the time. She sees them at the grocery store, around town, and pretty much anytime she goes outside. She is always the "*bōmori-san*" to them, she reports, so she really has no privacy. She grew up in this temple (her husband, the younger son of a temple family in Kyoto, was adopted into her family as the successor when they got married), so she knows all of the parishioners' names and faces very well. She lamented that her own son and daughter-in-law are not as familiar with the parishioners as they live across town now, but they eventually will move back to the temple when the elder Higashis retire. "The younger generation doesn't have the same manners about living in the temple as we do. Just look at my son, and you'll see that. He has a different way of doing things. I try not to say anything about it, because it will be his job soon. But I do worry about how much his wife will help out. She doesn't seem interested. We keep telling them we're going to retire soon, but they keep saying, 'Give it just one more year,' or, 'Just two more years.'"

Throughout our interview, Michiko repeatedly brought up the fact that it was hard for her ever to leave the temple. "People around here would complain if I left the temple unattended," she observed. "In fact, the few times they have called at the temple and no one answered, for whatever reason, they did complain to my husband later." Her parents were always very insistent on this when she was growing up, she explains. "Never leave the temple unattended," they would tell her. "People can't come in if you're not there." I asked the Higashis if anyone else could help out by looking after the temple when they needed to go out. They could hire a third person to stay home when they were out, she and her husband agreed, but they would not have direct communication with the laity that way. The stay-at-home party would just be like an answering machine—they would just have to tell the parishioner "Yes, I'll tell the *jūshoku* that"—and Mr. Higashi would feel bad for the parishioners in that situation.

Michiko's husband offered his opinion about the importance of his wife's role: "First of all, it is much easier to talk to a woman than a man, and that is important to our parishioners. You know, the home (*katei*) is important. Men move about (*ugoku*), but women are important at home."

"It's like that everywhere, though," interjected his wife, "Not just at the temple."

"Propagation activities (*kyōka katsudō*) are important to what we do at the temple," Mr. Higashi continued, "but it can't just be the *jūshoku*. The *bōmori* has to do it too." By this, he apparently meant propagation activities that did not require her to "move about." In other words, by providing a constant and inviting human presence at the temple, and by being an accessible and good listener to the laypeople who visited it, she could promote connections (*en*) between the laity and the temple in ways befitting a housewife.

I asked what Michiko did when parishioners dropped by, and she answered that she would simply serve them tea. This was when people would often talk to her, usually wanting to tell her about their problems. She always tried her best to put out tea when someone came to the temple, although recently, with her ailing legs and back, she has often thought about stopping this. "Just let them come without hosting them, I say—they can still come and visit the altar. But in this town people would complain," she explained. I asked her if she tried to talk to parishioners about the Shinshū teachings on these occasions, and she quickly demurred. "I don't know much about that. I usually just listen to whatever they want to talk about." Finally, after about twenty minutes of patiently cooperating with my interview, Michiko excused herself. "My husband knows everything that I know. If you don't mind, I have to take this chance while he is at home to go out and do my shopping. I can't leave when he is out, you see."

There is much to unpack in this exchange between Mr. and Mrs. Higashi. In some respects, they echo the gendered division of labor propounded by the Japanese state since the Meiji period. Mr. Higashi's understanding that men move about in society while women are active in the home echoes Meiji-period gender discourse nearly verbatim. In the Shin Buddhist world, in publications such as the Buddhist women's journal *Katei,* for instance, one finds the following 1902 commentary on women's responsibility for running the home as if it were "a small society."

> The home is certainly a small society. If the lead actor [the husband] is the Prime Minister and the Foreign Minister, then the wife is the Minister of Education and Domestic Affairs. The country has responsibility for the education of citizens and at the same time the housewife must take care of the home economics and the education of the children; it is precisely by being an individual in the "small society" that she must contribute to the "great society." The men must be active in the broader society, and so the women have responsibility for everything in the home.[2]

In the Meiji period and thereafter, masculinity in Japan has been pinned to a husband's role as breadwinner. As recently as 1989, 85 percent of Japanese families were found to agree with the statement that "men should be out working, women should be in the home."[3] This "hegemonic form of masculinity" in postwar Japan has been embodied by the figure of the corporate salary man (*salariman*) (Hidaka 2011, p. 112). Recent anthropological scholarship has revealed increasing contestation of these roles, by both men and women, with mixed results.[4] In temple families, however, the gendered division of labor remains relatively entrenched.

For male *jūshoku,* performing the masculine role in the domestic-clerical partnership means being the one to leave the temple to perform ritual services, such as monthly visits to parishioner's homes, known as *omairi,* or to attend workshops to learn or teach about doctrine or social issues. Some temple families also require outside income to supplement their earnings from temple operations, and in these cases, too, it is the *jūshoku* who goes out to work. In these situations, the *bōmori* is left at home alone to guard the temple. When a parishioner or other visitor comes by, it is often she and not her husband who is there to receive them. Both Mr. and Mrs. Higashi seemed to affirm this gendered division of labor and space, even in their twenty-first-century temple.

In some cases, the pressure for a temple wife to stay home and refrain from working outside the temple stems from the family's economic relationship with their parishioners. For a *bōmori*—or even a temple daughter-in-law who has not yet assumed the duties of a *bōmori*—to work at a part-time job risks sending the message to parishioners that the temple family is so economically strapped (or perhaps greedy) that they must resort to sending a woman to work outside of the temple. Such was the case for an anonymous poster to the young *bōmori* message board on Mixi, a popular online social network in Japan. Although she wished to continue working after moving into her in-laws' temple, her mother-in-law would not allow it. Eventually, as the daughter-in-law lived in the temple longer and grew more sensitive to her parishioners' expectations, she came around to her mother-in-law's position: "Now, I can see what my mother-in-law was saying. Even though we're being relieved of economic hardship [by the support of the parishioners], you would hear them saying, 'Look at that young temple wife who's working out of the house!' I think she was just considering the way it would look."[5]

Much can be said about this relationship of economic and spiritual interdependency between the temple family and the laity implied in this young *bōmori*'s statement; I delve more deeply into this topic in chapter 3. Here it is most important to note that an appearance of gratitude for gifts given by the laity is achieved simply by keeping the young *bōmori* at home. Her physical presence inside rather than outside the temple makes a statement that the family is comfortable and content with the economic support provided by the parishioners.

Temple wives need not *always* stay at home, however. Now as in the past, the division of labor among temple family members can be quite fluid, so if there are more than one female family member at the temple, like a mother- and daughter-in-law, one woman may be able to go out while the other stays at home. These days, many younger or urban *bōmori* engage in numerous activities outside the temple whether or not anyone stays home, and some even brag that new technology such as call forwarding to their cell phones has allowed them to come and go more freely than their mothers' generation. Yet the ideal scenario of an unlocked temple with a constant human presence to welcome visitors looms large, and many women are apologetic for their frequent absences from the temple. My friend and informant Sachiko, who hosted the tea with her *bōmori* neighbors previously described, once joked self-deprecatingly that she should be called *sotomori,* a made-up term that would translate as "guardian of the outside," rather than *bōmori,* "guardian of the temple."

Most hospitality that a *bōmori* provides while staying at home is informal. Once when I was lunching with an informant at her temple in urban Kyoto, the doorbell buzzed no less than three times and her telephone rang twice in the span of about an hour. When the doorbell or buzzer would ring, indicating that someone had entered the temple foyer, she would excuse herself and go to the front entrance. Once she was gone for nearly fifteen minutes before darting back in to boil some water for tea. "It's a parishioner who's having a problem. I'll be just a minute," she explained. As she headed back down the hall toward the temple area, I heard her voice again. Apparently the parishioner, realizing she had company, had risen to leave. "Oh no, I'm not busy, you don't have to leave. Here, I've just made you some tea. Sit down." She returned to the kitchen ten minutes later without a mention of the parishioner, and without seeming to have missed a beat in our own conversation.

As the caretaker of the temple as a public entity, the *bōmori*'s stay-at-home responsibilities include receiving deliveries, paying contractors and vendors, and generally acting as a receptionist. More important from the perspective of her religious duty, however, are the occasions on which the call to be answered is from a parishioner. There are a few different reasons why parishioners may drop by the temple: first, they may just want to pay a visit to the Buddhist image in the main hall, dropping a coin in the coffer or lighting some incense or a candle, and perhaps offering a prayer. Second, if the temple hosts a cemetery or reliquary, they may be there to pay a visit to the remains of an ancestor.[6] In either case, the visitor may ring the bell and deliver a greeting to whatever temple family member happens to be at home. A layperson may also come by specifically to talk to someone, but more commonly conversations arise spontaneously as the tea is poured.

Encounters with the laity, in other words, arise from the *bōmori*'s simply being present. This can be seen in the following story told by a young *bōmori* at a workshop for temple daughters-in-law in Hyōgo Prefecture. She explained to her fellow participants in a small-group discussion how she had provided refuge to a troubled middle-school student who was avoiding a bully at her school:

> Once, a middle-school student came and rang the bell at the temple out of the blue. I looked outside and saw a girl dressed in the uniform of the local junior high school. She said, "I can't go to school. Can you let me stay here today?" At that time I had a little baby at home with me and I wasn't going anywhere, so I said, "Okay, why don't we talk?" Before I asked her why she couldn't go to school, I went ahead and let her inside. When I started asking her questions, she admitted she was being bullied at school, so she didn't want to go. When I asked her if her mom and dad knew about this, she

answered, "Well I told my mom about it once, but I don't want to make her worry...if I tell my mom, she'll be sad."

I was really happy that she came to the temple. We talked until the afternoon, and I worried the whole time about what to do—should I call her parents, should I contact the school? I thought, well if I can listen to her for one day, she might feel relieved. At lunchtime we had a *bentō* together. Then in the afternoon, she said, "Okay, I'm going to tell my mom, I'll tell her I spent the day at the temple." She told me where she lived, so I said, "Why don't I walk you home. I won't go in, though, you can tell her yourself." Later her mother called me, and said, "Thank you for taking care of her today."

For someone like that who had no place to go and was troubled, I'm really glad that she chose my place as a place she could come and be listened to, even though she had never been to our temple.... Rather than the temple being a place that's inaccessible, I'm really happy that she thought, "Oh, maybe I can go in there." It was one of those situations where she couldn't tell anyone who was close to her—there are times when you can help precisely because you're outside of things. I wish everyone felt that way about the temple, but it's hard to make an appeal about that. To put a sign up or something—that just seems strange. Well, not strange, I guess, but it's really hard to do that. It would be wonderful if people just thought that way about us.

This young woman's story was met with admiration and praise from the other young *bōmori* and the staff member from the sect who was leading the discussion. They congratulated her on making the temple an open place that people in the neighborhood could feel safe going to, and for making this connection with the community. However, the woman's passivity and reluctance to aggressively promote the temple or insert any talk of Buddhism directly into her conversation with the young girl is also noteworthy. This reluctance was not countered by any of the responses to her story. Temple residents share an implicit understanding that if the *bōmori,* and by extension the temple, is simply *present,* then the laity will know where to find it and at some point may seek it out. If the encounter between the laity and the temple is handled correctly, a lasting connection may be made.

Propagation in the Jōdo Shinshū: Forging Connections

Shinran (1185–1262), the founder of the Jōdo Shinshū, was skeptical about the ability of priests to effect any kind of salvation whatsoever on behalf of his followers. There is no efficacy ascribed to rituals performed by Shin priests—in other words, no merit is produced or redirected through ritual action. On his own unimportance as a priest, Shinran is quoted in the *Tannishō* as saying: "As for myself, Shinran, I do not have a single disciple. If I could make others say the *nembutsu* through my own devices, they would be my disciples. But how arrogant to claim as disciples those who live the *nembutsu* through the sole working of Amida's compassion. If the karmic condition is to come together, we shall be together; if the karmic condition is to be separated, we shall be separated" (Unno 1996, p. 9). Shinran disavows his own ability to "make" others say the *nembutsu*—or by extension, to make them attain faith—because assurance of rebirth in Amida's Pure Land is attained through the arising of true faith (*shinjin*) and nothing else. Any kind of intentional or calculated practice is rejected, and all is left to Amida's compassionate bestowal of faith on the believer as she utters the *nembutsu*.

Rennyo (1415–1499), who is known as the "restorer" or "second founder" of the Shin Buddhist institution, gives another useful formulation of Shin Buddhist soteriology. In one of his letters, Rennyo describes five conditions through which salvation occurs. First, one's karmic conditions from the past unfold in this life, allowing you to encounter the Buddhist teachings. Second, you encounter a teacher: as the dharma does not transmit itself, someone must explain it to you. Third, you are grasped by the teachings and you start to understand the truth of them. Fourth is the attainment of faith. And fifth is the urge to utter the name of Amida (the *nembutsu*) out of gratitude for your salvation. This whole process is decidedly passive on the part of the believer, and at no point is ritual intercession called for. The only need for religious professionals is so that people who are karmically disposed to listen to the teachings will have an opportunity to hear them. As Rennyo puts it, "without meeting a good teacher through the unfolding of good from the past, birth [in the Pure Land] is impossible" (Rogers and Rogers 1991, p. 187).

By viewing the temple as a physical and social space through which people's karmic conditions (*shukuen*) from the past may bring them to have a crucial encounter with Amida and the Pure Land teachings, the function of religious professionals becomes more obvious. The duties of temple residents would seem to be twofold: first, they must act in constant gratitude for and dutiful stewardship of their material blessings, as everything they have is a gift from Amida; second, they are responsible for taking care of "Amida's home," where connections between the faithful and Amida are apt to be made (or karmic connections from the past are apt to play out). The temple wife is well positioned to perform both of these functions, as we will see. The former will be explored further in chapter 3. Now I will examine how the *bōmori* works to play host to the establishment of connections between Amida and the laity.

A temple's image of Amida with *buppan* (the Buddha's rice) arranged in front of it.

The Honganji-ha's 2009 survey of the sect asked lay respondents what they wanted from their temple's *bōmori,* providing a list of activities from which they could select several that were important to them. The highest percentage of parishioners (75 percent) responded that they wanted their temple's *bōmori* to "open-heartedly receive parishioners" at the temple; 65.5 percent wanted her to "do her best to protect the temple"; and 56.2 percent wanted her to "kindly care for the parishioners."[7] From such responses, it is clear that the personal relationship between the *bōmori* and parishioners is highly valued, and that laity primarily desire the temple wife to be accessible, caring, and provide a warm reception for them at the temple.

The act of hospitably receiving the laity at the temple is an important part of the vocation of religious professionals in the Shinshū. In sermons since at least the fifteenth century, one finds that hospitality is one of the obligations of those living in the temple and one of the activities they should engage in to repay—and pay forward—the gift of faith and other blessings they have received from Amida. For instance, Rennyo is recorded as having said:

Lay followers are the most honored guests of the Founder Shinran.
Nowhere among the people of the world is there a guest so fine as
this; we must treat our laity just this honorably (Rennyo 1997, p. 607).

If we consider that even by giving a person some wine, even giving
him a single thing, his feeling of gratitude will be hastened, and it
may allow him to hear the Buddhist teachings, and allow him to
attain faith, then we can think of all of these things as our grateful
repayment of our debt to the Buddha (Rennyo 1997, p. 584).

Ideally, tea or sake or food served in the temple is not just a refresh-
ing treat but an opportunity to make the layperson feel a connection to the
temple and to Amida, and may even hasten his attainment of faith (*shinjin*). Staying at home and welcoming laypeople is both a spiritual obligation
for those who share Amida's home and a form of propagation with a potential religious benefit. This perspective helps us to understand why Michiko
Higashi would have been scolded by her mother and subjected to criticism
from the townspeople if she had blithely gone out and left the temple locked.
An empty, unattended temple represents the waste of a potentially valuable
opportunity for it to fulfill its religious mission.

In an early-nineteenth-century sermon for *bōmori,* a scholar priest
from Higashi Honganji admonished his audience of temple wives as follows:
"The first priority of the *bōmori*'s service to the Buddha and Shinran is to make
the parishioner's visit to the temple into an opportunity to hear the Buddhist
teachings—this is of the essence, and she must rush to do it" (Tokuryū 1891,
pp. 9–10). Tokuryū's urgent admonition for *bōmori* to propagate the teachings
to visiting parishioners is suggestive but somewhat ambiguous. What does it
mean to "make a visit into an opportunity to hear the teachings"? Should the
bōmori be the one to preach the dharma? Is she prepared to do so? Certainly,
in Tokuryū's time no formal religious education was available to temple wives,
although they may have learned much about the teachings from their fathers
or husbands. Recalling the story—applauded by the other religious professionals to whom it was recounted—of the young temple wife who shared a *bentō*
at the temple with the teenage victim of bullying, the ambiguity of this form of
propagation, which is decidedly passive, continues even today.

The informal pastoral role of listening to laypeople's concerns, with
or without offering advice, is usually referred to as conferring (*sōdan*). A
2009 survey conducted by Nishi Honganji asked temple parishioners to select
the kinds of problems about which they were most likely to seek advice from
temple family members. They reported going to *bōmori* to ask about funerals,
the Shinshū teachings, religious questions, and questions of etiquette. The
jūshoku's advice was as likely to be sought on these issues, but *bōmori* were

overwhelmingly preferred over *jūshoku* for problems involving family relationships or conflicts with neighbors, childrearing or education, and the like.[8]

There is obviously a substantial degree of overlap in the areas in
which these married religious professionals are consulted by parishioners.
Less obvious from the data, however, is the gendered nature of listening. In
my interviews, many informants, including *bōmori* and resident priests both
male and female, volunteered their opinion that laypeople find it easier to talk
to a woman than to a man, and are much more likely to open up to a *bōmori*
or even a female *jūshoku* than to a male priest.[9] It is a pervasive feeling among
temple residents that laypeople may find a male priest too intimidating or
may assume that he has more urgent things to do than listen to their mundane concerns. The temple wife by virtue of her gender is better suited to play
the role of religious professional in a domestic key.

Thinking of Tokuryū's entreaty to turn even a casual visit to the temple into an opportunity to hear the teachings, I often asked my informants
whether they try to use such encounters with parishioners to bring up the Shin
teachings. Nearly all said that they do not. Although most seemed to think that
they should try, many did not feel confident enough to talk about the Buddhist
teachings and would rather leave that to the *jūshoku* or a visiting preacher
who would come and give the dharma talks. The *bōmori* with whom I spoke
were largely hesitant, too, to use words like "counseling" to describe what they
do, although guidance is certainly given on occasion, and indeed counseling
and clinical psychology have recently become popular topics at neighborhood
bōmori association meetings and workshops. The overwhelming consensus
was that parishioners primarily just needed someone to listen to them.

A more assertive or educated *bōmori* may venture to bring the Shin
Buddhist teachings into her casual conversations with the laity, pointing out
lessons that Rennyo's letters or the *Tannishō,* two popular texts in the Jōdo
Shinshū, may have to offer to their condition. But the vast majority of my informants insisted that they consider themselves unqualified to "teach" parishioners anything about doctrine. However, the *bōmori*'s constant presence at the
temple, and her approachability as a wife and mother, often result in her forming closer relationships with parishioners than does her husband. Though a
bōmori may think of her parishioners as if they were a second family, it is often
noted that the temple wife should try to be somewhat careful and professional
in their company. Remaining slightly removed from the parishioners also
allows her a neutral place from which to listen to their problems and concerns.

Connecting the Inside with the Outside

Alongside, and sometimes in tension with, the stay-at-home role is the ideal
that temple wives will be leaders in the temple community and beyond. The

Honganji-ha's 2009 survey to inquire into the community involvement of *bōmori* found that roughly 10 percent hold positions in their local PTA, and 12.3 percent hold a position in some other community organization.[10] The actual number is likely higher, as only one representative per temple was able to respond to the survey, and involvements like the PTA are generally undertaken by the younger generation of *bōmori* (known as *waka bōmori*) while their mothers-in-law are young and able enough available to look after the temple in their absence. Common wisdom holds that in her capacity as a propagator for the temple and the tradition, the *bōmori* must use her identity as a woman, wife, and mother, to connect the community and the temple's parishioners in ways uniquely befitting these roles.

Within the temple community, some *bōmori* are active in hosting one of their temple's parishioner groups. As their primary method of educating the laity and bringing them to the temple outside of ritual events and funerals, most temples sponsor a number of parishioner groups (*kyōka soshiki* or "propagation groups"). These are composed primarily of the temple's registered parishioners and are often distinguished by age or sex. For example, some common groups are the Women's Association (*fujinkai*), Young Women's Association (*wakafujinkai*), Young People's Association (*seinenkai*), and the Children's Association (*kodomokai*). In recent years, the Honganji-ha administration has actively encouraged priests to form a children's group called "Kids Sangha" (*kizzu sanga*) at their local temples. Many temples in both of the major Jōdo Shinshū sects have a long-running tradition of hosting a Sunday school (*nichiyō gakkō*), which may meet once a month and is often led by the temple wife, or sometimes cooperatively by both the *bōmori* and the *jūshoku*.

The *fujinkai*, whose members are usually women over fifty, is the lifeblood of many temples. This is especially true for temples in the Honganji-ha, which boasts a strong national and even international federation of Buddhist laywomen's groups. Not only do *fujinkai* represent the most active and earnest of the temple's followers, regularly attending monthly study groups, dharma talks, and pilgrimages to the head temple in Kyoto, they also frequently comprise the base of volunteers from which the temple draws to perform much of the manual labor such as cooking and cleaning for major yearly events. The *bōmori* is the obvious point person for such groups, being a woman who is often close to the members in age. Her relationship to the *fujinkai* is often described as being very important. Although she does not usually play the role of a formal teacher (an outside lecturer is usually brought in to give talks or lead study groups), the *bōmori* will nearly always greet, host, and chat with the women at these events, and she manages their volunteer efforts on the day of major rituals. Further, if they go on a pilgrimage to the head temple in

Kyoto, or make some other kind of group trip, she will attend and will likely be instrumental in its organization.

Many *bōmori* who are involved in social causes or are seeking their own religious education outside the temple have come to feel the tension of their position acutely. In a 1995 roundtable discussion among temple wives in the Ōtani-ha, *bōmori* leader Hiroko Kondō pointed out that, although she is often congratulated on her many involvements, it is difficult for her to leave the house. She often regrets being away from the temple so much. On the other hand, what she learns from her experiences outside of the temple allows her to ground her relationships with parishioners in the Buddhist teachings. Kondō explains:

> The wife of a temple is supposed to stay in the temple, and when the parishioners come around she serves them and listens to them talk. She must listen to what kind of problems which family is having, all of that. But, if she doesn't listen with the Buddhist teachings at the base, then it's no more than "idle gossip" (*idobata kaigi*), and if she doesn't learn about various things for herself, then she can't suffer together with the parishioners. You know, she oughtn't sit in some elevated place and say, "It's like this, it's like that," dispensing of them with token responses.[11]

But *bōmori* who endeavor to expand their role beyond that of the more passive temple guardian by studying for ordination or engaging in social work or community groups, as Kondō describes, immediately encounter a conflict with the need to maintain a presence in the temple at all times. Keiko Mochizuki, a leader in the Ōtani-ha's women's movement of the 1990s, once confronted the head of her district's parishioner association (*montokai*) about his contradictory expectations for *bōmori:* "He said he wants the *bōmori* to be there in the temple. I asked him if that meant it was okay for the *bōmori* not to study, and he said no, I want her to study. I told him she can't study if she stays at home—but in the end the parishioners do think of the *bōmori* as someone who stays in the temple" (Mochizuki 2006, p. 132).

Mochizuki's account recalls an underlying contradiction found in Shin Buddhist rhetoric regarding the role of *bōmori* dating back to the Edo period. *Bōmori* are idealized as temple professionals who may lead the laity in studying and listening to the teachings, occasionally serving as religious instructors themselves. But they are also expected to provide a constant welcoming presence at the temple, a requirement that severely restricts their ability to cultivate themselves for a teaching role.

Hospitality at Yearly Rituals

The gendering of religious labor never appears more clearly than it does on the day of a major ritual event.[12] In particular, what some have called the "front and back regions" of the social world of the temple become strikingly evident, with women operating in the latter and men in the former (Giddens 1984; Orsi 1996; Munro and Madigan 1999). The notion of the parishioners' shared ownership of the temple space is exemplified when it comes time for a major event, as the lay volunteers prove to be the unseen oars that propel the event forward. As I will show, this voluntary labor is as gendered as that of the religious professionals themselves. Often one or more layperson acts as an officially appointed helper (*sewakata*), liaising between the temple family and the lay guests, the assisting priests, and the visiting preacher who will deliver the dharma talk after the ritual. The *bōmori* is frequently the manager of these volunteers' efforts, directing the traffic of people, robes, candles, incense, flowers, cushions, food, tea, gifts, and the like.

From a Shin Buddhist doctrinal perspective, rituals are efficacious only insofar as they are opportunities for hearing the teachings. They are counted along with other propagation activities as opportunities for laity to be brought into contact with Buddhism, to utter the *nembutsu,* and to feel gratitude for the unbounded compassion of Amida. Yearly ritual events are the primary occasion for the laity to come to the temple as there are no weekly services, and most funerals and memorial services are held either at a funeral hall or in the member's home. As such, they are of the utmost importance in connecting the laity to the temple. It is for this reason that so much emphasis is often placed on the *otoki* or communal meal that they will be served. Many temples incorporate an *otoki* of some kind into all the yearly events on their ritual calendar, but it is a centerpiece of the *hō-onkō* celebration. The *hō-onkō* ceremony is unique to the Shinshū, and, as a ceremony of gratitude to the founder Shinran, is the most important yearly event for most temples.[13]

On the day of any major ritual, it is generally expected that the *bōmori* will be in charge of coordinating most aspects of the event that do not take place on the ritual stage (though, of course, she has frequently helped to clean and prepare the altar too, before the day of the ritual). Primarily, her work entails reception of visitors. While it may sound like a simple task, an extended episode from my fieldwork will illustrate the dizzying complexity of the hospitality that takes place at the temple on the day of a ritual. The following event, which took place in a rural temple in Niigata Prefecture in northwest Japan, illustrates the multiple layers of "guests" that the hosting temple family must receive on such an occasion, and also the competing pressures that a *bōmori* may feel as a domestic religious professional on these event days.

Hō-onkō *at a Rural Temple*

I first met Rina Terasaki, thirty-four at the time, in Kyoto at an event in anticipation of Shinran's 750th memorial celebration in October 2010. We were similar in age, and after exchanging only shy greetings during the first few meetings of our volunteer activity, we finally found some time to talk on a long bus ride up to Mount Hiei, where our group would be taking a hike to revisit some of Shinran's places of practice before he had left the Tendai monastic center there. Rina has a knowing, friendly countenance, and like other temple women, she dresses sensibly, usually wearing hiking shoes or otherwise comfortable footwear, nothing flashy or expensive. She wears little to no makeup and does not dye or style her hair, preferring to wear it pulled back in a simple ponytail. In addition to her warm and quiet demeanor, she also has a keen sense of humor. She was often slow to answer my questions, pausing pensively before speaking, and sometimes again in the middle of a sentence. At the time I met her, she was living in her husband's family's temple in the Kansai region, but she repeatedly described with great fondness the large rural temple in Niigata Prefecture near the Sea of Japan where she had grown up. Upon learning about my research interests, she insisted that I join her for the *hō-onkō* event at her home temple that summer.

The timing of the *hō-onkō* is determined by each temple, depending on the convenience of their parishioners and the availability of nearby priests to assist with the ritual performance. The sects' respective head temples (Nishi Honganji and Higashi Honganji) hold their *hō-onkō* events in November, December, and January, and this is generally considered the *hō-onkō* season. But in Niigata, the event is occasionally scheduled for June. According to the *bōmori* of Jōdoji, the temple whose event I describe here, this unique timing was dictated by both the region's weather and the convenience of parishioners: the majority of laypeople were farmers, and many would be busy in October with the rice harvest. After that, Niigata's snowy winter would set in, and gathering laity at the temple would be impractical. So the *hō-onkō* is held is June, with services and communal meals on three consecutive days, so that as many laity as possible can attend.

We set off in Rina's car at dusk on Friday, arriving after midnight in a medium-sized city in Niigata, where she deposited me at a hotel downtown, explaining apologetically that the rooms the temple usually used to house guests would be filled up with visiting priests and family members that weekend. She picked me up promptly at six the next morning in the midst of torrential rain, carrying an umbrella and a pair of galoshes. "It's a bit muddy out at the temple," she apologized. On the way, Rina commenced her work as my capable guide and narrator, quizzing me on each of her family members' names, which she had taught me the night before on our long drive from Kyoto.

Her mother, Kyōko, was the *bōmori* of the large rural temple, and her father was the *jūshoku*. She had two older brothers, both of whom were married and had young children. Tomonori, her thirty-five-year-old middle brother, was the assisting priest, or *fuku jūshoku*. According to Rina, he was poised to remain in this position for the rest of his life, while his older brother would eventually succeed to the head priest position. His contentment with this supporting role often drew discouragement from other temple priests and even parishioners, who thought it more appropriate for him to seek out his own temple at which he could be the primary priest. But, as Rina explained, Tomonori's wife Aiko was from a lay family and was unconvinced that she could handle becoming the *bōmori* of their own temple. Currently the couple and their two young children enjoyed living independently a few minutes away from the temple so that Aiko was able to come and immerse herself in temple work only during large events such as the *hō-onkō* and New Year's festivities. Rina's elder brother Shin'ichi was in line to inherit the temple when their father retired. His current title was the "junior resident priest," or *waka jūshoku,* and he lived in the temple together with his parents, his wife, and their two elementary-school-aged children.

When we arrived at the temple, I let myself in while Rina parked the car. To my right was the *kuri,* the traditional term for the temple kitchen. It also refers by extension to the temple family's residence, usually located on the second floor of the industrial-sized kitchen, which is used both for the temple family's private meals and for temple events. The walls of the family's dining area were lined with shelves holding all manner of serving dishes, trays, and other entertaining supplies. The family's own trinkets, maps, train schedules, children's progress reports, school and temple newsletters were pinned to the wall. Over the doorway separating the kitchen from the dining room hung six computer-printout calendars, each with a personalized picture of one of the *jūshoku*'s grandchildren. Beyond the dining area was the gigantic kitchen that was outfitted with four restaurant-sized sinks, three refrigerators, and three industrial-sized rice cookers.

Rina came in and handed me an apron still in its package, assuring me that I would be allowed to help when things heated up. As the temple family finished their breakfast, the children (Rina's nieces and nephews) began to disperse throughout the sprawling temple-home complex, excited by the presence of a foreign visitor and racing up and down the halls with their mouths still full of breakfast. Rina's father, the *jūshoku,* was around sixty years old, and as he walked through the receiving room where I sat he nodded an embarrassed greeting to me. He was still wearing his white under-robes and had a toothbrush in his mouth. Twenty minutes later he rushed through again while running an electric razor over his face. Rina's two brothers, wearing dark-blue cotton workers' robes, were also busily shuttling goods between this side of the temple complex and the main hall.

While we waited for the preparation to begin in earnest, Rina gave me a tour of the temple, introducing me to the various venues where the event would take place and to the people who would be involved. First, she took me down a long hallway, past the public bathrooms to the main hall. When we entered, Rina knelt briefly in front of the main altar and performed a few *nembutsu* before continuing our tour. The hall was vast compared to the Kyoto temples to which I was accustomed: it could probably accommodate several hundred guests, although today only about three dozen floor cushions and ten chairs (for those with knee or back problems) had been laid out for anticipated attendees of the ceremony.

The main hall was to be the venue for the most public, formal events of the day. Tomonori, who had just returned from relief work in the areas of Japan stricken by the recent Tōhoku earthquake and tsunami disaster, would give a talk at 10:00 a.m. relating his experiences in the disaster zone to the Shin Buddhist teachings. The two formal liturgies would take place at 11:00 a.m. and 3:00 p.m. At that point, a total of eight priests dressed in their formal robes of varying colors would file in and arrange themselves at both the slightly elevated inner altar (*naijin*) and the outer altar (*gejin*) to perform the *hō-onkō* liturgy, which includes a chanting performance (*shōmyō*) of various Shinshū scriptures and prayers, such as Shinran's *Shōshinge* and *Jōdo wasan,* followed by a reading of one of Rennyo's letters. During the chanting, two incense boxes would be passed around among the parishioners so each attendant could dribble some sand on top to add to the room's fragrance as they bowed their heads to the image of Amida at the center of the altar.

At the entrance, where laity would begin to enter the hall in another hour or two, a reception desk was set up for receiving and recording contributions for the ceremony. A group of male volunteers, men who formed the long-standing core group of the temple's parishioners, would kneel here to collect attendees' names and write down the amount of their contributions, giving them a receipt if requested. The contribution was voluntary, but a baseline amount was around two thousand *yen.* Many parishioners who were farmers still brought their contributions in the form of rice from their fields, the volunteers explained to me later. Some would bring money in a special envelope in addition to rice or produce from the farm. Thus, a large empty barrel had been placed at the entrance where laity could deposit their rice, and next to it bags of freshly harvested root vegetables, corn, greens, and tomatoes would accumulate throughout the day. Rina explained that in a few minutes these male volunteers would gather in the reception room to be instructed on the day's activities by the *jūshoku* and the successor *jūshoku*—although most of them had served as volunteers for many years, and little was likely to have changed. The orientation session was primarily a chance for the hosting priest to greet and serve tea and snacks in gratitude to the volunteers, who were also the lay leaders of the congregation.

At this stage I could discern two layers of guests participating in the ritual. First, the most distant from the family are those general laity who come in and give a basic contribution to attend the ritual, hear a dharma lecture, and attend the communal feast afterward. Next are the lay volunteers and congregational leaders (the designated "helpers"), both guests of the temple family and personnel who help carry out the event. They enjoy a special intimacy with the temple family due to their collaborative work in preparing, executing, and cleaning up after the event—indeed, this is recognized by a special meal served at the end of the weekend in which the volunteers are invited to dine together with the entire temple family and assisting priests; they are also owed a special debt of gratitude for their efforts.

Rina then brought me back down the hallway toward the temple family's residence and showed me the banquet room, a long room with tatami floors surrounded on two sides by floor-to-ceiling sliding glass doors overlooking the temple's garden. After the 11:00 a.m. ritual, the general attendees and male lay volunteers would file down the hallway from the main hall and settle onto floor cushions here placed there for the communal meal. They would be joined for the meal by the *bōmori* and the *jūshoku*, who would give brief greetings and thanks to the attendees, followed by a somewhat longer greeting and announcements by one of the male leaders of the congregation (usually the *sōdai,* or parishioner representative to the temple's board of trustees). All would join together in reciting the Shinshū's pre-meal prayer of gratitude (*shokuzen no kotoba*). Later, a midday dharma talk would be followed by a second performance of the ritual, and finally another, nearly identical communal meal would be served for attendees of the afternoon's events.

As Rina oriented me to all the different venues for all the various activities of the day, I began to understand what a dizzyingly complex feat of hospitality this event was. Her mother Kyōko's job was, in part, to be a welcoming hostess to all of these different kinds of guests. But we still were not finished with the tour: Rina then took me upstairs to the priests' changing room. Although the room was unoccupied at this point in the morning, there were two sets of priests' robes hanging on the wall and a long floor table where empty teacups, clean ashtrays, and packages of wet napkins had been laid out in anticipation of the arrival of the third type of guest, the assisting priests. At the morning performance of the ritual, there would be five assisting priests in addition to Rina's father and two brothers. One of these was Rina's cousin, and two were *jūshoku* of nearby temples, who were also old friends of her father. Two others were friends of Tomonori (one had joined him in the recent volunteer trip to Tōhoku). I asked if these priests were paid, and Rina said they were, discreetly, in elegant gratitude envelopes. This kind of honorarium for ritual performance is called a *hōrei*. The amount usually depended on the seniority of the priest, but also whether he had his own temple or not. Rina explained that assistant or floating priests like Tomonori relied on their income from such ritual work to support themselves, whereas those with their own temple would have other regular sources of income, and this was taken into account when determining their honorarium. However, Rina paused thoughtfully after giving me this account of the priests' compensation. "Actually, the visiting *jūshoku* usually bring us a gift too when they arrive at the temple," she noted. "Usually it is an expensive bottle of sake or something like that. I suppose it cancels out what we give them," she laughs, having considered the exchange in monetary terms for the first time, and noting its irrationality when looked at from such a perspective.

As the priests were to be served food and drink in this room before and after performing each ritual, I asked Rina who was in charge of serving them. As she began to place bottles of beer and tea in the room's refrigerator to cool, Rina paused to think before answering me. Straightening the place settings on the table while she talked, she said: "I am usually the one to serve them. I guess the other women think I have more to talk about with the priests than they would, since I have my ordination too. Actually, I think most of the women are embarrassed to come into the room with the priests. They say they are too dirty from working in the kitchen. Of course, some of the women volunteers are older, and their knees could not handle going up and down these stairs." Indeed, I joined Rina for much of the day in her hospitality duties among the male priests, and we must have scaled the harrowing stairwell leading up to the priests' room at least three dozen times, often carrying trays full of food and drink.

By 8:30 a.m. my tour was finally complete, and Rina deposited me back in the kitchen area where I would join the female lay volunteers for an intense morning of food preparation for both the morning and afternoon feasts. Rina's mother Kyōko greeted me warmly as she glided past carrying a cylindrical tower of freshly cooked rice on a brass tray down to the main hall, where she would place it on the altar in front of the Buddhist image. I sat down and unwrapped my apron, joining the eight laywomen who had already arrived. They were all housewives and seasoned *hō-onkō* volunteers who had brought their own aprons. We sat on the floor of the dining room, whose tables had been pushed back against the wall after the temple family's breakfast had been cleared. Each woman had a cup of hot green tea in front of her, and a lacquered tray of rice crackers and a plate of homemade pickles circulated among us. About twenty feet and two sets of sliding doors away in the reception room, the male volunteers were receiving their own orientation from the male members of the temple family.

Kyōko held up a diagram she had made on the blank side of a large sheet of paper discarded from the wall calendar, which showed the meal they would be preparing that day. An overhead view of the *bentō* box that would be distributed was drawn with each section labeled and numbers tallied along the side showing the number of servings for the noon and evening meals, respectively. Although she wore an apron in solidarity with the volunteers, Kyōko was dressed slightly more formally than her lay counterparts, as she would be running out to greet various guests as they arrived. The common wisdom among temple women is that *bōmori* of this midwestern region of Japan (called Hokuriku) are treated as slightly more eminent than those in other regions. In other areas, it may be more acceptable for a *bōmori* to get gritty with physical labor even on the day of a big event. On the other hand, in places such as Hokkaido, it is expected that she will sit in the front of the congregation during the ritual, holding her liturgy book and prayer beads as an example for the laity. Such variations in the image of a *bōmori*'s role at a ritual event are determined by a combination of regional, familial, and individual differences. Rina's mother exuded a warm and professional friendliness as she moved about in elegant clothing and played the part of the consummate hostess throughout the weekend. Of course, she never once stood idle, her hands full of gifts received from—or food to be served to—the temple's visitors; and at the end of the day when all of the laity had departed, she spent many hours in the kitchen washing dishes and sorting the trash after the laity and the priests had enjoyed their feasts and gone home to rest.

While Kyōko spent much of the day busily darting back and forth from one end of the temple complex to the other, the activities in the giant and bustling kitchen were directed primarily by two other women. One was a laywoman in her late eighties or early nineties who had been the unofficial head chef of the *otoki* feast for decades. She was in charge of the "flavor," and most questions concerning preparation, seasoning, and achieving the proper taste for each dish, many of which were perennial offerings, were brought to her. She was provided with a chair in the back of the kitchen, where she sat hunched over various pots of foods, squeezing the excess water from cooked spinach or peeling potatoes for the vegetable stew (*oden*). As is customary, the feast was entirely vegetarian (*shōjin ryōri*)—although the priests who supped in the changing room upstairs would be served a special plate of horse sashimi (*basashi*), a regional delicacy, as an expression of special thanks for their efforts.

The wife of the successor *jūshoku* oversaw the other logistics in the kitchen, such as plating and serving the feast. Kyōko's elder daughter-in-law's official title at the temple was *waka bōmori* or young temple wife,

Members of the *Bukkyō fujinkai* help at a temple event. Photo by Daniel Friedrich.

and she lived upstairs in the temple residence along with her husband, her three young children, and her parents-in-law. Today she carried her youngest child, a cherubic eighteen-month-old girl, strapped to her back for nearly the entire day. The younger son Tomonori's wife, Aiko, also worked alongside the other volunteers, although she was occasionally beckoned away by one of her two children, who were three and five years old, respectively. The five temple grandchildren had basically free run of the premises, although at various points when their presence became obstructive they were shooed upstairs to the residence to do homework or watch TV; this is also where they enjoyed their midday meal.

In contrast to the bustling and feminized atmosphere of the kitchen, the priests' room upstairs was a din of priestly masculinity. Cigarette smoke, boisterous laughter, and empty beer bottles would fill the room throughout the day. I helped Rina serve the priests a light snack and tea upon the arrival of each; after serving, we would usually linger and chat until a conversation that included the newest arrival had taken hold, when we would return to the kitchen to retrieve another dish or assist with the food preparation. After the performance of each ritual (morning and afternoon), the priests would file back into the room, smelling of sweat and incense, and take off the outer layers of their clerical garb as they lit up a cigarette. Beer was poured from tall bottles and sake was offered as well, although the priests usually would not drink too heavily before they had performed the final ritual in the late afternoon. Rina and I brought up a sampling of the *otoki* feast arranged in fine ceramic dishes, along with an arrangement of the aforementioned horse sashimi, and returned to the kitchen with our arms full of dirty dishes and emptied drink containers. Although none of the male priests participated in the food preparation or cleanup as far as I observed, Rina's father did wander into the kitchen at the end of the night, after the male priests had been taken out to a restaurant for their final meal of the day, and asked his wife if he could do anything. Kyōko quickly shooed him away, and he gladly left the five of us women (Rina, her mother, her two sisters-in-law, and myself) to the laborious task of garbage sorting and dishwashing.

In the process of explaining to a newcomer the events of the hō-onkō, in which she had taken part since she was a young child, Rina seemed to be seeing them in a whole new light. She would sometimes stop in mid-sentence as she noticed how clearly the labor was divided along gender lines, turn to me, and shrug apologetically: "It's not like anyone *says* the women all have to stay in the kitchen, they all just put on their aprons and go there." Or, "We don't tell the women volunteers that they have to eat standing up in the kitchen, it's just that they're embarrassed to go into the banquet room in their dirty aprons, and there aren't enough chairs in the kitchen for them to all sit down there."

The most poignant moment of this kind occurred when she tried to explain to me why she herself did not take part in the ritual performance. "Actually, I have taken ordination too. It's just that ever since we were young, my brothers just sort of took care of the ritual side of things. I used to ask my father if I could do more, if I could go with my brothers to the chanting training camp (shōmyō kōshū) at Higashi Honganji, but he said it wasn't necessary. I guess I tended to believe it when I was told things like that—I thought, 'Well, I guess it probably isn't necessary.'" Once, she made a point of joining her brothers in the service, donning robes and chanting alongside them during the Friday night performance. However, Friday is the most sparsely attended of the rituals, and she recalled there being only two laypeople in the audience. "I wanted there to be more, I wanted more people to see me doing it," she recalled. One might be tempted to ask why a woman who was so obviously conscious of gender discrepancies and wishing to expand her role at the temple would not push harder for equality within the temple family—indeed, I believe Rina expected me to question her on this issue. But after taking in the staggering complexity of hospitality that surrounded the ritual event, I was inclined to agree with her decision to remain backstage and help her mother and the other women. There was simply more to do in the kitchen than in the main hall.

The Double Bind

Each temple wife must navigate for herself what her place will be on the day of a major temple event. She must determine whether her hospitality role will take precedence over her duty to participate in the more overtly religious dimensions of the day's activities. If she has taken ordination, this could include suiting up and assisting her husband and the other priests with the sutra reading, although as we have witnessed, this is rarely allowed by the myriad of tasks pulling her back into the temple's kitchen, or her constant duties of greeting and hosting the arriving volunteers and guest speakers. Her identity as a role model for the lay adherents may also mean that she should make an effort to sit in the main hall and listen while the visiting teacher gives the dharma talk. After all, hearing or discussing the teachings (an activity known as *monbō*) alongside one's fellow companions is one of the primary religious activities of Shin believers, in which temple family members should be exemplary. However, it is impossible to be in two places at once, and the *bōmori*'s obligations as a behind-the-scenes coordinator and hostess often demand her physical presence outside the *hondō*, where the main religious events of the ritual and dharma talk are being staged.

A recent address by a professor emeritus at Ryūkoku University at a sect-sponsored gathering for new *bōmori* highlights this tension, which dates back at least to the Edo-period sermons for *bōmori* noted briefly above. The eminent professor lightly remonstrated some *bōmori* for not always fully living up to their duty to listen to and spread the teachings (*kyōka no nin*): "You could say there are three types of *bōmori* [*laughs*]: the one who never comes out—even when requested, she is never seen. Then there is the one who just puts out the tea for the teacher [who delivers the dharma talk], but then slips back into invisibility. Then there is the *bōmori* who stays in the *hondō* and listens to the entire talk. What kind of *bōmori* are you?"

The professor indicates here that the ideal for *bōmori* is not to stop merely at completing their hospitality duties, but rather to actively seek to learn about the teachings by sitting alongside the lay guests to the temple to listen to the dharma talk. While he does not apparently question that she should also serve tea to the visiting teacher, he implies that this is *not enough,* and that ideally she should do more.

During the small group discussions following the professor's talk, one woman raised her hand straightaway: "The professor said that there are three kinds of *bōmori,* and we should reflect on which kind we are. Well, I want to listen to the dharma talk, but the phone will ring, or they'll need me in the kitchen, and of course someone has to serve the tea to the other priests. I have to come in and out—usually I can just hear the first few minutes and the last few minutes. What am I supposed to do about that?" The male facilitator of the discussion, a staff member of the district office hosting the workshop, nodded knowingly and tried to suggest a solution for how she might become this sermon-listening kind of *bōmori:* "Who brings the tea to the visiting priests at your temple? Sometimes there is a special helper among the parishioners [a *sewakata*]—do you have one of those?" "No," she replied, "At our temple it is the *bōmori*'s job."

Another woman jumped in at this point, "Actually, I am always troubled about what to do about greeting the dharma speaker. I don't want to ignore him, but I don't know what to talk about when I go in there [to the room where he's drinking his tea]. So, I just bring him his tea, and say something about the weather, but…does he just want to be left alone? I worry that I'm bothering him by just chatting about silly things." All of the young *bōmori* leaned forward in their seats at this point, expressing similar anxieties about how to be good hostesses—particularly those from lay households who had no idea how to meet the social expectations of a traveling dharma speaker. Not having had a formal education in the Shin teachings, they were perceptibly insecure about their ability to serve as stimulating conversation partners to a religious teacher.

It is clear from these women's anxieties, and from the scale of activity required to carry out most temples' yearly events, that the *bōmori*'s most immediate responsibility on the day of a major ritual is to be the event's manager and to serve as the friendly face of temple hospitality. This job requires coordinating the labor of the lay volunteers and ensuring that everyone contributing to the effort (lay or cleric) is shown proper appreciation and hospitality. We have seen in the described examples how simply creating a space for listening to the teachings—or more generally just for coming into contact with the temple—invites the human connections that are foundational to Shin propagation. It is easy to understand how a *bōmori*'s work on such occasions may remain invisible, particularly to those (like the professor above) who have their eyes trained on the ritual stage and dharma-speaking podium for instances of propagation.

A tension therefore inheres in the necessity for a *bōmori* both to passively stay at home and to actively work to turn the parishioner's visit into "an opportunity to hear the teachings," as the nineteenth-century sermonizer Tokuryū had advised. How, as Keiko Mochizuki pointed out, is she supposed to teach others about the Buddhist teachings without being allowed to leave home to learn about them herself? How is she supposed to execute the major feat of hospitality that is hosting a ritual event *and* also attend the dharma lecture in the main hall? Indeed, there is reason to believe that the *bōmori* would have fewer opportunities to hear the Buddhist teachings preached than any other type of practitioner, for her most intense hosting duties coincide precisely with those times when Buddhism is preached at the temple.

Public Work in Domestic Spaces

I have shown how the life of the *bōmori* as an individual woman and housewife is intricately interwoven with the life of the temple. In her own daily rhythm and life cycle, she cannot easily extricate herself from the temple's pull on her, though she may sometimes wish to. As a result of the gendered division of labor within the temple family, the *jūshoku* is often out of the temple to perform ritual duties or to work in a part- or full-time secular position to support the temple family; in these cases *bōmori* find themselves in the position of being the sole body at the temple during the day. This means that if a layperson drops by, she must act as the representative of the temple that will be there to greet her and answer her questions. Indeed, it is in her capacity as a welcoming presence, a listening ear, and a warm body in the temple at all times that the *bōmori* is most valued as a temple professional who helps the laity make connections with Amida and the Shin Buddhist teachings. I call this phenomenon, which lies at the intersection of Shin Buddhist spirituality and modern Japanese gender roles, a "propagation of hospitality."

In the terms given by Jonathan Z. Smith, who locates religion "here, there, and nowhere" (2004, p. 325), the *bōmori* as a religious professional stands astride the "here" (household religion) and "there" (temple religion). Ferrying gifts and food up and down the hallway between the kitchen ("here") and the main hall of the temple ("there"), the *bōmori* continuously opens and closes the sliding door that putatively cordons off the public, religious space of the temple from the private, domestic space of the family's residence. In Smith's terms, we might even say that the *bōmori*'s "here" is in fact the "there" of the rest of the temple community. Her domestic life speaks to the truism, originating in the Meiji period "cult of domesticity," that the housewife's work was not only of domestic import, but was of tremendous social and political significance as well.

In the world of religious professionals, the *bōmori* challenges our tendency to divide public religious roles from private ones. Accounts of women in society often appraise women's status or value based on how public their activities are and how well they have been able to break free of domestic constraints and "enter the public world" (Rosaldo 1974, p. 36). Analyses of female religious professionals are no different. Scholars' tendency to idealize those activities construed as public has resulted in a disproportionate amount of research on nuns to the neglect of other types of female practitioners. Of such scholarship Nirmala Salgado observes that "Often, the public sphere is associated with a freedom of renunciation that is seen ideally (in the sense of textual precedent) and practically (in terms of lived realities) as a male domain. Such studies depict female renunciation as a feminist act...making possible a resistance to subordination, conventional familial norms, and the private sphere" (2013, p. 51). Nuns are often the object of scholarly attention because they are seen as feminists of sorts, rejecting the constraints of home life—"the area in which women, tied to domestic chores and child care, are restricted"—in favor of the freedom to pursue religion in the "public" domain of a monastery or temple (2013, p. 52). It is difficult to argue with the fact that the domestic duties of the *bōmori,* in some cases considered absolute, act to restrict her movements and prevent her from pursuing interests outside the temple (even if those interests relate to Buddhism). Several of the *bōmori* I profile articulated this feeling of being bound by the temple. On the other hand, we cannot foreclose the possibility that their activities may indeed be invested with a great deal of religious significance, even though they take place off the ritual stage.

Applying the insights gleaned from the lived religion of temple wives about the interpenetration of domestic and religious operations also helps to push our own notions of Buddhist doctrine (in Japanese, *kyōgi, buppō,* or *oshie*) and propagation (*kyōka*) beyond the strictly textual. In the world of temple wives, we see Buddhist teachings taking shape in material objects, encounters over tea, and communities forged over shared manual labor in the kitchen. Following the activities of the temple wife brings to light these domestic modes of Buddhist doctrine and practice that may be obscured by an overreliance on public/private and sacred/profane dichotomies. The next chapter continues this examination of the intersection of domesticity and religiosity in the *bōmori*'s daily life by focusing on her practice of home economics and care for the temple's material objects.

Home Economics

Stewardship of the Buddha's Goods

For temple wives, who were born in a temple and married into a temple, from the time when they were in the womb they have had a connection with the Buddha [Amida]. Everything, beginning with the toys they received when they were young children, could only be bought thanks to the Buddha. Because you are a body who was brought up in this way by the Buddha, you must tirelessly offer the *nembutsu* of gratitude for these blessings…However, the wasteful consumption of the Buddha's goods by donning ostentatious clothes or decorations is positively despicable, resulting from a lack of faith and a failure to think about the deep blessings of the Buddha….As for the things that you receive from the laity, commenting on whether it is ample or meager, or whether it is good or bad, means that you do not understand that these are gifts received from the Buddha. Everything that you receive, you should receive it and use it while intoning the *nembutsu*.

Sōboku, Bōmori kaisoku no hōgo

AS THE CUSTODIAN OF THE TEMPLE'S DOMESTIC sphere, the *bōmori* largely oversees the transfers of material goods between parishioners and temple family members. The management of lay donations—which may include rice and produce from the farm, snacks and souvenirs from travels, seasonal gifts, and of course money—falls under the temple wife's purview as home economist. Even the uncooked rice that will be used both for the Buddhist altar and for the temple family's breakfast is often still received directly from parishioners, especially in rural areas. The reception and preparation of this sustaining gift is among the daily duties of the temple wife. The *bōmori* also holds the proverbial purse strings of the family, and is in many cases the manager of the temple's own finances. In the early modern scholar-priest Sōboku's (1718–1762) sermon, quoted above, the privilege of subsisting on these gifts was a manifestation of the *bōmori*'s karmic connection to the Buddha. On the other hand, her failure to be a grateful and prudent steward of the temple's goods was linked to a lack of faith.

Giving and receiving among temple residents, the laity, and Amida takes place within a complex matrix of factors that contribute to the meaning of the transfer: gender roles, social relationships, calendric cycles of gift giving, religious doctrine, rituals and sacred space, and, of course, monetary value. In many cases, objects such as rice, tea, flowers, ritual implements, and the image of the Buddha serve as markers of intimacy between Amida and the human inhabitants of his household; as such, material items become important media for relationships among human beings and between humans and divinities. Focalizing the material practices overseen by *bōmori* renders visible the domestic spaces in which practitioners encounter Buddhist ideas in non-textual and non-liturgical forms.[1] This chapter takes two decidedly non-textual foci—domestic labor and voluntary donations—to help us understand lived religious experience from the perspective of women's roles at the temple.

First, I describe the community-making functions of the *bōmori*'s handling of material objects, highlighting the intimacy of the temple family and their parishioners as they come together in stewardship of the Buddha's temple and its ritual objects. Next, I outline the prescribed meanings of the temple family's economic dependency on the laity in the Jōdo Shinshū before profiling a contemporary *bōmori* who narrates in clear terms the religious meaning inherent in her material reliance on the generosity of the laity. While in many cases across the Buddhist world it is this mutual material dependency that defines the relationship between laypeople and religious professionals,[2] the threat of commodification of religious goods and services is also a source of anxiety for practitioners. The final section examines the often uncomfortable overlap between temple economics and the market economy and practitioners' attempts to maintain a distinction between different types of exchanges.

Intimacy and Community in the Buddha's Home

During his fieldwork at a Catholic shrine in Chicago, Robert Orsi observed "how minor a part of the total religious experience *words* are" (2005, p. 164; emphasis mine). I found the same to be true in contemporary Jōdo Shinshū temples. The purpose of this section will be to show that material practices can be just as efficacious in bringing about a sense of belonging and familiarity with the Buddhist tradition as are Buddhism's more discursive expressions in texts, sermons, and liturgies.[3] Their efficacy is borne out both by doctrinal formulations (as in Sōboku's sermon with which this chapter opened) and by ethnographic observation. The *bōmori*'s activities draw our attention to forms of physical labor and friendship that have been shown to be powerful catalysts of religious sensibilities (Furey 2012; Moore 2015). Indeed, the relative informality of the domestic sphere lends itself ideally to the forging of such bonds.

During the summer of 2010, I joined the Nagai family (whom we met in chapter 1 of this book) for their annual deep cleaning of the inner altar by removing and polishing the shrine's brass items. The task is called *omigaki,* a polite form of the noun for "polishing."[4] This polishing session took place on a hot July day roughly a month before the August *obon* ceremony. The Nagais' two older daughters were both at daycare, as was my daughter. Naoko, the elder *bōmori,* greeted me when I arrived, gestured for me to get comfortable with the other volunteers in the main hall, and went to fetch me a glass of cold tea.

As I entered the hall, I immediately noticed that the inner altar had been emptied of its brass decorative objects, which had been spread out on top of newspapers, on top of a rug, on top of the tatami floor. I sat down with the three volunteers from the temple's membership (at least two of whom also regularly help with the cooking on ceremonial days). Before us had been laid out piles of old towels and gardening gloves and a half a dozen cans of polish.

I chose a ring-like candleholder that broke down into four different pieces and asked the woman next to me what I should do next. She handed me a towel and showed me how to apply the varnish.

"You sit on your knees very well," she commented, and admitted she was embarrassed that she could not do so herself, owing to her bad knees. "Every day I practice in the bath, though. I hold on to the sides and stretch my legs slowly underneath me. They pop if I sit down on them just like that."

The other ladies seemed relieved to find that I spoke Japanese and noted that they had seen me on a temple trip a few months ago. One of the women asked where my daughter was—she had seen me with her at the equinox ceremony in the spring. I replied that she was at daycare. "Oh you must be so busy," she remarked, "but you still came to help!"

After a while Hiroko entered the main hall carrying her youngest daughter, Chie-chan, who was just six weeks old. She placed the infant into a bouncy chair on the floor to nap and took a place in the circle. Like Naoko, Hiroko was dressed in clothes fit for doing manual labor, and she tied a sweat-absorbing towel around her neck as she dipped her head in thanking each of the volunteer temple ladies. The ladies cooed over the baby for a bit, and Hiroko picked up a piece and began to polish, checking with her mother-in-law about how to do it properly. Another volunteer arrived, the only man who would join us, and Naoko asked Hiroko to go get him some tea. Naoko asked the man about his wife, who had apparently broken her hip and was in the hospital undergoing rehabilitation. Although the others imagined that he must be too busy caring for her to come volunteer at the temple, he admitted to being glad to have this break from the hospital.

In a few more minutes, Akira joined us, tying on his own neck towel and bowing his head to each volunteer as he thanked them for coming. We were making fast work of the polishing by now, and a few volunteers commented that it was difficult to work the polish into the small corners of the pieces. There were a few toothbrushes floating about, and we took turns using those, each of us marveling as we learned that the implement we were holding broke down into a surprising number of tiny pieces. At one of the women's request, Akira explained the significance of the mythical Chinese creatures from the Pure Land sutras that comprised the shrine's decorations and gestured toward the altar as he explained where each implement would be placed once they were cleaned.

The male volunteer, looking up, asked about the calligraphy displayed on the back wall. He gestured at a hanging scroll on which the phrase "This is fate" (*kore wa goen desu*) was painted in elaborate script. Akira answered that one of the temple's parishioners taught a calligraphy class twice a month and encouraged the retired volunteer to join them at the next lesson. "Well, I do need a new hobby," the man said thoughtfully.

As we each picked up a last implement to complete the polishing, Akira remarked enthusiastically, "This will be a beautiful *obon* ceremony. It's going so quickly this time around, thanks to so many people coming."

"Yes, there's power in numbers," replied the smaller dark-haired woman.

The woman with the bad knees added, "The talking makes it more fun, so it goes by quickly. Anyway, if I were at home I would just be watching TV by myself, so this is much better!" she laughed.

As the last implements were placed on the fresh spread of newspapers, the polishing nearly complete, Akira disappeared and returned a few minutes later with a tray of iced coffee in tall glasses and cold individually wrapped cream-puffs, a simple snack that probably cost 1,000 yen for all of us but was perfectly timed and much appreciated by the overheated volunteers.

The communal effort of *omigaki* did more than make the temple's altar area shine. It also made a community: for one hot, sweaty afternoon, the distance between the temple family, who were the custodians of the "special space" of the altar, and the temple's parishioners was removed. By touching and rubbing and working the Buddhist implements into face-reflecting clarity, lay volunteers gained a sense of ownership and intimacy with the components of the usually off-limits inner altar. Those in attendance visibly enjoyed working together side by side with members of the temple family, chitchatting in a casual atmosphere with the resident priest, and asking him questions about the arrangement of the altar, what it is like to work with these implements during ceremonies, and how he himself had learned all of these things.

In this domestic setting laypeople can encounter the world of the Buddha and the promise of their salvation literally with their own two hands, without the mediation of a chanted scripture or a prepared sermon. An afternoon spent polishing an altar's decorations with fellow parishioners and the *jūshoku* and his family offers elderly and unemployed parishioners friendship, laughter, and a sense of being useful, but it is also a site for what Justin McDaniel has termed "emerging doctrine."[5] A casual question about the meaning of a calligraphic character on the wall, or an observation about the gleam or curve of a mythical beast said to populate the Pure Land, are as likely to engender familiarity, understanding, and perhaps more importantly, affinity to the Buddhist teachings as would an academic lecture or sermon. Sharing domestic labor generates intimacy among religious practitioners and a connectedness to the Buddhist tradition in a way that attendance at a more formal liturgical event may not.

Other-Power (*Tariki*) and Shin Buddhist Economics

In 2010, I attended a lecture given to *bōmori* by Ikeda Gyōshin, a scholar, priest, author, and at that time the chief administrator (*shūmusōchō*) of the Jōdo Shinshū Honganji-ha. He explained that all temple residents must consider the special obligation to society that results from their tax-exempt status. Why, unlike ordinary households, are temple households granted tax exemptions? Because they are expected to contribute to society, he explained, and to serve a social function. Walking out of the closing ceremony of a two-day training event for temple wives at Nishi Honganji, one woman commented to me: "What I was most moved by out of all the lecturers' talks was what Ikeda-sensei said about temple households being tax-exempt. Like he said, if you think about why we are tax-exempt, it means that society expects us to serve a social function. We aren't like other families because we don't pay taxes, so we shouldn't act like other families." The chief administrator's admonishments urging temple wives not to lapse into thinking of themselves as regular housewives had clearly left an impression. The responsibility of her special position as a *bōmori* was crystallized in this reminder of her economic dependence on society.

It might seem strange that out of a two-day retreat filled with lectures on Shin doctrine, ritual practice, and social reform, a remark about taxes would have had the strongest impact on this woman. And yet the chastening effect of being reminded that one is a member of a class whose well-being is dependent on donations rather than salary, and whose service to others in the form of doing "spiritual" work rather than ordinary labor, is nothing new. Although the distinction Ikeda refers to here—namely, that income received for religious services is tax-exempt—is a legal fact of postwar Japan, Shin priests, as householding clerics, have long had to defend their legitimacy as priests and therefore their right to receive donations from the laity and tax exemptions from the government.[6] The early modern scholar-priest Tokuryū (1772–1858) of Higashi Honganji was clearly conscious of potential critiques from the broader society in his sermons for temple priests and temple wives, respectively. After acknowledging that Shin priests were different from those in other sects because they were permitted to marry and raise a family while running a temple, he went on to explain the special obligation of the Shin priesthood from a labor-economic perspective:

> [Shin priests] have no profession as a warrior, farmer, craftsman, or merchant like those in lay households do. Instead, they have the status of priest (sōryo), whose duty is to serve the Buddhas and the patriarchs and to work for the sake of the laity's great concern in the next life; in so doing, they should remember that they receive all of their clothing and food from that which is given to the Buddha.[7]

This passage refers to the organization of Edo-period society according to one's profession. Tokuryū and the abbot of Higashi Honganji whom he represented were careful to remind temple residents of their special exemption from contributing anything other than spiritual labor to society. Shin temple family members were urged to grasp their unique position as householders whose sole occupation is to serve the Buddhas and the patriarchs of Shin Buddhism by spreading the teachings. Tokuryū emphasized that it was the distinctive material privilege of Buddhist clerics to live within a household and yet subsist on the generosity of the laity without having to "earn" their subsistence in the same way that members of other sectors of the workforce must. Nearly 150 years later, Ikeda Gyōshin's speech shows us that a very similar message continues to be transmitted to temple family members in the Jōdo Shinshū.

In order to understand the dynamics of giving and receiving in Shin Buddhist doctrine, we must understand the concept of other-power (tariki), which is central to Jōdo Shinshū soteriology. The founder Shinran held that the achievement of rebirth in the Pure Land—the soteriological aim of Pure Land Buddhism—was accomplished solely by Amida's vow and not by self-powered practice (known as jiriki) or the ritual intervention of religious specialists, which was just another futile form of calculated effort. In principle, then, Shin clerics are not supposed to possess a religious status superior to that of the laity. As James Dobbins puts it: "Ultimately, Amida is the magnetic force drawing a person to his vow. The particular teacher communicating this message is merely the agent" (2002, p. 72). According to prescriptive sources, the donations of the laity cannot be given to obtain spiritual advantage: that is all in Amida's hands and has nothing to do with ritual intervention by priests. Donations are given simply out of a sense of gratitude to the teachings and a wish to extend the gift of salvation to others. One expression used for this sense of religious practice—which applies not just to donating goods or money, but to any activity undertaken out of gratitude—is the phrase *button hōsha,* literally, to repay one's debt to Amida.

The ideal transaction goes something like this: when a practitioner attains faith and thereby feels assured that Amida's compassion accomplished their salvation long ago, their natural response is a desire to repay their spiritual debt (*hō-on*) to Amida. The laity therefore give various things (rice, money, time) to the temple out of a sense of gratitude. Temple residents become the custodians of these gifts, which are described as none other than the Buddha's blessings. Temple residents, in turn, engage in activities of propagation out of gratitude to Amida and their Buddhist teachers, the foremost of whom is Shinran. As we have seen, propagation can include sermonizing or more informal activities as long as it provides an opportunity for followers to form a karmic connection with Amida. In other words, in a spiritual sense, these exchanges of services, goods, food, money, and teachings are conducted *among* humans *on behalf of* the Buddha Amida. The circulation of spiritual and material gifts is thus one of the ways in which the central premise of the Shin Buddhist doctrine of *tariki* is enacted.

The division of labor surrounding home economics at the temple is bound up in the demarcation of gender roles in modern Japan. The Japanese term for "economy" (*keizai*) is itself a late-nineteenth-century neologism coined to describe one of the duties of the newly emerging professional category of housewife (*shufu*). As in English, the term "economy" originally had a distinctly domestic quality. Jordan Sand observes from early Meiji sources that "An older 'economy' rooted in conceptions of household governance distinct from the modern discipline of political economy still informed the textbooks used by girls and women in the early period of the Meiji education system.... 'Economy' in these texts encompassed the maintenance of a self-contained system, the 'managing of the interior,' which was primarily the mistress' domain of authority.... The unifying component in these texts was an injunction to frugality" (Sand 2003, p. 81).

Beyond the more general injunctions in Meiji educational literature for women to be frugal, Shin Buddhist authors of the Meiji period hoped to inculcate in their female readership a particularly *spiritual* sensibility about their management of household resources. The women's journal *Katei,* which was published out of the Kōkōdō publishing house founded by Kiyozawa Manshi, featured an unattributed article entitled "Economic Principles of the

Buddhist Household" (Bukkyō katei no keizaihō). The author's desire to protect the stewardship of household resources from being reduced to "ordinary"
economic principles is striking:

> The principle of ordinary economics is to measure what comes in
> and regulate what goes out, transmitting what is appropriate to
> your position. This surely requires quite a great deal of knowledge,
> and yet for those who believe in the Buddhist law, this law of eco-
> nomics is hardly adequate....
>
> How should a household that serves the Buddha consider its law
> of economics? Rennyo has taught us something about this in the
> Goichidaiki kikigaki....Rennyo said that clothing, food, and shel-
> ter are all things that are entrusted to us by the Buddha, so we
> must never be wasteful or extravagant in their use (*Katei* 3[10]: 5).

This author finds resources for imbuing the practice of frugality with religious
significance in the writings of Rennyo (1415–1499), the fifteenth-century
leader of the Jōdo Shinshū institution. The impulse to assert a distinctly Buddhist meaning regarding apparently quotidian tasks is notable. It is a tendency that remains strong in contemporary Shin Buddhist discourse.

The daily dealings in money, rice, flowers, and the like usually come
under the temple housewife's purview. Depending upon their age and the cli-
mate of their temple, *bōmori* may be more or less acutely aware of the obligation of temple residents to manage the Buddha's goods as if they actually
had no ownership over them. A *bōmori* born in 1938 whom I interviewed at a
Kyoto temple-wife study group recalled the same message being clearly con-
veyed in her own prewar upbringing: "My father always taught us never to
waste anything, that everything we had belonged to the Buddha, and that the
temple was the Buddha's home. We were taught that the parishioners were
the Buddha's guests, Shinran's guests. That may sound strange, I suppose, but
it's just the way I was brought up."

Many temple family members, while they observe the cultural imperative of treating gifts as special objects, stop short of fully internalizing the tri-
adic relationship between themselves, their parishioners, and Amida. I asked
Sachiko Hino, an Osaka temple wife whom I profile in chapter 6, how she felt
about the saying that the temple family's material belongings are really "the
Buddha's goods." Did she consider her temple to belong, ultimately, to the
Buddha? She replied:

> "The Buddha's home"? Yes, I hear that kind of thing, I hear peo-
> ple saying that, especially older *bōmori*....It stays right here in

my head [*motions to a spot at the top of her head*]. But I think,
"Can you really do that?" At some point, it just drives you to feign
being a good person, doesn't it? Even if you aren't good, you want
to be sure people think well of you. So when I'm talking to an older
bōmori, of course I always watch how I behave.

While Sachiko claimed to dismiss this as an unattainable ideal, she also simultaneously conceded that this expectation for temple people to live as if their
belongings were not their own still exerted an influence on her behavior. We
must recognize that temple residents, sometimes despite their best efforts,
do not universally achieve a feeling that their material belongings signal their
participation in a spiritual economy with Amida at its center. It does remain,
however, an aspirational sensibility for most.

"We Must Do Something to Give Back": Noriko's Vocation

I first met Noriko at a gathering of *bōmori* near the beginning of my fieldwork. Talkative and outgoing by nature, Noriko approached me immediately
after a group interview, asking a steady stream of questions about America,
why I had come to Japan, and how I had learned to speak Japanese so well.
When I contacted her nearly a year later, asking to visit her temple so I could
interview her individually, she quickly invited me to attend an upcoming children's group meeting (*kodomokai*) at her temple.

   When I arrived, she greeted me cheerily at the front gate with a small
yapping dog in each arm. Noriko's demeanor is bright and jolly: she has a
warm and boisterous laugh, and her round face and ample cheeks betray her
love of cooking and eating (although she told me that she forced herself to go
to the gym at least once a week to try to take off some of her extra weight). She
wears red glasses, and her ear-length hair is dyed a reddish tint—a fashion
choice of which more conservative or rural *bōmori* might disapprove. Her two
dogs joined us for the interview, and one of them frequently jumped up on to
the leather couch to lick my hand as I tried to take notes. Noriko just smiled
and gently scolded the dog to get down, laughing at Shin-chan (named after
Shinran) with motherly forgiveness.

   It had recently become hot and muggy outside with the start of Kyoto's rainy season, so Noriko brought us cold green tea and delicious red-bean
cakes, a Kyoto specialty. As we drank our tea, Noriko explained the events
that had led her to marry into this tiny temple, an aging wooden structure
squeezed in between a ramen shop and a gift store in the shadow of Higashi
Honganji. She had grown up in a temple of the same sect in an adjoining prefecture, in a somewhat more rural setting. When I asked her if she was glad
that she was born into a temple, she replied:

My answer to that question now is, yes, definitely. But when I was young I would not have answered yes. Before I got married, I wasn't crazy about living in the temple, and I didn't think I needed religion. I was content not asking myself those kinds of questions. But when I considered living in a secular household, I realized it would be lonely (*samishii*). Something would be missing. I believe it's important for people to have something their hearts can rely on, to have a religious life. I mean, if you don't have a religious belief in something greater than yourself, you could feel justified in killing someone if you wanted to, couldn't you? That cannot be right. So I'm glad that I was born in the temple and I have this opportunity to live amidst these religious teachings, to have a strong religious life.

When she was in her early twenties, Noriko's younger sister introduced her to the man who would become her husband, and she moved in with him and his family as soon as they married, some twenty-four years ago.

Noriko explained that her own strength in propagation was working with children. When her children were young, her in-laws were still alive and living in the house with them. She did not want to be with her in-laws all the time: "You see things you don't need to see and realize things you don't want to realize about people when you live together," she explained with a smile. So she actively sought involvements that would take her out of the temple, becoming active in the PTA at her children's school and making connections that now allow her to recruit local elementary school students for her temple's children's group.

Once a month, Noriko stands in front of the gate of a few different elementary schools in nearby neighborhoods and hands out flyers for her temple's children's group. "Sometimes the kids will say, 'Who are you? Some kind of strange old lady?' [*Noriko laughs.*] I tell them, 'Just take the flyer home and show it to your mother. Tell them the temple wife gave it to you. They'll know I'm not strange.'" She used to lament how few opportunities people of any age had to come to the temple. Previously, yearly rituals would be the only opportunity for people to gather there. So she started a parishioner group (*dōbōkai*), in which mostly older parishioners would gather once a month for crafts, study, and socializing. Eight years ago she started the children's group. Unfortunately, Noriko explained, younger people tend to have a prejudice: they imagine that the temple is only for funerals. She wants very much to change that perception. Out of all the things her temple does, it is the children's group about which she is the most passionate. Noriko has a degree in early childhood education, and she worked at a nursery school before her children were born. Further, as she explained with another boisterous laugh, leading a children's group allows her to take advantage of her loud voice.

After our interview was finished, no children had yet arrived for the children's meeting, so she gave me a tour of her aging temple. It was less than a block from Higashi Honganji, and when the latter burned down in 1864, she explained, her temple had burned as well. But all of the resources and donations from the faithful had gone to rebuilding Higashi Honganji, and her temple was left on its own to scrape together the wood to rebuild. As a result, she pointed out, the beams supporting the main hall are puny, perhaps even thinner than what one would see in a regular household.

The hall itself looked like it had not seen much renovation since it was rebuilt at the end of the nineteenth century. The floor was covered with removable carpets to protect the tatami mats while the hall was being used for crafts and group meetings. Photographs of Noriko, her husband, and their children's group at a camping event with a group from another temple hung on one wall. A bookshelf filled with comics (*manga*) for young people to read was crammed in the back corner. There were also samples of the crafts that her elderly parishioner group had made in their monthly gatherings: straw sandals, boxes made from milk cartons covered with handmade paper, and origami boxes.

After we had stood in the empty *hondō* and talked for another thirty minutes, it became clear that no children were coming to her children's group that day. "Kids are so busy nowadays with their weekend commitments, club sports, and lessons," she explained apologetically. "Some weeks we get a dozen or more, especially if we do an activity like cooking. I'm sorry you couldn't see it today for your research!" It seemed that this week, despite her best efforts at recruitment, other extracurricular involvements had drawn the neighborhood children elsewhere.

Noriko seems to have done an admirable job of imparting her love of the temple to her own children: all three are now in college, and all have said they would be willing to inherit the temple. "It's a mystery!" she said, declining to take any credit as a temple mother for her children's attitude. "Most temples have trouble finding someone who is willing to take over, but we have the opposite problem. What shall we do if all three really decide to take over?" she laughed. Her youngest son is the only boy and has been treated affectionately by the parishioners and his grandparents as the "young successor" since he was born. He seemed to enjoy this special attention, Noriko observed, and he went along willingly enough when it was time for his ordination at the age of nine. It was helpful that many of his friends were also temple sons and were all ordained at the same August administration of the ceremony at Higashi Honganji, like a summer camp for young successors. He is now in college. Her two daughters both assume that they will live in a temple themselves someday, whether their own or that of their future husbands, and have said they intend to become ordained too.[8] Her oldest daughter sometimes accompanies her father on his monthly visits to perform a monthly service at parishioners' homes, but only as a novice. "She says she wants to receive a payment for helping out with the services, and that's why she wants to take ordination," Noriko laughed. "But I've told her that's an impure motive, and I won't allow it!"

At this point, Noriko revealed to me the ethos that informs her sense of vocation as a temple professional and prompts her to instill the same ethic in her children. She explained her family's economic dependency on their parishioners and on Buddhism as being at the root of her very strong conviction that *bōmori* have a special obligation to propagate the teachings.

> Here in the temple, the only reason we are here is because of the contributions (*fuse*) of our followers. These are not the same as a salary. In a regular household, someone goes to work in order to earn money, and then they come home and support the family with that. But for us, we just sit here and teach when we have the opportunity, and host people when we have the chance. But we are able to subsist simply because people are generous enough to contribute to the temple. We don't work to *earn* their money. I mean, it comes in whether we lift a finger or not—look around, there are certainly temples where no one but the *jūshoku* does much of anything, and even the *jūshoku* just goes through the motions and does the funerals or what have you. But we don't really earn our subsistence in the way other people do—the money just happens to come in. I just feel that we *must* do our best, at things like *bōmori* associations or other volunteer activities. We must actively propagate. Even if it's not giving lectures or performing rituals or whatever—whatever you can do, whatever your strengths are, you must do your best at that. We must do something to give back. When I hear about some *bōmori* who, when it comes around to them to serve as an officer in the *bōmori* association, say, "No thanks, I'm not interested"—I think they're missing the point of their position. They haven't really thought about what makes their life possible.

Noriko's interpretation of the temple family's material blessings as manifestations of her debt to Buddhism and to Amida, a debt she must strive to repay, is in tune with the message of Sōboku and other Edo period sermonizers who encouraged Shin followers to consider their material belongings as the blessings of Amida. Her insistence that a priest's income "is not the same as a salary" suggests that the Shin tradition has been successful in protecting religious labor from commodification: according to Noriko, the transaction wherein the layperson gives the priest money, for instance, on the occasion of his reading the scriptures and teaching the dharma, should not be understood as a "payment for religious services," but rather as a gift.

In Noriko's understanding, the temple family's dependence on both the laity and the Buddha translates into an obligation to serve Shin Buddhism by undertaking propagation in various forms. Her sense of vocation as a religious professional arises directly from her material dependency on the gifts of the laity. For some temple residents—including Noriko, the women at Ikeda Gyōshin's lecture at Nishi Honganji, and those listeners who were persuaded by Tokuryū's early modern sermons—it is precisely their material relationship with the laity and the Buddha that *constitutes* them as religious professionals. And yet, the need for temple residents to subsist on gifts from the laity, who must earn financial capital by working in the general economy, raises the risk of commodifying what Noriko and others see as a properly spiritual transaction. This speaks to a much larger issue of authenticity within Japanese Temple Buddhism, to which I will briefly turn in the last section of this chapter.

Temple Economics and the Market Economy

Contemporary Japanese Buddhism has an image problem.[9] The reality that the religious economy of Buddhist temples and the broader political economy are interrelated is something that temple residents across Buddhist sects in Japan are acutely aware of, as they are confronted with the problem of earning a living in a hyper-capitalist society without betraying the ideals of their religious tradition. As Stephen Covell puts it: "Critiques regarding [priests'] economic activities often assume a clear division between the sacred and profane, between world-renouncer and householder. They fail to acknowledge how thoroughly enmeshed these realms are in everyday life. Such critiques bring to light scholarly and popular assumptions about what is, or is not, properly religious or Buddhist" (Covell 2005, p. 142). The question of whether religious "production" should be measured in the terms of the market—for example, how or whether to assign fixed prices to ritual services or temple membership—is one that troubles contemporary clerics. This tension profoundly affects not only temple families and their local parishioner communities but also sectarian institutions.

Shimazono Susumu (1998) defines the "commodification" of religious giving in contemporary Japan as a transformation from a more all-encompassing, communal oblation into more discreet and individualized exchanges. Often this kind of transaction is associated with new religious groups in Japan, but Shimazono asserts that it is becoming equally characteristic of giving to traditional Buddhist institutions. The push for commodification in the form of a set list of prices for religious goods and services has come as much from laypeople eager to be sure they are not being disrespectful by paying too little, or being swindled by paying too much, as it has from priests trying to make a profit from temple work.[10] The image of Buddhist priests in popular media in Japan, however, often attributes such commodification to priestly greed and corruption.

Contemporary priests struggle to walk the line of accepting and even soliciting contributions in exchange for religious goods and services without being seen as abandoning their spiritual vocation and succumbing to what one Japanese Buddhist author has called "the commercialization of the soul" (Ashida Tetsurō, cited in Covell 2005, pp. 161–162). Most of Stephen Covell's informants, who are Tendai priests, report that they are uncomfortable designating a set price for ritual services, hoping instead to inculcate a "spirit of donation" in their parishioners. This is a subtle but significant distinction. His informants lament that "in many cases [parishioners] perceive donations less as religious acts than as a price for membership. . . . Donations are often seen as acts necessary to the care and maintenance of ancestors who are buried and memorialized at the temple, rather than as funding for the promotion and support of the sect and its goals" (p. 145). In other words, views of the proper spirit of donation held by the laity and the religious professionals are in misalignment. What the priests and Tendai institutional officials view as properly "religious" giving would be for the laity to offer up voluntary and generalized support for the propagation of the Buddhist teachings. On the other hand, an exchange of a fixed monetary donation (which we could call a fee) for an expected service (interment and memorial services for ancestors, and membership in the parish) feels too commodified, at least for the religious professionals with whom Covell spoke.

Often, or perhaps always, the purchase of a religious product is made for complex reasons. In his ethnographic study of changing burial practices in contemporary Japan, Mark Rowe (2011) examines the motivations of laity in consuming Buddhist "products" in intimate detail. What emerges is a clear view of the reality that religious actors are motivated by a variety of concerns, some of which defy categorization as *either* religious *or* economic. For example, his informant Naoko decided to purchase an eternal memorial grave for herself and an expensive, handcrafted Buddhist statue for the protection of her daughter's pregnancy, but denied the assertion that either purchase was motivated by religious sentiments. In analyzing Naoko's consumption of these religious products, Rowe highlights her desire for control over the uncontrollable (in this case, death) as a motivating factor that cuts across various other categories we often use to analyze people's behavior. These purchases, Rowe writes, speak "to a concept of religion that does not allow a clear distinction between those elements one might consider strictly religious (e.g., prayer, ritual, or soteriology) and those that have traditionally fallen under the purview of economists and social scientists" (2011, p. 96). Religious lives are plainly not undertaken in isolation from material and economic realities, and individual decisions are not easily classified as one or the other.

These examples also show that even when there is a relatively clear context of remuneration in Temple Buddhism, most adherents feel a need to maintain some degree of "specialness" in the transaction that characterizes it as more personal, voluntary, and spiritually driven than exchanges of commodities. This comes through even in the narratives of priests who have devised nontraditional institutional models in order to accommodate Japan's shifting demographics, decreasing parishioner base, and the increasingly commodified view of religion held by laypeople. One of the Buddhists profiled by Rowe is a good example.

Takizawa Kazuo is a high-ranking Sōtō Zen priest and abbot of Tōchōji temple in Tokyo, where "business and Buddhism" are intermingled in ways that challenge scholars who might want to "distinguish the commercial from the spiritual" (Rowe 2011, p. 114). Despite Takizawa's success at building a modern-looking, highly popular, and even profitable alternative grave association for Tokyo urbanites that redefines the temple–parishioner relationship, he clearly has his limits in making concessions to commodification. Rowe tells us that "when people began asking if they could make donations (*fuse*) to the temple through bank transfer (*furikomi*)," Takizawa felt ill at ease: "Though he has not banned the practice, Takizawa is concerned that allowing offerings, which for him are a fundamental element of Buddhism, to be electronically automated will set the tone for all future interaction[s] with the temple" (p. 127). In other words, the *manner* of giving—and presumably receiving—is one area in which he hopes to preserve a personal relationship of some kind. Though Takizawa employs a large staff of non-monastic workers to communicate with the temple's members and guide them through the process of taking lay precepts and handling the burial and memorial arrangements for their relatives, he also insists that these staffers be part of the sangha, or Buddhist community. Rowe cites Takizawa's explanation here: a staff member should be "a follower of Buddhism, as people who live a life based on the Buddha, they must be believers. Otherwise it is just business" (pp. 127–128). Though Rowe's study of changing burial practices offers many more insights on the intricacy and diversity of Buddhist responses to the threat of commodification, one that we can take away here is that a strong feeling continues to prevail that there *should* be some difference between Buddhist temple economics and "just business." As priests like Takizawa insist, the human interaction that accompanies an act of giving to the temple continues to be in some way integral to the exchange.

Here, the activities of temple wives can add intimate texture to the discussion of the relationship between business and religion. The temple wife's role as the household manager who frequently handles in person the receipt of gifts from the laity—and also sometimes serves as the temple's accountant—invites us to view the intricacies of practitioners' material relationship to Buddhism. Focusing our ethnographic attention on a particular donation can help to crystallize the relationship between giving, intimacy, space, and consumption at a Shin Buddhist temple. When I visited Noriko's temple for the first time in several years, I brought a package of coffee, some cookies, and handmade jam from California where I had been living most recently. In the course of our conversation, I asked Noriko to describe what she did with gifts that laypeople brought to the temple.

"I give them to the Buddha," she explained simply.

"But what does that actually mean?" I asked.

"Here, would you like to give this coffee to the Buddha?" she offered.

"Yes, of course," I replied.

She took the bag of Peets coffee into her temple's modest main hall and placed it just in front of the altar, which housed an image of Amida. She knelt in front of it and brought her hands together in prayer. After a moment of silence, she leaned forward in a bow and uttered a few *nembutsu* phrases (*namu Amida Butsu*). After pausing at the low point of her bow for another long moment, she came back up, paused again with a lowered head, and then turned around to me and said: "There. Now we've given it to the Buddha. And now we can drink it if we like."

Observing the lack of formality with which the coffee was "given" to the Buddha, I realized that the temple family's relationship with the Buddha, whose home they share, is better characterized by intimacy than awe. After all, they also share the Buddha's breakfast every morning, with the first scoop of rice being carried from the family's rice cooker to be placed on the Buddha's serving dish and taken to the altar in the main hall.[11] The temple wife as home economist and hostess oversees the object's transformation from a commodity to a good that belongs to the Buddha. Her prescribed role is to receive the gift graciously from the parishioner and acknowledge the two parties' mutual obligation to one another. Ideally, she should recognize both the interpersonal relationship between her family and the parishioner and the original, cosmic motivation for this gift, and all gifts to her temple—namely, Amida's great compassion. As she places the gift in front of the Buddha's image and intones the *nembutsu,* she affirms the relationship of her family to the Buddha, that they live under the same roof and share the same material goods. This is one of the routine ways in which the Jōdo Shinshū doctrine of *tariki* can be enacted and affirmed at a bodily level.

Sociologists and anthropologists have struggled to distinguish different types of exchanges and economies.[12] Practitioners clearly do the same, and most are not unaware of the multilayered complexities of economic transfers outlined in scholars' analytic models. Though reciprocity is frequently emphasized as being a quality inherent in "gift exchanges"—in contrast to the one-time transactions of self-interest that characterize commodity exchanges—the term "reciprocity" would be misleading here, as Nicolas Sihlé (2015) has shown it to be in the vast majority of Buddhist contexts. In Jōdo Shinshū thinking, though the language of *on* or debt is used, it is not possible ever to "repay" one's spiritual debt, which ultimately is owed to Amida. In its ideal form, giving at a Shin Buddhist temple exemplifies what has been theorized as "generalized circular giving" (Sahlins 1996 [1978]) and is both a response to and performance of one's faith. Shin Buddhist piety as repayment of one's debt to the Buddha is conceived as a gift arising out of gratitude, for which one expects no return. The original gift, the act of generosity that gave rise to gratitude, was Dharmakara's (the bodhisattva who would later become the Buddha Amida) vow to save sentient beings, even evil ones, by the creation of a Pure Land where anyone could be reborn merely by uttering his name. Crucially, all of these transfers and contributions involve practitioners in a gift community together with the Buddha Amida.[13]

Finally, we can see how daily life in a temple is supposed to be a constant performance of gratitude for one's involvement in that spiritual economy. Recall Noriko's comment in the previous section about the difference between a temple family's income and a salary: "Here in the temple, the only reason we are here is because of the contributions (*fuse*) of our followers. These are not the same as a salary....But we are able to subsist simply because people are generous enough to contribute to the temple. We don't work to *earn* their money....We must do something to give back."

It is difficult to imagine a more cogent articulation by a religious practitioner of the qualities of morality, spontaneity, and lack of self-interest thought to characterize a moral economy, in contradistinction to a more commodified transaction (e.g., Cheal 1996 [1988]). While it is easy to appraise the material practices of a temple resident as being somehow "religious" when they take place on the highly ritualized occasion of the *hō-onko* (as seen in chapter 1), for temple residents the cycle of giving and gratitude ideally pervades the everyday. The temple wife's domestic role in this regard unveils the potential for temple economics themselves to catalyze the appropriation by practitioners of the Shin Buddhist concept of *tariki* on an intimate level.

In prescriptive accounts such as Sōboku's sermons, the gifts and donations that sustain the temple and its residents are emphatically not like goods obtained through ordinary labor in the general economy. They, at least according to the sermonizers, are the "goods of the Buddha." The *bōmori* is supposed to keep in mind that she is sustained for her entire life by the Buddha's blessings, and in this way her karmic condition is inscribed in her material conditions. This fact makes home economics another important thread in the tapestry of the *bōmori*'s identity as a religious professional. Recalling Sōboku's admonishment, cited at the beginning of this chapter, that temple wives should "receive and use" everything that belongs to the temple, from food to clothing to toys for their children, "while intoning the *nembutsu*," we realize that the spiritual stakes of home economics can be quite high. Acting at the intersection of religious piety and home economics, temple wives bring into view the domestic life of the material–spiritual exchanges that take place at Buddhist temples.

In many cases temple wives and other family members struggle to reconcile the two economies in which the temple family trades. Engagement in the commodity economy is seen as inauthentic and inappropriate for a Buddhist cleric, yet it is indispensable for the institution's survival. But dwelling solely and for one's entire life in the spiritual economy of Amida's gifts is an ideal that is difficult to achieve. In reality, a sense of possession tends to creep in, and as one informant pointed out, the ideal can have the effect of making temple residents just feign virtuous behavior.

Finally, the work that women perform in daily life as stewards of the Buddha's goods highlights the important role of quotidian, nondiscursive interactions with Buddhist forms that subtly but surely engender practitioners' sense of belonging to the Buddhist tradition, and even a feeling of intimacy with the Buddha. As David Morgan argues, "materiality *mediates* belief...material objects and practices both enable and enact it. Handling objects, dressing in a particular way, buying, displaying, and making gifts of particular commodities, attending certain events are all activities that engage people in the social relations and forms of sacred imagination that structure their relations to the divine" (2010, p. 12). If this is so, then the domestic labor the *bōmori* performs alongside her parishioners—as in the bustling kitchen on the day of a *hō-onkō* feast, or the long, hot morning spent meticulously polishing the decorations from the temple's altar—involves parishioners intimately in Amida's community. It also induces a sense of belonging, gratitude, and faith as much as—and potentially even more than—her husband's more formal sacerdotal labor in front of the altar.

Social Networks and Social Obligations in the Disciplining of *Bōmori*

I'm not sure when I became [a *bōmori*]. That is the reality. But as for when I lived at the temple, and began doing the things a *bōmori* does—what you probably think of—it's been thirty years.

Vice President of the National Federation of
Bōmori *Associations (Ōtani-ha)*

I HAVE ALREADY PROFILED SEVERAL TEMPLE-BORN WOMEN in this book (for instance, Michiko and Rina in chapter 2 and Noriko in chapter 3), highlighting the ways in which their domestic activities and family relationships define their relationship to the Buddhist tradition. But what about women like Hiroko Nagai, the temple wife and daughter-in-law whom we met in the introduction to this book? By the time I interviewed her she had been married to the *jūshoku* and living in the temple for almost ten years, and yet her sense of embarrassment and shame about her lack of authority and authenticity compared to those of her mother-in-law was still so strong that she burst into tears in response to my simple question about her role at the temple. Lay-born women now comprise roughly a third to a half of current *bōmori* in both of the major Shinshū denominations.[1] This chapter addresses the question of where and how such women, who grew up in a secular household and might never have met a *bōmori* until they became one themselves, acquire practical and doctrinal expertise, and, ideally, the interior disposition of a Buddhist adherent and a temple professional.

Few lay-born *bōmori* start out by aspiring to become religious professionals—some are not even particularly Buddhist at first. Rather, they marry a Buddhist priest, begin engaging in the upkeep of the temple and the cultivation of relationships with parishioners and in-laws, and only later achieve the interior disposition of a Buddhist devotee. The attainment of faith, if it does occur, may come only after many years of service at the temple. In many ways, a *bōmori*'s path from being a laywoman raised without a Buddhist emphasis to being a temple resident with a strong Buddhist faith resembles the pedagogical process identified by Dorinne Kondo (1990) in her study of students at an ethics center outside of Tokyo. She describes the strenuous rote practices undertaken at the ethics center as a means of forging a sincere and ethical self through bodily practice, a pedagogy described by a teacher at the center as "entering through the form" (*katachi de hairu,* pp. 106–107).[2]

In the education of a *bōmori,* bodily, practical learning tends to precede more intentional, discursive forms of training. Pierre Bourdieu's notion of cultural mastery helps elucidate the learning process: mastery of the role of *bōmori* "is transmitted in practice, in its practical state, without attaining the level of discourse" (1977, p. 87). In other words, *bōmori*-in-training (temple daughters-in-law) are often most motivated to imitate behaviors that are never explicitly articulated but nonetheless appear important to successfully performing the role of *bōmori.* Along these lines, Talal Asad describes ritual mastery as "apt performance," which "involves not symbols to be interpreted but abilities to be acquired according to rules that are sanctioned by those in authority: it presupposes no obscure meanings but rather the formation of physical and linguistic skills" (1993, p. 62). For *bōmori* born in lay households (and sometimes those born in temples), the explication of religious meanings is often a secondary, nonessential element of their training. If she wishes to understand the religious doctrine of the temple into which she has married, a temple daughter-in-law must make an effort to attend workshops and training courses at the sect's local and national offices. Depending on the attitude and resources of her affinal family, she may be either encouraged or discouraged from studying outside the temple.

In this regard, it is important to highlight the nexus of interpersonal relationships that facilitate the acculturation of new *bōmori.* A young temple daughter-in-law's cultivation of the discipline and sensibility of a "temple person" is inextricable from the relational structures in which a young Japanese bride is situated. These relations need not always be dictated or even recognized by the central religious institutions themselves, but they are nonetheless pivotal in a *bōmori*'s training.

In the first two sections of this chapter I profile two temple daughters-in-law who are learning the ropes of their new position. Kayoko and Mari's experiences demonstrate that a temple wife's education may occur at a variety of sites: for example, at home in the form of mentoring within the temple family or through exchanges with peers at local meetings of temple wife associations. Though many women begin their residence in the temple with feelings of trepidation or ambivalence, by the time they reach middle age most come to embrace their identity as Shin Buddhist adherents and their position as religious professionals. Once they do, they often begin to narrate their having "randomly" met and married a Buddhist priest as evidence of their karmic predestination for a life lived as a devout Buddhist. In narratives of successful *bōmori*, a woman's resolution to take up her role as a temple professional with zeal and dedication is bound up with her attainment of Pure Land Buddhist faith (the emic term for which is *shinjin*, sometimes translated as "true entrusting" in Amida's saving power). In the final section, I describe national *bōmori* conferences and training retreats hosted by the head temples in Kyoto or their district-office venues for training *bōmori* that are far from their home temples. In these various sites where *bōmori* acquire practical competence, doctrinal knowledge, and self-awareness as religious professionals, I will show that the structuring forces of Buddhist doctrine and family obligations often converge in the cultivated docility of temple daughters-in-law.

On-the-Job Training: Kayoko's Story

The *bōmori's* practical training, like other aspects of her job, is highly localized. In an informal survey of nineteen Ishikawa Prefecture *bōmori* association members conducted on my behalf by their chief officer, all nineteen said that they primarily learned their jobs either from their own mother or their mother-in-law and husband. This is consistent with my findings from interviews with *bōmori* across generations and from various regions throughout my fieldwork. The story of Kayoko Hirata, the thirty-three-year-old wife of the assistant *jūshoku* of a rural Kyūshū temple, offers a fairly typical example of a young laywoman's journey to becoming a temple wife. Kayoko began as a blank slate: until she became one herself, she had never even heard of the term *bōmori*.

"When my husband and I started dating, the temple didn't really come up," Kayoko told me over lunch one day. "I grew up in a regular household, and I went to a two-year women's college near Ryūkoku University [the affiliated university of Nishi Honganji], where my husband went. One night I went out to a drinking party with my friends and some guys from Ryūkoku, and he and I hit it off. As we started dating, I learned that he came from a temple. I thought that sounded like an interesting way to grow up, but we didn't discuss the future very much."

Even after she and her husband married, they did not move into her in-laws' temple right away. Instead, her husband got a job working at a branch office of Nishi Honganji located in a nearby town in southern Kyūshū.

For historical reasons, the temples in this area are generally large and boast remarkably zealous congregations.[3] As a result, Kayoko's husband's family temple sprawls over a large lot of land in the middle of a sleepy agricultural village, whose livestock was being ravaged at the time of my visit in 2010 by hoof-and-mouth disease. The temple also runs its own public day-care facility (*hoikuen*), which is the most common side business for Shinshū temples.[4] Thus, with a large number of parishioners and a side business, the income of the temple is secure, but the priestly and administrative duties the family must manage are considerable.

While they were living an hour away, Kayoko would visit her husband's temple when there was a major ceremony or seasonal cleaning event. Somewhat like an internship, this allowed her to help out while shadowing her mother-in-law and two sisters-in-law who, not yet married, were still living at home and performing the work of the temple's junior female religious specialists, or *waka bōmori,* and getting acquainted with her future parishioners. During this period she began receiving her practical education as a *bōmori.* She accompanied her mother-in-law when she cleaned the main hall, prepared the daily rice offering for the Buddha, arranged the flowers on the altar, maintained the grounds, and received visitors and business calls for the temple. On the day of a major event, she learned how and when to serve tea to the visiting lecturer (*kōshi*) when the temple hosted a dharma talk. Very little of this instruction was explicit, however: "Rather than my mother-in-law explaining to me what to do, it's more like I watched and tried to remember how she did things," Kayoko explained. All the while, she continued to read the cues from her mother-in-law and parishioners to discern what was expected of her in terms of demeanor and comportment. As a certified nursery school teacher, she had the interpersonal skills and nurturing qualities that can help a *bōmori* be successful at her job; on the other hand, she got the impression that her copper-dyed hair, so common in urban Kansai where she grew up, should be toned down if she were to look more like a temple person. Because of her duties behind the scenes at the temple and the business of raising her own two young children, she told me that she did not plan to work at the temple's day care as a teacher, despite her credentials.

On the days of major rituals, Kayoko served as a kind of runner, taking instructions from her mother-in-law in the kitchen, relaying messages, and running errands as she helped the lay volunteers prepare for, execute, and clean up after the event. Often she would join the laywomen's association members in the kitchen and learn from them the customary way of preparing the communal feast. Although the laity were welcoming enough, she reports being daunted by the task of remembering all their names and faces—there were so many of them, and only one of her. The language barrier between her and her new community was also unexpectedly strong: the local dialect in Kagoshima Prefecture is famously difficult to understand, and Kayoko had spent her whole life in Kyoto. In addition, she found that the temple's parishioners possessed a religious fervor and an expertise in the Shinshū teachings that made her ashamed of how little she herself knew.

In her quest to learn more about her future profession, Kayoko became involved in the district's temple wife association, or *bōmori kai,* where she met both older and younger *bōmori* than herself. By talking to peers from other temples, she learned that there were a variety of situations for temple wives, often dependent on local customs or the division of labor within a particular temple family. Appraising the precedent set by her in-laws, Kayoko also noted that all of the women in her husband's family had their ordination, and they often made the temple's monthly home visits to parishioners' homes. Though no one expressed the expectation explicitly to her, she surmised that she should be prepared to do the same when she moved into the temple.

Although initial ordination (*tokudo*) in the Jōdo Shinshū Honganji denomination technically only requires a ten-day retreat followed by a ceremony at Nishi Honganji, Kayoko was intimidated by how little she knew about Buddhism. She decided to undertake a full year of study at Nishi Honganji's central seminary in Kyoto, although this is not a formal requirement for ordination. Kayoko's feeling was that children who grew up in a temple must have unconsciously absorbed an understanding of the Buddhist teachings since they were young. "I've tried asking my husband to explain things about Buddhism to me, but he's lived in a temple his whole life, so he can't explain it. He can't tell the difference between what's obvious and what people from the secular world have no idea about." As a woman who grew up in a lay household, Kayoko found even basic Buddhist concepts surrounding suffering and salvation to be mystifying. Her husband, who grew up living and breathing all things Shin Buddhist, had trouble explaining such things to a non-Buddhist. In sociologist Pierre Bourdieu's terms, Kayoko's husband's "practical sense" as a temple son, from which flows "the pre-verbal taking-for-granted of the world," puts him in a fundamentally different relationship to the Buddhist teachings than that of his wife (1990, p. 68). Kayoko's approach to learning doctrine was by necessity more deliberate and more cognitive.

In order to attend seminary, Kayoko moved back into her birth parents' home in Kyoto and enrolled her two young children in Nishi Honganji's preschool while she went to study full-time. The seminary's curriculum is designed to solidify or augment the informal training that temple sons and daughters have received from their parents (see table 1). In practice, it is one of the places where temple-born twenty-somethings go to meet a potential spouse who also comes from the temple world. When I interviewed Kayoko near the end of her year at seminary, I asked if she felt prepared to be a *bōmori* yet. She answered equivocally: "I still don't feel like I've learned enough about the teachings—a lot of it is really hard to understand, and having to take care of my kids at night I was usually too tired to study. The teachers were nice enough to let me pass anyway. It was mainly worthwhile because of the people I met there. I plan to keep in touch with them."

Kayoko's feeling of being incompletely prepared despite having attended a Shinshū seminary full-time for a year is extremely common among lay-born temple wives. Many women blame their lack of formal training for their ignorance, but in Kayoko's case she continued to disclaim any expertise in the tradition even after a year of formal study. Regardless of the level of formal or informal training temple daughters-in-law have received, the narrative of incomplete preparation is nearly universal. The lack of a clear start and finish to a *bōmori*'s training is aptly reflected in the quotation with which this chapter began, spoken by a national leader among temple wives in the Ōtani-ha: "I'm not sure when I became a *bōmori*."

A few weeks after graduating from seminary, Kayoko departed for Kyūshū again to finally move into the temple and begin occupying the role of junior *bōmori* full-time. Her sisters-in-law had married and moved out of the temple, and her mother- and father-in-law were making rumblings about wanting to retire within the next three years. "They're still quite healthy, I don't know why they need to retire so soon," she confided to me. Despite her feeling of still being an amateur, particularly with regard to the Buddhist teachings, the full mantle of temple wife would soon be hers alone.

Acting out of a desire to be an able assistant in her husband's family business, Kayoko has transformed herself into a religious professional. She plans to take basic ordination when her children are old enough to be without her for the ten days of the training retreat. Her practical knowledge of what a *bōmori* is supposed to do has primarily been obtained through a much more informal and local process of being mentored by her husband, her mother-in-law, and her parishioners.

Mother-in-law as Mentor

Although Kayoko's experience is relatively typical, she was fortunate to have been able to live separately from the temple for so long before, to have kind and patient in-laws, and to have been able to spend an entire year studying Buddhism in a formal setting. Another of my informants, Mari, a temple wife in her early thirties, was having a similarly privileged experience as a temple daughter-in-law when I met her Kyoto, but she wanted me to know that not all young *bōmori*-in-training were so lucky.

Mari is quiet, intelligent, and studious, but like her peers at the Honganji-ha seminary, she also enjoys a good night out drinking. She met

Theme	Subject	Content
Jōdo Shinshū	Shinshū	Explanation of the fundamentals of Shinshū teachings and faith
	Scriptures	Overview of Shinshū scriptures such as the three Pure Land sutras
	Shōshinge	Reading and explanation of Shinran's Shōshinge, fundamental Shinshū texts and the tradition of the seven masters
	Wasan	Explanation of Shinran's three major collections of Japanese hymns
	Tannisho	Reading of the Tannisho and explanation of its major principles
	Fundamentals of Shinshū seminar	Discussion-style study of the Shinshū teachings
Buddhism	Basic Buddhism	Fundamental doctrines of Buddhism
	Buddhist sects	Explanation of the basic teachings of each sect
	Fundamentals of Buddhism seminar	Discussion-style study of the Buddhist teachings
Religion	Religion	Overview of religion
History	Buddhist history	Overview of Buddhism's history in India, China, and Japan
	Shinshū history	Overview of Shinshū history
Propagation	Essentials of propagation	Explanation of propagation (dendō)
	Propagation practicum	Instruction in giving dharma talks
Ritual (gonshiki)	Ritual	Explanation and instruction in daily liturgies
	Chanting	Explanation and instruction in chanting
	Ritual practicum	Practice in performing rituals
Laws	Sectarian bylaws	Basic explanation of the Honganji-ha's bylaws
Applied Shin Buddhism (Jissen Undō)	Lecture series on applied Shin Buddhism	Practical aspects of working toward a cooperative society based on Shin Buddhist principles (On-dōbō no Shakai wo Mezasu Undō)
Culture	Calligraphy	Practicum
	Buddhist music	
	Flower arranging	
Physical Education	P.E.	

Source: Chūō Bukkyō Gakuin website. http://www.chubutsu.jp/lecture/summary.html (accessed May 16, 2017).

her husband at the elite university they both attended in Tokyo more than ten years ago. As she tells it, they were just close friends for many years during and after college because her husband had promised himself he would not get married. The reason he gave was that he did not want to condemn someone to suffering the hardship of becoming a temple daughter-in-law, and then a temple wife. Eventually, he overcame his aversion to marriage—though he was sure to warn Mari of what she might be in for. The two wed in a large ceremony at his temple in Hiroshima, with hundreds of people in attendance. "I didn't know who most of them were," Mari recalls. "They were people from the temple world—parishioners, other temple priests, and all of his relatives."

At the time of my research Mari and her husband were living in Kyoto and pursuing careers unrelated to temple work. They returned home to her husband's temple only for major events when the temple family needed extra help. Mari knows there is a time limit built into her life in Kyoto, however, and she laments that there are probably no jobs in her professional field in the rural area where her future temple is located. She knows she will be required to give up her profession in favor of full-time temple work, and this is why she chose to complete a year of study at the Honganji-ha's central seminary. As part of her course, Mari attended the ten-day ordination training retreat with her peers at Nishi Honganji's Nishiyama Betsuin facilities outside of Kyoto and then returned to the head temple to undertake initial ordination.

I asked her over dinner one evening in Kyoto how her mother-in-law was preparing her for what her job would be when her husband eventually took over as *jūshoku.*

> In the beginning, I really had no idea what I was getting into with the temple work and temple life. But my mother-in-law has been kind enough to ease me into it, just a little at a time. [My husband and I] go and help out at the temple during busy times, like *obon* and *hō-onkō,* and she has me do just a little bit at a time. She doesn't want to overwhelm me. You see, there are two types of women who have suffered at the temple. One tries to inflict the same kind of suffering on her daughter-in-law, and the other tries to spare her the same suffering. I'm very lucky my mother-in-law is the second type.

Mari's mother-in-law had had her own difficulties as a young temple wife—it is safe to assume that nearly every temple wife has—and hoped to spare her daughter-in-law from such a trying mentorship. This was what had also motivated her husband to swear off marriage: he did not want to be responsible for bringing another daughter-in-law into the temple only to reproduce the cycle of hardship he had seen his own mother endure. At this stage in her long-distance internship, Mari was able to consider trips to the temple in Hiroshima as something like a vacation. She tended to shrug off my questions about the difficulty of being a temple daughter-in-law with assurances that her situation was actually quite privileged, and that she was being spared the difficult crash-course in temple manners that some young women had to undergo.

However, when I met her and her husband for dinner near their apartment in Kyoto over a year later, Mari was late meeting me at the bus stop. As she hurriedly pushed her bike up the street, I saw that she was carrying a tall spray of flowers wrapped in paper in the front basket. There was a perceptible grimace on her face as she explained that her mother-in-law had "suggested" that she take flower-arranging lessons in preparation for her future career. It was a necessary skill to be able to arrange the flowers in the temple's altar, her husband's mother had explained, and the temple would be willing to pay for it. After all, it was a useful way to spend her time while she was still living in Kyoto. Today, her lesson had run late because her teacher, perhaps sensing that she was distracted and looking forward to another appointment, had told her she was not concentrating properly and required her to begin her arrangement again. I asked Mari if she enjoyed flower arranging, and she replied, "I'm not particularly interested in it, but I guess it is an interesting exercise in patience." Despite her mother-in-law's gentle touch as a mentor, the reality of Mari's future as a temple wife, and the ways in which her own desires and inclinations would have to be curtailed to conform with the role, were beginning to sink in. As an intelligent and hardworking woman who strives to perform well in her first career as a Japanese language instructor, Mari will likely continue to take the same approach to her future career as a temple wife.

Most of the *bōmori* I spoke to agreed with Mari's characterization of the two "types of mothers-in-law." Women who treat them harshly may be trying to "break in" their daughters-in-law through hardship, just as they once had been by their own mothers-in-law. This aspect of temple family culture is consistent with the broader Japanese sensibility about ethical cultivation. Dorinne Kondo comments that "In Japanese society in general, hardship is considered one pathway to mature selfhood" (1990, pp. 108–109). During her fieldwork as an employee at a confectionary, Kondo's coworkers used expressions such as "*kurō ga tarinai*" ("he hasn't experienced enough hardship") or "*kurō saseta hō ga ii*" ("he needs to be made to suffer") to describe what needed to happen to their young, cocky coworker in order for him to achieve maturity (p. 109). In the case of temple wives who marry into their husband's temple, it is often the mother-in-law who assumes this task of mentoring—some would even describe it as hazing—the younger woman into maturity.

The structural position of the daughter-in-law in Japanese households is a difficult one. Scholars such as Allison Alexy have noted that the traditional concept of the daughter-in-law as the "family's bride" (*uchi no oyo-mesan*) continues to wield influence, even among urban women. The young women Alexy interviewed in her fieldwork on marriage and divorce in urban Japan continue to feel tied to the idealized standard of a docile daughter-in-law who puts the needs of her in-laws before her own. The stereotypical dynamic between daughter-in-law and mother-in-law, in which the latter brings the former into line with the ways of doing things in her new household, borders on abuse. Alexy writes: "Because mothers-in-law are commonly understood to be responsible for teaching a [daughter-in-law] the ways of the family she's married into, the stereotypical mother-in-law harshly critiques a bride's every move, forcing her to second guess her most basic actions" (Alexy 2011a, p. 249). To the extent that nuclear families have replaced three-generational households in Japan, the experience of living under the mentorship—or tyranny, as the case may be—of one's mother-in-law is not as universal as it once was in the life cycle of Japanese brides.[5] Temple daughters, however, continue to experience it acutely.

Making a young wife her mother-in-law's apprentice can lead to

A *bōmori* and her daughter-in-law, the *waka-bōmori*, follow along as the *jūshoku* performs the morning service. The young successor watches from his mother's lap.

rocky relations, fraught with generational tensions, jealousy, or territoriality. The most wrenching stories of frustration, and sometimes despair, about relations with mothers-in-law come from young wives who have completely moved into the temple and live under the scrutiny of their in-laws from morning till night. The below statement was posted to an online community of temple daughters-in-law on Mixi, a popular Japanese social networking site, by a young woman who appears to be suffering at the hands of Mari's "first type" of mother-in-law:

> Sometimes I think horrible things about [my mother-in-law], thoughts unbefitting a temple person. It's so awful....I just want my daily life to be more peaceful. I want to spend more of my days smiling. Every day is so hard, just seeing her face is so painful I can't stand it.[6]

While this woman's desperation might be somewhat extreme, her post is followed by a number of sympathetic notes from other temple wives who offer commiseration and advice.

There may not be anything particularly Buddhist about this generational clash other than the fact that it takes place in a Buddhist temple and is a fairly common process in the acculturation of daughters-in-law into their new temple household's domestic practices and ritual decorum—for instance, how they arrange and clean the temple's altar, and what relations they maintain with their parishioners. It is often the case, though, that a distinctly Buddhist narrative takes shape around the soteriological meaning of such hardships. The social givens in a person's life—especially but not only one's parents and spouse, and one's obligations to them—are often cinched together with the idea of one's spiritual indebtedness to the Buddha. Shin Buddhist doctrine, if it is available to a young temple wife, can be a resource for understanding not only hardship but also family relationships as being the social conditions through which one's karmic destiny comes to pass.

The Karmic Ground of the *Bōmori*

In the fifteenth century, *bōmori* who read the letters of Rennyo (1415–1499) or listened to sermons based on his epistles would have encountered messages such as this one:

> Those who become wives of [Shinshū priests]...should be aware that this happens because past conditions (*shukuen*) in their previous lives are not shallow. This awareness, however, will come about after they have realized that the afterlife is the matter of

greatest importance and [have] undergone a decisive settling of faith. Therefore, those who are to be wives [of the priests] should, by all means, firmly attain faith.[7]

The message continued to be reiterated, often verbatim, in sermons for Jōdo Shinshū priests' wives until around the middle of the twentieth century (Starling 2013). In other words, in the classical doctrinal view, the social conditions into which a *bōmori* was born—or married—were evidence of her karmic predestination, resulting from a profound connection to Buddhism in her past lives.

The concept of *en*—which can be translated variously as "opportunity," "connection," "affinity," or "fate"—is crucial for understanding notions of causality and agency in the Jōdo Shinshū tradition and in Japanese Buddhism more generally. In Buddhist doctrinal terms, *en* refers to the conditions (Skt. *pratyaya*) that aid the fruition of one's past karma. In common Japanese usage, the Buddhist meaning may be more or less explicit depending upon the person using the term, but the view of causality that it invokes is certainly of Buddhist origin. Ian Reader summarizes the contemporary Japanese view of karmic causality as follows:

> The recognition that physical events have spiritual causes is intrinsic to traditional Japanese views of the world.... Karma (Japanese: *innen*), the notion that all events and actions have repercussions, often referred to in Buddhist terms as the law of cause and effect ... may be transmitted and shared—recognition, indeed, that people do not stand in isolation but are closely bound, especially through blood and familial ties, with each other, existing as a result of a series of interconnected causal relationships and defined through them, rather than in more individualistic terms.
>
> Karma need not have negative connotations: the word *en* (affinity, karmic relations) which is frequently used in terms of relationships has distinctly positive nuances. When two people join their *en* together (*en o musubu*) they are getting married, and *en* may bring people into contact with each other [as in, "the Buddha's *en* has brought you to this temple"]. The whole field of relationships that develop between people and [gods], Buddhas and ancestors is closely connected to the concept of *en,* to the process of creating it and causing it to continue for the benefit of the living. (Reader 1991, pp. 47–48)

While *en* is a polysemous term employed in a broad range of contexts to account for the relational conditions of a person's life, the concept's association with love and marriage in Japan is especially strong. Anne Dutton has documented the activities of two particular temples that served as divorce temples or "temples for severing karmic relations" (*engiridera*) during the eighteenth century (Dutton 2002). In these cases, the expression for karmic relationship is used metonymically to refer to legal marriage. More recently, several ethnographic studies have shown how maintaining *en*—sometimes translated as "bonds"—between family members during life and after death has become a central concern driving the transformation of funerary practices in Japan (Rowe 2011; Boret 2014).

Beyond the general Japanese Buddhist view of karmic causality and interconnectedness, Jōdo Shinshū doctrine also contains a sense of the all-encompassing efficacy of Amida's Primal Vow. The notion of *tariki* or other-power—a radical insistence that salvation is achieved through "grace alone" (to borrow terminology from Protestant Christianity)—is an important part of the identity of the Jōdo Shinshū as distinct from other Buddhist schools. "Grace," as I use it here, refers to the mechanism by which a believer is caused to be reborn in the Pure Land and ultimately attains the Buddhist goal of enlightenment. For Shinran, a person's religious striving (what one might call "works") can have nothing to do with it. To live authentically as a Pure Land believer means to live "naturally" (*jinen*) or "without calculation" (*hakarai ni arazu*) in acceptance of the supreme power of Amida's vow. Within such a soteriology, individual agency is radically de-emphasized.

Today the term *en* is frequently heard in discussions among *bōmori* in relation both to building lasting connections between parishioners and the temple and to their own path in having come to live in the temple. One common expression when describing one's life path or current circumstances is *go-en o itadaita*, or, "I received this connection/opportunity." For example, a woman who contributed an essay to Nishi Honganji's biweekly newspaper *Honganji shinpō* explained her experience of marrying a temple *jūshoku*, whom she met at her own father's funeral, when she was middle-aged and going on to become an ordained Shinshū priest herself: "I've truly received a mysterious connection" (*hontō ni fushigina go-en o itadakimashita;* Hasegawa 2009, p. 7). The implication is that one's life course is the result of unknowable events in past lives, in particular the mysterious workings of Amida's limitless compassion in providing opportunities to encounter the Pure Land teachings. A *bōmori*'s connection to her husband is thus one of the most significant among the "field of relationships" encompassed by the term *en*.

The way my informant Mari first introduced herself to me provides an excellent example of the term's Buddhist connotations and their strategic deployment in certain contexts. I was having lunch with a group of female students from Nishi Honganji's central seminary in Kyoto, most of whom I was meeting for the first time. Out of the five young women gathered, all were temple daughters except for Mari, who came from a lay family. Each woman briefly introduced herself to me in front of the group, and when Mari's turn came, she explained: "I'm from Tokyo, and I really had no relationship to Jōdo Shinshū or temples or anything. But then I married a priest, and [*smiles*]—I mean, I had an *en*, and so I decided to come to [the seminary] to study more about Buddhism before I go and live in the temple."

Mari's shift in wording seemed to be a self-conscious recontextualization of the path that had led her to the seminary. She had begun by presenting her connection to her husband as mere happenstance: she *happened* to meet and fall in love with a Shin priest while she was a young woman in Tokyo and had entered the seminary simply to prepare herself for the lifestyle that now lay ahead. She then revised her wording—presumably for the benefit of her listeners, all of whom were all Shinshū seminary students except for me, an American researcher presumably here to learn about Buddhism— to reflect a more Buddhist worldview: meeting her husband represented an *en,* an opportunity brought about by a mysterious karmic connection to Buddhism, and to the Shinshū in particular. She had then chosen to pursue this opportunity by seeking her own ordination and education in the teachings.

I had to inquire among older, more seasoned *bōmori* before I found women who were more confident in narrating their marriage and careers using the Buddhist vocabulary of karmic predestination. When I attended a large gathering of *bōmori* at Higashi Honganji in 2011, each local group of women carried a flag into the Amida hall with a slogan they had chosen to communicate to their fellow *bōmori,* who had gathered from around Japan. The group from Tokyo carried a flag that read, "Receiving a fortuitous connection" (*Tama tama no go-en o itadaite*). Intrigued, I sought an interview with women from this group at an event the following month. Two officers, one temple-born and one lay-born, gladly answered my questions in between lectures at Higashi Honganji's conference facilities.

> *Temple-born Woman:* Until recently, it was common for women to marry from a temple into a temple.
> *Lay-born Woman:* But just yesterday [here at this conference] out of nine women [in our small group], only one had been born into a temple. Everyone else was a laywoman (*zaike*).
> *Temple-born Woman:* That's where this theme, "Receiving a Fortuitous Connection" comes from. From women who married in from outside a temple. The lifestyle is totally different, and quite possibly they married in without knowing anything about the Shinshū. So, when we heard that experience from people, that was the departure point for "this is where the encounter with Shinran begins."

Lay-born Woman: Usually a woman [marries in] from a lay
Shinshū household, but in my case my mother and father
were lay followers of the Sōtō Zen school. I went to a
Sōtō-affiliated university, and got a regular job. It was really
quite random that I made a connection with my husband
(*hontō ni tama tama no go-en*). It was quite mysterious....

Temple-born Woman: So, it's something you couldn't have chosen for yourself, but you do choose it....You did not choose
it yourself, but—

Lay-born Woman: —it's what is in front of you—

Temple-born Woman: —so you choose it.

Interviewer: And yet you did choose it. That is, you knew that
your partner was a priest, and you married him.

Lay-born Woman: But I didn't think, "I want to be a *bōmori*."

Temple-born Woman: Particularly when you are young when
you meet your partner, you don't think about it.

Lay-born Woman: I was a bit older, I had been working for a
while. And when I randomly (*tama tama*) met my husband,
and he said, "I've got this kind of place [a temple], how
would you like to come here [get married]." I thought, that's
the kind of place I could marry into, and I accepted. *From
there* I encountered Shinran. That was my departure point. I
didn't intentionally choose it, but in the end I suppose I did
choose it.

Temple-born Woman: So in the end, it's *tama tama* isn't it?

Once a woman has embraced her position as a *bōmori* and grown
more comfortable using a Buddhist vocabulary to narrate her path, she may
begin confidently to link her karmic predestination and the compassion of
Amida to her marriage. Although I have translated *tama tama* as "accidental,"
"fortuitous," or "random," it may just as easily be rendered "predestined," as
the women who are reconciled to the Shin Buddhist understanding of Amida's powerful compassion would consider even seemingly "random" events
and encounters as part of Amida's destiny for them; and indeed the sense of
karmic predestination is present more or less explicitly in the common Japanese usage of *tama tama*. Though there is a strong sense that a person's life
circumstances are mysteriously preordained, these circumstances are clearly
framed as opportunities rather than as a static destiny. In some ways Amida's
and the practitioner's agency work in tandem to bring the woman's accumulated karma (*shukugō*) to fruition.

Most women who live the majority of their lives in a temple manage
eventually to reconcile their interior disposition and their ascribed identity

as a *bōmori,* but the harmonization of interior and exterior is not automatic, nor universal. I asked the two women above about their peers who were unenthusiastic about their role or resistant to the Buddhist teachings. One of the women replied, "That's a temporary problem, and I think they will mysteriously come around at some point." Her use of the adverb "mysteriously" (*fushigini*) suggests that karma and Amida's compassion are the causes of the change. Her friend, who had been raised in a lay family but married a Jōdo Shinshū temple priest and was now in her fifties, agreed: "As they gain in years, it will happen. When you're young, it can be harder....All *bōmori,* though they may be *bōmori,* do not have the same intensity. Those women who are here today, at this venue, they are comparatively enthusiastic about the teachings." Her temple-born friend added: "Even here [at the *bōmori* conference] there are those who disliked the teachings in the beginning. Upon encountering them, though, it was like, 'Ah-ha!' and they were made to realize something about their current position."

In these women's explanation, which is a very typical one, the realization and embodiment of one's social position and the truth of the teachings can—and ideally do—occur in conjunction, either in a single epiphanous moment or more gradually. A temple wife should embrace two things simultaneously in order for her to achieve successful identification as a *bōmori* and faith as a Jōdo Shinshū adherent. The first is her "position" (*tachiba*) as a temple wife: this implies an outward performance of filial and religious duties contingent on her social relationship to in-laws and parishioners. The second is the Buddhist teachings themselves. When these two sources of meaning and efficacy converge, my informants tell me, the result is a *bōmori* who has "intensity."

Sometimes this Buddhist narrative of a woman's karmic trajectory, which ties together her romantic, filial, and religious identity, coheres only after years of outwardly performing service to the temple and carrying out the duties of a filial daughter-in-law. During this time, a *bōmori* may be acting like a Buddhist "in form only" (*katachi dake de*). A laywoman who has ultimately become a *bōmori* with intensity, like the lay-born woman in the above exchange, will emphasize in retrospect, as my informant did, that "*From there* I encountered Shinran." In other words, moving into the temple with her husband was a starting point for her religious journey. This process illustrates a move from physical performance (exteriority) to faith and resolution (interiority) in the inculcation of a *bōmori*'s subjectivity.

Outside the Temple: Temple-Wife Networks

While the everyday toiling that trains the young *bōmori*'s body and character in the lessons of temple life take place at her home temple and in the context of her family relationships, the acquisition of an intellectual familiarity with the tenets of the Jōdo Shinshū is not explicitly built in to a *bōmori*'s local training. Both Mari and Kayoko sought an independent education at seminary to fill in the gaps of their knowledge. It is in large part at more central sites of instruction, like *bōmori* association meetings hosted by the sect's district or national offices, that most women receive a doctrinal education in the frameworks of meaning that scholars generally associate with Buddhism. In the case of the Jōdo Shinshū, these frameworks include the doctrine of *tariki* and the resulting desire to repay one's debt to the Buddha.

Temple-wife associations (*bōmori kai* or *jizoku fujinkai*) began forming over a century ago when Buddhist and other kinds of women's associations were proliferating in the late Meiji period. [8] The Honganji-ha's first modern temple-wife association was formed in Tokyo in 1889, and the Ōtani-ha's was formed in 1928 (Chiba 2002, p. 125; Obata 2016, p. 121). Temple-wife associations, like the rest of the sectarian institution, are organized in a hierarchical structure, the smallest unit being local or neighborhood temple clusters.

In some cases, like the central Kyoto district, these neighborhood clusters may consist of a few dozen temples within a few miles of each other, but in more sparsely populated areas like Hokkaido, the temples may actually be an hour or more apart. Nearly every cluster has a *bōmori* association (although some may be currently inactive), which holds events of varying frequency (an average of three times a year) at a nearby meeting place. They may use the facilities of the district administrative office (*kyōku kyōmusho*) or a branch temple (*betsuin*) of the sect's headquarters if one is nearby, or they may rotate the hosting responsibilities among the members' own temples. [9]

Each local *bōmori* association is led by three to four officers, who usually serve three-year terms before the responsibility rotates to another member. While it is possible for an uninterested *bōmori* to duck this responsibility and remain uninvolved in the association's extracurricular activities, if she wants her temple to remain in good standing with its neighbors—an important consideration, as many temple communities rely on each other to provide priestly support at major rituals—she must commit at least a minimum of effort to participating in the association. Not all *bōmori* eagerly seek to participate. Some find it an unwanted demand on their time that they can hardly spare in addition to their work at the temple and raising their children or taking care of elderly in-laws. However, for many women, the *bōmori* association provides a community of peers and opportunities for study and social involvements that prove critical to their thriving as *bōmori*. This is most obvious in the case of young women from lay families, who may start out with little self-confidence, a sense that is reinforced by their lack of expertise in the tradition. Local *bōmori* association study groups and lectures can begin to provide the education that these women crave, as well as providing a group of peers or elders in the profession outside of their somewhat complicated relationship with their mothers-in-law.

Generally speaking, officers of the local association elicit ideas for curriculums from their members or decide among themselves on a topic they find interesting and construct a program based on these requests. They bring in a teacher to give a lecture or workshop for the members, usually a male professor from a nearby Jōdo Shinshū-affiliated university, a social worker or clinical psychologist, or sometimes a professional Shin preacher (*fukyōshi*). Typical topics in the Kyoto group whose meetings I frequented included methods of grief counseling, the temple's role in the community, the relationship between Shinran and his wife Eshinni (1182–1268?), and various topics on discrimination and human rights (such as gender equality, leprosy, and outcastes), in connection with the sect's Dōbōkai Movement (see chapter 6).

Local networks can provide opportunities for women to become involved in the social activities supported by the sect. Their meetings may also serve as a social forum for staying in touch with their *bōmori* colleagues. Beyond these local associations are district (*kyōku*) and regional (*renku*) workshops, which are held roughly once a year. Known as *benkyōkai* or *kenshūkai,* these overnight retreats are attended by the officers of each level of *bōmori* association and any other interested *bōmori*. In the Honganji-ha, the highest level of bureaucratic organization of *bōmori* associations is the district association; but in the Ōtani-ha, the various regional *bōmori* associations are joined in the National League of Bōmori Associations (Zenkoku Bōmorikai Renmei), which is overseen by the sect's Organizations Department (Soshikibu).[10]

Having the opportunity to travel to the sect's Kyoto headquarters— the bureaucratic and symbolic center of the Jōdo Shinshū—can have a strong influence on the identity formation of *bōmori*. Women are invited to articulate their individual accounts of becoming a temple wife in the presence of other temple wives who are doing the same. This is a forum that explicitly urges a woman to reflect on herself in the context of the temple, the Shin Buddhist tradition, and as a Buddhist in Japanese society. Each individual woman is also, of course, a number of other things besides a temple wife—a housewife, a mother, a daughter or daughter-in-law of the elder temple priest and wife, a role model or point person for her temple's laypeople (especially its *fujinkai* or laywomen's association), a member of a neighborhood, a PTA member—and she likely plays other roles as well. At a national convention, however, each woman must define herself *as* a temple wife among her fellow temple wives, sifting through all of her multiple identities in answer to the question—posed explicitly by her elders—"Who are you as a temple wife"? This moment of truth may catalyze the cohesion of a narrative that would otherwise remain unarticulated.

Because all the attendees at the national conferences of the League of Bōmori Associations are leaders of their local *bōmori* associations, one might assume that they would exude confidence and assuredness with regard to their position as *bōmori*. However, when I began talking to individual women at one Higashi Honganji conference about why they came to the conference, nearly all of them protested that they had been "roped into" (*hippareta*) being an officer rather than seeking out the position, which they explained was simply rotating and eventually came round to them. Their universally deferential accounts indicated that they did not yet feel confident claiming the title of *bōmori* or serving as representatives of "*bōmori*" in a study being conducted by an American scholar.

One woman in a small group discussion that I attended reflected on the significance of networks to her own evolution as a *bōmori* in a way that was telling. This laywoman of about forty had married a priest but lived apart from her in-laws' temple and knew nothing of its activities until, after a sudden death in her husband's family, she was thrust without any ceremony or preparation into the role of *bōmori*. She responded to the discussion group leader's question, "How are you coming along as a *bōmori*?" as follows:

> In my case, last year's conference was my first time to come to the head temple [Higashi Honganji], and at that time the question also came up about "you as a *bōmori*." In truth, before that I had no concept of myself "as a *bōmori*." When I took over as *bōmori*…it was quite out of the blue. There was absolutely no transition, and I knew absolutely nothing about how it had been done before I got there. So, still acting like a regular salaryman's wife, I just jumped right in. In fact, I was still living in the same home as before and was just commuting to the temple, so I had even less sense of "protecting the temple" or that I had "become a *bōmori*." So I just went to the temple, cleaned, and if I ran into parishioners I would greet them. And that was it. Of course, when there was a yearly event I managed all of that.
>
> Last year, though, when I participated in this [the national *bōmori* conference], I thought, "Oh I guess I have to think about this "as a *bōmori*" thing too. Slowly but surely, I heard about how things are different in different places, [and I realized that] because there are different situations, people have different ways of thinking, and there are different ways of doing things. So now I think going forward I will have to figure out how I can be a *bōmori* in my own way. But at this point, I still don't have *any* consciousness of myself as a *bōmori*. Seriously, I really don't—I don't know how I can do it. That's how it is. Nothing comes to mind when someone says the word "*bōmori*" to me—it really doesn't. It's just like, "I'm doing temple work."

As this woman's account suggests, the experience of deepening one's self-awareness as a *bōmori* by plugging into networks, whether local or national, is not necessarily a universal one for temple wives. This woman initially identified herself only locally, in relation to her husband, her predecessor (mother-in-law), and her parishioners, and gathered what she could about her job from these local cues. Only when she attended her first conference did she begin to conceptualize *bōmori* as something abstract and universal and try to fit her individual instantiation of it into that broader category. Nonetheless, by her own account, two trips to the sect's headquarters to converse with *bōmori* peers and listen to lectures have thus far been inadequate to fully bring her into the role. Whether as a result of resistance, inexperience, or other obstacles, she still does not confidently identify herself as a *bōmori,* despite performing the outward duties of the position and representing her *bōmori* peers as an officer in her district's *bōmori* association.

A National Conference for Young *Bōmori*:
Accepting the Blessings of Hardship

Like my two informants Mari and Kayoko, many *bōmori* who were raised in a lay family begin their careers with the rather modest goal of simply not disappointing their husband or in-laws. Learning Buddhist doctrine is usually on their to-do list—many express acute anxiety that a layperson will ask them a question about Buddhism that they will be unable to answer—but there is little opportunity to do so in their everyday lives. They therefore solicitously seek out clear explanations both of their duties as a *bōmori* and about sectarian doctrine. There could be no more authoritative site for such instruction than the sect's headquarters in Kyoto. Although the Honganji-ha does not have a nationally confederated *bōmori* association, a national gathering of *bōmori* does take place during the twenty-four-hour training preceding the *bōmori* initiation ceremony (*bōmori shiki*) held once a year at Nishi Honganji.

Since 1999, the Ōtani-ha's League of Bōmori Associations has hosted a yearly gathering known as the National Young Bōmori Conference (*Zenkoku waka bōmori kenshūkai*). In May 2010, I attended one of these gatherings at Higashi Honganji. On the first morning of the conference, sixty-six women arrived in Kyoto from all over Japan, depositing their bags in their assigned dorm rooms and picking up their conference materials and white service group (*hōshidan*) sashes to be worn while using the Dōbō Kaikan retreat facilities. Seventeen of the sixty-six brought their children, who would be looked after in the childcare room on the first floor of the retreat building, and the sounds of wailing infants desperate for their mothers could often be heard upstairs in the lecture hall. Occasional mention was made in remarks and lectures during the conference of the "young successors" who were playing downstairs.

The attendees of the two-day event were primarily temple daugh-ters or daughters-in-law who participated at the local level in *bōmori* associ-ation workshops. As I asked them about themselves, however, most women were thoroughly dismissive of their qualifications as *bōmori* and unsure how to explain their exact positions at their home temples. Common replies were: "I'm actually just a temple daughter, and I'm not even married yet, so I'm not really a *waka bōmori*"; or, "I still don't live in the temple, but my husband is in line to inherit it, so I thought I would make an effort to get involved with our local association." These deferential accounts indicated the ambiguity of these women's positions at their home temple, and their reluctance to claim the title of *waka bōmori*.

The conference materials distributed at check-in described the aim of the gathering as "Verifying together those tasks that are being asked of each of us, as individuals living in a temple in modern society." Beneath this motto, the aims of the retreat were expanded upon:

> Having received a karmic connection (*go en o itadaite*), we have placed our bodies in a Shinshū temple. As one who has married into a temple, as one who was born into a temple, as we engage with various problems and concerns, we are called "*waka bōmori*." We all have various thoughts, from challenges and hopes to trou-bles and uncertainties: "What can I do as a *waka bōmori*? How and what can I get involved with? What is expected of me? In what direction should I be headed?"
>
> Even if our customs and surroundings are different, we are all the same in that we are treading the path of *bōmori* amid the same Shinshū teachings. That which can't be seen by one person, may become visible through our connections to one another. Haven't our elders (*senpai*) also experienced concerns and uncertainties? How are our elders engaged with the temple?
>
> We hope that this study retreat will be an opportunity for you to take your doubts and uncertainties, get closer to your *senpai*, and reexamine the way you yourself are living.

Workshops in the Jōdo Shinshū are informed by Rennyo's entreaty to "Get together and discuss the Buddhist teachings" (*Goichidaiki kikigaki* 201, SSZ 3: p. 581); they generally feature large-group lectures interspersed with discussions of the lecture held in smaller breakout groups. The National Young Bōmori Conference was carried out on these two planes. First, an eminent teacher delivered a series of lectures in the main hall; and second, participants dispersed into small groups of their peers (with whom they also roomed overnight) to discuss the lecture and share their individual experiences at the temple. These two elements combined to weave a distinctly Shin Buddhist narrative that dealt with the common plight of young temple wives and the religious meaning of their existence at the temple.

In the five years or so leading up to Shinran's 750th memorial celebration (which would be observed in a series of events throughout 2011), the themes of workshops held at the head temple were overwhelmingly related to this major event of the sect. In the case of the May 2010 convention, however, the conference lectures (two ninety-minute sessions over the two days) were given by a *bōmori* elder, who focused on her own experience of learning to be a *bōmori*. Fujiwara Chikako, a distinguished woman in her seventies, is the retired *bōmori* of an eminent temple in Ishikawa Prefecture as well as a teacher, author, and wife of a well-known professor. The title of her talk was, "As Someone Who Places Her Body at the Temple: Living a Connected Life" (*Tera ni karada o oku mono to shite: Tsunagari no inochi o ikiru*). Part of her talk involved a simple explanation of some basic Shinshū doctrinal concepts, and for this she referred her listeners to the *Shōshinge* and the *Tannishō*, texts that are contained in the standard red book of Shinshū scriptures the women had been instructed to bring with them. However, the young women were clearly more excited to hear about her own experience of having married into a temple herself and how she had overcome her own difficulties. She shared such stories generously.

Fujiwara had grown up in a lay Shinshū family outside of Nagoya and married a man she met at Waseda University in Tokyo. Her husband was the successor to an important Shinshū temple in Ishikawa Prefecture, and when she moved back to the Hokuriku region with him, she seemed to have one embarrassing or troubling experience after the other. Far from home, she had frequent misunderstandings with her parishioners as a result of her ignorance of the local dialect. Her listeners laughed at these anecdotes, releasing a bit of their own tension in the process. Some of her experiences back then were truly difficult, she confided, but even though she saw it only as hardship (*kurō*) at the time, she now knows that she was truly brought up by the people of Ishikawa, both her in-laws and her parishioners. She thus now feels nothing but gratitude for those adversities. She asked her listeners: "When you find yourself living with your in-laws, don't you sometimes long for the blue skies of your hometown? It is hard to accept the blessings of these hardships, isn't it?"

As a role model for her young listeners, by divulging her own journey through culture shock, adversity, and a gradual embracing of the role of *bōmori*, Fujiwara offered some assuagement of their nagging sense of being out of their depths at the temple, and also a story line of maturation to which they could aspire. The softening of the young audience's worried expressions was visible each time the teacher reminded them, in an authoritative yet reassuring voice, that all they needed to do at any given time was the *very least* of their job description, and that they need not do everything perfectly from the start. Fujiwara frequently repeated the reassurance, "It's okay to only achieve zero percent. As long as you try." In particular, notes were rigorously taken whenever she gave her listeners some concrete idea of what that "very least" might be: for instance, greet parishioners with kindness and equanimity when they visit the temple; offer guests cold tea in the summer and hot tea in the winter; do their best to keep the Buddhist altar somewhat tidy and decorate it with a basic sense of propriety; and put the Buddha's rice out every morning without making any egregious errors.

After the lecture, the participants broke into small groups for discussions. They were encouraged by staff members to try to relate the teacher's lecture to their own experiences at the temple. In the small tatami rooms, gathered in a circle around low conference tables, the women took turns offering comments on the lecture's relevance, or lack of relevance, to their life at the temple. At many conferences I attended at both Nishi and Higashi Honganji, I was able to join these small group sessions as a guest, and after some initial attention paid to my presence, women often settled into their normal practice of disclosing personal experiences, including poignant or bitter emotions. This time, however, my contact at Higashi Honganji, in her letter granting me permission to attend the workshop, asked me not to attend the small-group meetings. She explained that the young women often burst into tears there; as it might be the first time they had been asked to speak of their feelings about becoming a temple wife, they tended to be acutely vulnerable.

Small-group discussion at a workshop for young temple wives. Photo courtesy of Shinshū Ōtani-ha Bōmori Renmei.

The next morning at 9:00 a.m., however, the conference program began with presentations by women representing each of the small groups, so I was able to get some idea of what they had discussed. When it came time for the women to present, it became clear that there were still some young adults bordering on adolescence among the attendees: some women had lightened their hair—a statement of urban or youthful fashion in Japan—and they were largely not confident public speakers. Several women rushed through their speeches in shaky voices, struggling with the polite sentence constructions required in public speaking, and frequently looked down at their prepared scripts.

The first group representative nervously began by reporting that her cohort found the Shinshū teachings to be "difficult," that the language of the sutras seemed impenetrable, and that "even if they listen to sermons, they cannot understand." Some women even felt that the more they attended study groups in their local district, the less they understood. The more experienced young *bōmori* in their group and the elder *bōmori* association officer who had moderated the small-group discussion had reassured them that, if they wanted to understand, even if it was difficult at first, little by little they would get something from the teachings. The speaker, steadying her voice as she concluded her report, told the audience that, for her, the primary benefit of attending this conference had been that it made her realize there was no need to panic or do everything well right away. A second small-group representative reported a slightly less optimistic discussion among her group concerning a phrase used by Fujiwara-sensei: "the way to devote one's life" (*inochi o tsukusu hōhō*) to the temple and to Buddhism. They had felt resistant to this phrase, as none of her group members felt that they had the proper resolution (*kakugo*) to do this yet. They wished that Fujiwara could be present to assure them during the truly hard times they experienced at the temple. Much of the three-hour small-group discussion, the woman reported, was spent discussing the lack of clarity they felt about their job and how difficult it was to delegate labor with their mothers-in-law. This woman concluded her report by saying that, despite their having spent their time discussing difficulties, they all felt better now knowing that others had the same kinds of problems.

In sum, experiences of worries (*nayami*), uncertainty (*fuan*), and hardship (*kurō*) became building blocks in the narratives of young women working to construct themselves as *bōmori*. In the narrative presented at this workshop by senior *bōmori,* staff from the Ōtani-ha's Training Department, and the conference materials they had coauthored, the daughter-in-law's plight itself was understood as a necessary stage in a *bōmori*'s religious path: by suffering the hardships particular to the life of a young daughter-in-law, she may learn to turn feelings of desperation into gratitude, cultivating a uniquely Shinshū humility by embracing the contingent nature of her existence. [11] Conference attendees were repeatedly reminded during the retreat that they, like all other humans, were ordinary creatures replete with afflictions (*bonnō gusoku no bonbu*), whose every joy and sadness were gifts from Amida. Such suffering should be their teacher, in that it brings them closer to the humility necessary to accept their absolute contingency on Amida's compassion.

If she was able to accept this account, a young *bōmori* could feel assured that her suffering was part of a universal situation and was in the service of something—indeed, was something for which she should be grateful. A wife from a lay family who may feel particularly out of her element in her husband's family temple, by just listening to the lecture's narrative, will become more familiar with the religious language and worldview of her in-laws and may even begin to develop some facility in using this language herself.

A *bōmori*'s practical expertise is largely attained through her family relationships and her encounters with parishioners. The figure of her mother-in-law often looms large in this informal training. As seen in Fujiwara-sensei's story of adversity that was instantly recognized by the sixty-six attendees of Higashi Honganji's national retreat for young temple wives, the difficulties experienced by the young daughter-in-law in some ways constitute an informal initiation. The fact that the way things are done—for example, ritual procedures, altar arrangement and maintenance, and the division of labor among temple family members—is so very localized adds to some *bōmori*'s persistent sense of not being fully educated in an objectively "correct" way to execute their jobs. They therefore pay special attention and usually jot down exhaustive notes when they attend a conference at the head temple (Nishi or Higashi Honganji), whose standardized ritual procedure and doctrinal explanations are presumed to have absolute authenticity.

The young *bōmori* conference literature cited here pointed us to three concentric "sites" or social realities within which a *bōmori,* given the right resources and the experience of faith, can situate her bodily experiences—namely, the individual, the temple, and society. An "experienced body," points out Talal Asad, "is always sited in specific relations—even if these are changing, or contradictory—with itself and with other bodies, animate and inanimate, past and present" (1997, p. 49). A lay-born *bōmori*'s everyday training in new ritual procedures, manners of polite speech, domestic practices, and a new social position as a temple wife, is undertaken in the context of family relationships. When a temple wife travels to the center of institutional authority in her Buddhist sect, she is encouraged to locate her bodily experience in the context of the temple, society, and if possible, the all-embracing agency of Amida Buddha's compassion.

Depending on the degree to which she has access to education in the

Shin teachings, a *bōmori* may eventually learn to construe the adversity she encounters at home as an aspect of her existential situation as a Jōdo Shinshū follower. Narratives of successful *bōmori,* such as Fujiwara-sensei's autobiographical lecture, link the hardships a young daughter-law experiences to a path toward faith. Often, by the time a woman is in her middle age she will encounter some kind of stimulus to help her achieve a resolution and come to understand the Shin teachings in an existentially transformative way. Such an encounter, which is understood to take place through the grace of Amida, becomes the narrative of success for *bōmori.* The process is a humbling one wherein a *bōmori* strives to conform herself to various roles in relation to parishioners and in-laws. Although her first instinct may be to control or triumph over her difficult experiences through her own efforts or will (implying an unhealthy attachment to self-power, or *jiriki*), finally, realizing the futility of this, she comes to a better appreciation of the depths and power of Amida's compassion.

The twentieth-century Ōtani-ha doctrinal tradition in particular has emphasized introspection and acquiescence as being necessary dispositions for submitting to the salvation offered by Amida. This was the soteriological language used at the National Young Bōmori Conference. It is difficult to imagine a Buddhist explanation of "acquiescence" as a mode and a means of ethical cultivation that aligns more perfectly with the willful docility of participants in the Islamic piety movement studied by Saba Mahmood. Mahmood writes: "Although we have come to associate docility with the abandonment of agency, the term literally implies the malleability required of someone in order for her to be instructed in a particular skill or knowledge—a meaning that carries less a sense of passivity than one of struggle, effort, exertion, and achievement" (2005, p. 29). In the "acquiescence" implied by the ideal narratives related here, we see a similar will to transcend the individual, self-controlling self. For *bōmori,* this docility should be both filial and spiritual.

Wives in Front of the Altar

According to conventional custom, the leadership of our temples and churches has been limited to male priests only, and in the Shinshū there is no system of permitting so-called nuns (*nisō*). However, in the background we can imagine the strong work of women, so-called *bōmori*, who might well be called "untonsured nuns" (*uhatsu-ni*).

—*1929 article in the monthly journal of the Honganji-ha*

My father died in the war when I was four years old [in 1943]. My mother never had ordination and she despised doing rituals, but she had to after her husband died. The parishioners all recognized her, and still wanted her to come [perform services at their homes]. It seems there was no choice for women in those days—you hear stories about men coming in and offering to help with the temple, and then making off with all the money. So she did it herself, but as soon as I was old enough, I got my ordination and took over the ritual work for her.

—*Hisako, female resident priest in the Honganji-ha*

THE JŌDO SHINSHŪ DOES NOT HAVE A tradition of nuns. As a result, women have historically been affiliated with the tradition either as laywomen or as the wives and daughters of temple priests.[1] Today, temple labor is distributed among all of the temple family members, but its distribution is both fluid and unequal, just like the labor in any other household. As I showed in chapter 2, the physical demarcation of space along gendered lines at the temple is fairly clear-cut, at least in ideal terms. Men's work is "outside" and "in front": "outside" in the sense of leaving the temple to work, attend conferences, and visit parishioners' homes; and "in front" in the sense of being publicly visible as the performer of rituals and deliverer of lectures in the main hall. Women's work, complementarily, is "inside" and "behind." They remain inside the temple to greet guests who come by, and toil behind the scenes to clean, cook, and make preparations for rituals.

For instance, in chapter 2, I described a three-day *hō-onkō* ritual at a rural Niigata temple. Where were the female temple family members at this ritual? Two women, the daughters-in-law, were working in the kitchen while also attending to their young children. One, the senior *bōmori,* was running back and forth between the kitchen and the main hall, interacting with male and female volunteers, visiting priests, and lay attendees of the service. The wife of one of the assisting priests at the ritual was sitting *seiza* (legs folded beneath her) in the front row of the audience seating area. She had grown up in a temple in Hokkaido (the northernmost island of Japan), where the norm for temple wives was to be a model *monbōsha* (listener to the teachings) for the laity. On that day, none of the women in the temple family were participating in the ritual in a priestly capacity. This is the norm, but there are plenty of exceptions.

Rina, the daughter of the hosting temple family, told me that she had once tried to join the ritual as a priest rather than a back-stage helper. Freshly ordained and hoping to achieve some ritual parity with her brothers, she had timidly taken the ritual stage on Friday night for the first of four performances of the *hō-onkō* liturgy. As she sat next to her brothers and father on the elevated stage in front of the inner altar and looked out into the area in which the lay attendees sit, she was disappointed to see that there were only two laypeople in attendance. As she had gone to all the trouble of receiving ordination and convincing her father to let her perform the ritual, she wished there had been more people to see her. For the remainder of the weekend, when the more well-attended rituals were performed, she was busy with the domestic work of receiving and feeding guests, toiling alongside her sisters-in-law and lay volunteers in the kitchen and receiving rooms while her male family members performed the ritual work.

Despite this gendered division of labor within the temple family, the Jōdo Shinshū actually boasts the largest number of female priests, or *josei sōryo,* of any Buddhist school in Japan today. In the Honganji-ha, there are roughly 9,890 ordained women, and in the Ōtani-ha there are 10,640.[2] While this amounts to roughly one woman for each Shinshū temple nationwide, the majority of these ordained women are not serving as the resident priest of a temple. Only 3.8 percent of *jūshoku* in the Honganji-ha are female, and in the Ōtani-ha, only 1.3 percent.[3] Nearly all female priests in the Jōdo Shinshū are the wives, daughters, mothers, and widows of the resident priest. Many of these are *bōmori* who have chosen to ordain.

In this chapter, I explore the tensions that arise when a female temple family member attempts to move into a sacerdotal role. While many temple wives seek ordination and some become comfortable performing rituals—primarily monthly home visits, but also in some cases funerals and yearly events—alongside or in place of their husbands, the majority of temple wives must struggle to receive the recognition of the laity as having the same clerical authority as their husbands. In the event that a male priest is absent, however, a female family member is deemed a suitable replacement. This is a somewhat unexpected twist of the standard Japanese gender ideology: precisely *because* the wife must stay inside while her husband works outside the temple—or in an extreme example, goes off to war—she becomes the de facto religious professional of the temple, sometimes regardless of her ordination status. At no point in Shin Buddhist history was the need for temple family women to fill the clerical vacuum more widespread than during the Pacific War, when for the first time in history women in the Jōdo Shinshū were permitted to receive ordination in order to fill the clerical vacancies left by their husbands, fathers, and sons, who had been called off to war.

Nonetheless, in the past as today, it is only in the *absence* of a male body that a wife is deemed an acceptable priest. When a husband or a son that has come of age is available, the man in the family is consistently preferred as a ritual performer. However, there is another aspect of a temple priest's job for which a woman is more sought-after than a man, and that is connecting with parishioners on an intimate level. Part of a resident priest's job is often to make monthly visits to their parishioners' homes, in which they perform a sutra reading at the household Buddhist altar (*butsudan*)—but perhaps more importantly, engage in one-on-one conversation with their parishioners before and after the rite itself. My informants universally reported that women are better suited than men for the task of listening. In this chapter, I examine how gender works alongside ordination and inheritance as factors defining priestly roles and relationships with parishioners.

"Even the *Bōmori* Can Come": Negotiating Gender Roles at the Buddhist Altar

Currently, roughly half of *bōmori* in both the Honganji-ha and Ōtani-ha have taken *tokudo* ordination (a basic qualification to perform rituals), and a lesser number, between 10 and 13 percent, also hold the religious instructor or *kyōshi* degree (a qualification to become a *jūshoku*). These women are simultaneously *bōmori* and female Shin Buddhist priests. A major reason for this trend in ordination is that, as adult residents of the temple, *bōmori* may need to be certified to perform monthly home visits alongside the *jūshoku* or in his place. The most recent Honganji-ha internal survey estimates that 36.3 percent of current *bōmori* regularly perform rituals, although ritual participation varies by locality.[4]

How can we account for the increasing trend of temple wives taking on formal ritual duties? It may be a reflection of the advances women have made in Japanese society at large, slowly but surely penetrating professional positions that were once reserved for men. It has been suggested to me in numerous interviews, as well as in the pages of the gender-themed issues of the Ōtani-ha's academic journal *Kyōka kenkyū,* that the progress *bōmori* have made as ritual performers in the Shinshū is but a delayed response to the secular movement for the equality of the sexes.[5] On the other hand, it can also be read as an outcome of the gendered division of labor at the temple that dates back centuries.

Specifically, the role of breadwinner is a pillar of modern Japanese masculinity (Hidaka 2011; Goldstein-Gidoni 2012). In many smaller temples (for instance, those with less than one hundred registered parishioner households), income from religious activities alone is inadequate to support the temple family, and one member of the family is required to work outside the temple at a full-time job.[6] Japanese gender norms dictate that the husband must be the one to work at an outside job—despite the fact that he may have grown up in the temple, apprenticed to his father from a young age, become fully ordained after a year or two of study at seminary, and been registered as the temple's resident priest. When the resident priest takes an outside job, the *bōmori* is left alone (or with young children or elderly in-laws) at the temple all day. That means that when someone comes by or calls, it is she who acts as the representative of the temple, not her husband. In addition, when there is labor other than just passively guarding the temple that needs to be carried out during the week—monthly visits to parishioners' home altars, for example, or even memorial services—the wife often performs them. The reason many *bōmori* become ordained is to be prepared to act as an assistant priest in these situations. Even without ordination, however, an adult woman who lives in the temple is typically referred to as *otera-san* or "temple person" by parishioners, and has a certain amount of de facto clerical authority.

In this somewhat surprising transfer of religious authority, the woman becomes the priest by virtue of being a housewife. The fact that temple wives are the most logical or convenient choice to step in as priest during the week (or, as will be discussed in the next section, for a generation) does not mean that the transition from wife to priest is without its problems. While temple family women are seen as "good enough" to perform priestly duties in their husbands' absence, they are usually not parishioners' first choice.

Mochizuki Keiko, a feminist leader in the Ōtani-ha, points out that outdated images of a clerical partnership in which the woman does house-work while the man performs rituals still persist in the minds of parishioners: "When [the parishioners] have always thought that only a man could come and do the monthly ritual, it's only natural that when a woman comes, they feel consternation. In the old days, the *bōmori* would have been mopping the floor right before she came over" (Mochizuki 2006, pp. 136–137). In the *hō-onkō* ritual at the Niigata temple I described in chapter 2, the female volunteers themselves reported that their discomfort with entering the room where the visiting priests were received stemmed from the fact that their clothes were soiled from working in the kitchen all day. Mochizuki maintains that it is each individual temple wife's responsibility to shatter this stereotype by taking the initiative of becoming ordained and challenging the laity's outdated expectations.

In some regions, rituals performed by a female member of the temple family have been less valued monetarily than those performed by a male priest.[7] Variations in ritual honoraria are not solely determined by gender, however, and in some cases it may be customary to give a smaller amount for anyone who was not the *jūshoku,* or who had not yet been ordained, regardless of whether the replacement was a man or woman. There are some places, however, where the pay gap between husband and wife was explicitly gender-based. Mochizuki notes that in one case, the lukewarm reception she received from a parishioner was rooted in this traditional devaluation of women's ritual labor:

> I've also been told that it looks bad to their relatives [to have a female priest]. Once, after I did a memorial service, I was talking with the parishioners for a while at the communal meal. When the final round of alcohol was served, the parishioner asked me, "Why couldn't the *jūshoku* come today?" I had already told him the *jūshoku* was giving the dharma-talk at another temple. When I asked, "What's wrong with me?" he replied that his relatives might think that a woman came [instead of a male priest] because their contribution wasn't big enough! At that time, I received the same amount as the *jūshoku* would have. I replied without thinking, "Well, if that's the problem I can announce the amount of the contribution to everyone!" (Mochizuki 2006, pp. 136–137)

In Mochizuki's case, she possesses the same ordination degrees as her husband, and she expects to receive the same fee as her husband for rituals performed. Nonetheless, it seems that a stigma from this traditional practice of discounting the price when the wife performed the ritual may persist, limiting her desirability as a ritual performer.

In addition to centuries-old gender norms that idealize the temple wife in backstage roles rather than performing on the ritual stage, the strong momentum of the temple inheritance system also works against would-be female Shin priests. The custom of patrilineal temple inheritance, while cur-

rently the norm in all the Buddhist sects in Japan, is a model of priestly transmission that dates back to the Jōdo Shinshū's inception (Endō 2002). Today,
the position of *jūshoku* is almost universally passed on from father to son
(or some other male relative), and in fact the informal clerical "internship"
may begin when the son is as young as nine years old and receives his initial ordination. In the years that follow, the young successor may accompany
his father in home visits as he familiarizes himself with the ritual procedures,
texts, social routines, and names and faces of parishioners. The expectation
of the eldest son being the temple's next *jūshoku* is so strong among parishioners that they often affectionately call him "successor" (*atotsugi*) even before
he has taken ordination. This de facto clerical identity tends to trump factors
such as ordination in the eyes of parishioners. Although a temple wife may
now possess ordination (*tokudo*) and religious instructor credentials (*kyōshi
shikaku*) that are the bureaucratic markers of authority at Buddhist temples,
it is more difficult for her to physically embody parishioners' image of an
appropriate successor.

This type of clerical glass ceiling can be very frustrating for *bōmori*
who seek to share ritual duties with their husbands by obtaining ordination.
Sachiko, a temple wife in her sixties, worked hard to attain ordination and
facility in ritual performance but was still timid about performing rituals in
her husband's place. When she finally worked up the nerve, her parishioners
greeted her with discomfort and dismissiveness. Sachiko recalls: "The first
time I went to do a monthly ritual (*otsukimairi*) after getting ordained, it was
at our parishioner representative's (*sōdai*) house. I did the service, but later
the parishioner called my husband directly and said, 'If you were busy, you
could have just skipped this month. [Your wife needn't have come.]' I couldn't
believe it!"

Sachiko's eldest son, who is also ordained and is in line to inherit
the temple, has witnessed his mother's frustration and notes the disparity in
the way that parishioners receive him and his mother. They gladly welcomed
him when he would replace his father on home visits, even though he was
just a teenager: "Even if I would do a bad job, they said, 'It doesn't matter,
we're just glad you're here.' It was so different with my mother, though. They
told her she might as well not come. They didn't see her as a priest. Nonetheless, she worked hard to earn their respect, and I really admire her efforts."
This preference for a male member of the family to perform the priestly duties
is clearly not dictated by the individual's ordination credentials. Indeed, it
seems to exceed what is externally attainable for those who were not born
with the body of a (male) successor.

I asked three women who are part of a feminist group within the
Ōtani-ha[8] about the tendency for temple wives to be parishioners' second
(or third, if there was a male successor already in line) choice for ritual per-

former. They affirmed that it was often necessary for a *bōmori* to qualify or apologize for their visit because they were women, especially at first until the parishioners grew used to them in this role. One woman reported that when she first began to make monthly ritual visits in her husband's stead, she would volunteer an apology up front, saying, "He's otherwise engaged" or "He's not feeling well this week, so I'm sorry it will just be me today." Now when she arrives to perform the ritual she does not offer any explanation. If they ask why she and not her husband will perform the ritual, she tells them he has been called away to some other work. In her heart, she explained to me, she feels like this is bullying by her parishioners: they should be used to her as a priest by now, and should not even ask. Another woman from the feminist group agreed heartily, adding, "I detest saying, 'Is it alright if *even* the *bōmori* comes today?' Why do I have to say 'even'?" The women I talked to attribute such prejudice to vestigial societal norms dictating that women belong in the domestic realm instead of in front of the Buddhist altar in a position of sacerdotal authority. They are often irritated at the failure of their more conservative parishioners to recognize the possibility of the *bōmori* and the *jūshoku* working as equal partners in running the temple.

All this suggests that the absence of a male body is required in order for a woman to be seen as a suitable priest in the context of a family-run temple. For *bōmori* whose husbands or sons are alive and available, this translates into a less than enthusiastic reception from parishioners when they attempt to perform rituals themselves. As already mentioned, during the Pacific War the Shin sects suffered such a shortage of male priests due to conscription and overseas missionary work that they were forced to recognize temple wives bureaucratically for the first time as "proxy resident priests."

Guarding the Home Front: Filling the Clerical Vacuum during Wartime

The Honganji-ha first permitted women to become ordained in 1931 (Watanabe 1999). Female practitioners at that time were enjoying a high-profile moment in Shin Buddhist history, with a plethora of sect-sponsored events celebrating the contributions of Kakushinni, Shinran's youngest daughter, in helping to establish the earliest Jōdo Shinshū institution.[9] Multitudes of female practitioners, both temple wives and members of Buddhist women's groups (*Bukkyō fujinkai*), converged upon Nishi Honganji in Kyoto for a number of events in honor of the 650th anniversary of Kakushinni's death. The sect, eager to recognize and galvanize these women's enthusiasm, heaped praise upon female practitioners in publications and speeches. For example, in the 1929 piece quoted at the beginning of this chapter from the monthly magazine *Kyōkai ichiran*, the unsigned author lauded the behind-the-scenes contributions of temple wives through the years and even speculated that these wives should be more nobly titled "untonsured nuns" rather than just "temple guardians."

It is not clear whether the pending escalation of Japan's overseas military operations directly prompted the Honganji-ha's administration to allow wives to become certified as acting resident priests (*daimu jūshoku*), but it was certainly a factor in the case of the Ōtani-ha, the other major Shin sect.[10] The first *tokudo* ceremony in the Ōtani-ha to include women was held on March 3, 1942, and on the following day the status of *kyōshi* was first conferred on a woman. As war casualties increased and even young students were deployed to the fronts, Higashi Honganji authorized several special administrations of the exam as circumstances necessitated. In a special administration of the *kyōshi* exam for women on May 7, 1944, in Hokkaido, three hundred women are recorded as having taken it (Yamauchi 2006, p. 66, citing *Shinshū*). While in some cases female priests of this period trained and sat for exams alongside their male counterparts, as the ordination of temple wives and daughters was performed ever more explicitly for the purpose of filling the void left by male priests who had left for war, women's-only administrations of the *kyōshi* exam were given for these "temporary female *kyōshi*" (*rinji josei kyōshi*). Although such a sobriquet suggests that their status as priests was contingent upon the special circumstances brought about by the war, their credentials to act as the proxy administrator of their temple remained valid even after the war was over. Female priests in the Ōtani-ha were not granted permission to become full *jūshoku* for many more decades, however. In this sense, it was only in the capacity as an intermediary or placeholding administrator—whether as daughter, mother, or widow of the absent *jūshoku*—that women were seen as legitimate priests.

Commemorative photo of female participants in a special administration of the *tokudo* ordination, May 3, 1944. Photo courtesy of Shinshū Ōtani-ha (Higashi Honganji).

The Shin sects' struggle to find an appropriate place for women's service at local temples mirrored the ambivalence of the Japanese government during the early years of the Showa. In family-state ideology of the 1930s and 1940s, women were idealized for their fecundity and for their nurturing, protective roles as mothers. It was in the home, as a producer of children and protector of the stability of the stem-family (*ie*), that a woman was seen as a "crucial analogue to the male role of soldier fighting the 'sacred war' for the Japanese family-state" (Miyake 1991, p. 271). In Yoshiko Miyake's study of the abuses of female factory workers in 1940s Japan, one finds a striking analogy for the Jōdo Shin sects' approach to mobilizing women during the same period. As government officials debated the necessity of conscripting women for unarmed service from 1941 to 1944, "the contradiction between the two different tasks of preserving the family system and solving the labor shortage" became apparent (p. 288). Even when women eventually were conscripted in 1944, an exemption was retained for those "women whose roles as housewives and mothers were indispensable for family cohesion" (p. 289). Further, just as the increased presence of women in the workforce during the 1940s gave rise to more equal terms in postwar labor laws, so the precedence of women serving as fill-in *jūshoku* during the war provided an institutional foothold for women as priests that would eventually allow them to attain equal recognition (at least in theory) as full-time *jūshoku*.

Meanwhile, at a more intimate level than sectarian regulations and government policy, individual women were busy negotiating the role conflicts that were involved in simultaneously "preserving the family system and solving the labor shortage." In order to personalize the implications of the wartime shortage of priests and the institutional allowance for women to receive ordination, I include here a lengthy translation of a letter written by Katō Yano, a wartime temple wife who studied at the Osaka seminary to obtain her ordination.[11] The conflict this wartime temple wife experienced between having to guard the temple as a religious community (and a family business) and continuing to protect her young child is acutely evident in her letter. Katō wrote the letter to the teachers who had helped prepare her for the *kyōshi* examination. Her feeling of being simultaneously pulled toward and away from ordination and temple leadership by her familial obligations is quite poignant in her account. Her leader will lead us into a more detailed discussion of the complex interplay of filial duty, gender roles, professional aspiration, and religious sentiment that may have lead women to such an undertaking.

We can deduce from Katō's letter that her husband, the *jūshoku* of the temple she had married into, had either left for war or was deceased by 1941 when the Ōtani-ha began permitting females to take the *kyōshi* exam, and that he had no immediate surviving relatives. Katō had been managing the temple unofficially while caring for her young son when the announce-

ment was made that a women's training course and administration of the
kyōshi exam would be held at a nearby district office of Higashi Honganji
in January and February 1942. Although she leapt at the chance to become
ordained, she harbored significant reservations about the personal hardships
that such an undertaking would entail. On the other hand, if she managed to
complete the training course and pass the exam, the rewards would be great:
she would be officially recognized as the proxy *jūshoku* of her temple, and
the temple would be safely in her hands until her son was old enough to take
over. Although Katō does not mention it in her letter, one can easily imagine the uncertainty about the future that must have haunted her while she
managed the temple unofficially and visited parishioners' homes without having obtained official credentials. If another priest had wished to lay claim to
the temple, he would have had the legal right to do so, and Katō and her son
would have been forced to move out.

> When I heard the news in the middle of last November that a doc-
> trinal instruction center (*kyōgaku shidōjo*) would be opened at
> Namba Betsuin in Osaka and was seeking applicants for the *kyōshi*
> degree, I was delighted. I thought, "My prayers of late have been
> answered." But the season was then November, and [the training
> would take place in] January and February, which was the coldest
> time of the year. At that time my life at the temple, where I had
> lived together with my son in the seven years since the death of the
> *jūshoku* [my husband], wasn't particularly trying. But I worried
> about various things—for instance, wouldn't my seven-year-old
> son be lonely without his mother when he got home from school?
> Wouldn't I need to make more clothes for my family in this cold
> weather? What would happen if someone got sick? But I petitioned
> all of this to the Buddha, and despite the difficulties, I decided to
> enter the training course.
>
> Every morning I would wake up at 4:00 a.m. and get home at
> 4:30 or 5:00 p.m. We had a day off from school twice a week. On
> our early days I would use the extra time to make an evening visit
> to a parishioner's home [to do a service], and frequently I would
> run into someone on the way home and not even recognize their
> face [so harried was I].
>
> I felt so sorry when I would think about my son being all alone
> [after school], but thankfully the neighborhood children would
> play with him until late. I am so grateful for that.
>
> Beginning in January, I asked my birth father to look after
> things while I was out, so I could feel better about the house and
> the child while I studied.... [*After her child grows ill during the*

cold winter season] Saying prayers of gratitude, I imposed upon my seventy-four-year-old father to tend to the temple, leaving behind my child who was still not completely recovered as I headed to Kyoto....After our first day of training in Kyoto, I lay down to sleep, but it was no use. My father, my son's illness, the warnings from the teachers at that day's commencement ceremony, all of the uncertainties swam in my head like spinning lights. I couldn't sleep a wink on that first night. From the second day on, though, thinking of my own health, I calmed my mind and summoned myself to concentrate fully on my studies—because what would happen if I wasn't successful?

On the last day of winter, I made a request to the teacher and was able to return home. To say I was "grateful" is inadequate, but at any rate, [when I got home, I found that] my son was well, which put my heart at ease. However, when he said to me, "Mother, when I'm alone at night I start to cry," I felt so terribly sorry for him. But I hardened my heart and returned to Kyoto to listen to the teachings of Rennyo and Shinran.

I felt terribly when I thought about my elderly father, who had never had to lift a finger at our own home, doing all the cooking for me that winter—there was not a moment that I could feel at ease during that time.[12]

In the end, Katō was successful in her examination and returned home to her son, who had fully recovered. In this letter to her teachers she offers thanks for their instruction and guidance in helping her achieve her goals.

Katō's narrative of her experience is in some ways self-effacing: she cites her concern for her son and elderly father as the primary reasons why she found the experience of the training retreat so burdensome. Rather than crediting her own diligence or intelligence, she assigns all credit for her success in the *kyōshi* examination to her teachers and to Amida himself. This is a recognizably Shin Buddhist narrative of other-power (*tariki*) and gratitude. And yet the self-effacing nature of her narrative need not blind us to the objective significance of Katō's accomplishments under such trying conditions. The *kyōshi* exam was difficult, covering a wide range of topics (Shinshū doctrine, Buddhist studies, propagation, chanting, ritual etiquette, Japanese language, national history, and mathematics) and lasting for several days. While those who took it at the time are consistently deferential about the religious or social significance of their accomplishment, it nonetheless required a great deal of effort, ability, aspiration, and will to study for and pass these exams.

The other narratives that I collected from wartime female priests in the Otani-ha were similarly self-deprecatory. Most women expressed ambivalence about having stepped outside of the more traditional domestic role of the temple wife to rather uncomfortably don their husband's priestly robes. On the one hand, they felt required by the circumstances to continue perform-ing monthly ritual visits in their husbands' absence and to take whatever steps were necessary to protect the temple. They overwhelmingly cited practical necessity as their impetus for seeking ordination, and indeed many recalled being reluctantly compelled by their elderly in-laws to obtain the *kyōshi* degree in order to prevent the loss of the temple for the sake of the entire temple family. Many felt embarrassed about being seen in priestly robes, par-ticularly if they had to go outside the temple. Some women were confident enough about conducting daily tasks and carrying out the monthly home ser-vices for parishioners, but they still avoided conducting funerals. On these occasions they would ask for help from one of the few available male priests, sometimes their own elderly father or father-in-law. Such hesitancy suggests that most female priests in wartime still saw themselves primarily as wives and mothers rather than as independent priests; as such, they desired to con-tinue to embody the traditional norms for the *bōmori* who provides "domestic help" to the *jūshoku*'s more visible religious work.[13]

In short, wartime temple wives felt the double pull of both reproduc-tive and productive labor. As guardians of a home front that had been drained of male laborers, they often had to assume responsibility for both types of work. Some, like Katō Yano, were able to seize the opportunity to educate themselves about doctrine and ritual practice by taking the *kyōshi* examina-tion, which also ensured their legal right to hold the temple for a generation. And yet, in all of the cases I encountered, the role of temple priest was sought by women of this generation only temporarily: as soon as their husbands returned home or their sons came of age, they willingly passed the position of head priest back to the male successor.

Guarding the Temple for a Generation: Hisako's Story

The wartime years were exceptional in the number of temples that experi-enced a shortage of male priests, but the assumption of clerical duties by Shin temple wives in the absence of their husbands is certainly not limited to the early Showa period. In the introduction to this book, I presented the story of the Nagai family, whose matriarch Naoko had managed her husband's temple during his illness and after his death. Another of my informants is actually the third generation of women in her family to assume the duties of *jūshoku,* though she is the first to be officially registered as such. Her name is Hisako Yoshida, and she is a female *jūshoku* in the Honganji-ha.

As Hisako explains in the quotation at the beginning of this chap-ter, her father died during World War II when she was only four years old, at which point her mother swallowed her shyness and distaste for performing rituals in order to keep the temple running until Hisako, an only child, was old enough to take over. When I asked Hisako if the temple's parishioners had shown any resistance to an unordained woman performing their services, she quickly shook her head:

> The ones who were left at our temple were used to it. You know, my grandfather died young too, so my grandmother had done the same thing—she just grabbed my mother, who was a little girl at the time, and took her along with her [to conduct services at parishioners homes]. Women priests were not recognized [by the sect] back then, so of course she was not ordained. If one of the laity had had a problem with it, they would have left the temple and gone somewhere else—and a few of them did. But the ones who are left, they don't mind. Now they are used to it.

Hisako received *tokudo* at the age of twenty. She attended Kyoto Women's University for two years and then transferred to Ryūkoku University where she was able to receive the *kyōshi* degree as part of her college curriculum. She then got married and had two children, but divorced her husband soon after her son was born and has been her temple's *jūshoku* ever since. She was rather vague about the reasons for the divorce, but through my many conversations with her I was able to glean that her husband had been unreliable at best. He would sometimes go to parishioners' homes and perform a perfunctory monthly rite, accepting their contribution and keeping it for himself, never reporting it to the family and likely spending it on gambling.

Imagining that it must have been difficult for Hisako on her own with two children and the temple to take care of for all those years, I asked her how she managed. "My mother did not die until my son was seventeen, you see. So she would stay home with the children while I went out to do services. She really did most of the childrearing. By the time she died, the children were old enough take care of themselves." In this way, Hisako and her mother sorted out the labor of the temple in a way that resembled most husband-and-wife pairings of *jūshoku* and *bōmori,* with each family member sticking to her respective strength. As a result, she was unable to tell me exactly when she went from being a temple daughter, to a temple wife, to the temple priest—for her it was all one long life story of serving her parishioners, many of whom had known her since she was a little girl, and indeed are now some of her only friends in the world.

Hisako is now seventy-two years old and stands with stooped shoulders. She has undyed white hair and a modest demeanor, diverting her gaze from her interlocutor to such a degree as to almost close her eyes while speaking. Hisako's son, the presumed successor and current assistant *jūshoku,* is now in his forties and sometimes helps with monthly home visits and major ritual events, but he also works full-time outside of the temple. She told me she was eager for him to take over more of the temple work, but he did not seem in any hurry. "I've never gone abroad," she explained, "and I would really like to be able to before I get too frail. For many years I was running the temple while also working at Nishi Honganji to support us—those were hard years....At any rate, even when it's just the temple to take care of there is never a chance to go away for a long trip. We never know when a parishioner will call and need a service, or someone will pass away. We can't make our plans in advance."

Although Hisako was rather shy at first, particularly in her son's presence, I could sense a steady strength in her, and as we spent more time together a surprising feeling of kinship began to develop between us. Over tea, she would ask me many questions about life in America, Christianity, American attitudes toward religious affiliation, funerals, and the like—she even once asked me about mental illness, and whether I knew if there was a treatment for it. A parishioner of hers had recently committed suicide, she explained, but before that she had known hardly anything about depression (*utsubyō*). As I considered why she would be asking me, a foreign researcher of Buddhism, what I knew about treatment for mental illness so that she could better counsel her own parishioners, it occurred to me that Hisako was particularly isolated as a result of her rather anomalous identity as a divorced female *jūshoku*. She was not inclined to insinuate herself into the male-dominated world of other *jūshoku,* nor did she really belong in the community of *bōmori*. "I go to the temple wife study meetings sometimes," she explained, "but it's really more of a social club for them. So much gossip. I try not to get involved in that."

On three different occasions Hisako treated me to lunch after I visited her temple, and twice she ordered us glasses of wine with lunch. "So, do you like to drink?" I asked her. "Well, I like a little whiskey and beer," she answered, specifying which brands she liked and disliked. I had heard that drinking along with their parishioners was often a part of priests' role after they performed a funeral or memorial service, so I went on to ask, "Then you must be able to drink a lot at your parishioners' funeral banquets?" To my surprise, she shook her head.

"I don't join them for the banquet anymore, I just do the service and go home. I have to watch my behavior, you see. Whether it's drinking or eating, they are always watching what I do, and someone will say something. If I have something to eat, it's 'Look at how much the old lady can eat!' If I don't, it's 'Oh, the old lady eats so little!' So I just go home and have a quiet beer by myself to unwind." Although most of her parishioners have been family friends since she was a young girl, and perhaps know her better than anyone else, she feels she cannot truly let her guard down with them. She is a public personage in the temple community, and as such she has to be mindful of her behavior when in their midst. I came to see our friendship—in a sense, two working mothers separated in age by some four decades—as an indication of Hisako's isolation in her own community.

Although there are many aspects to her job as a *jūshoku,* the most regular encounter Hisako has with parishioners is the monthly visit to a parishioner's home altar, known as the *otsukimairi.* The *otsukimairi* technically requires basic ordination and is usually performed by the head priest, although depending on the situation of the temple it can also be performed by the *bōmori* or another ordained member of the temple family. In larger temples with a number of priests on staff, it could be one of those assisting priests. The visit is, in principle, a service to mark the memorial of a deceased relative and is often performed on the day of the month a household member passed away. A short, twenty-minute service is performed at the household altar, but a majority of the time is taken up with tea and conversation, which often ranges over a variety of subjects that include domestic, medical, or social concerns.

I accompanied Hisako one March day on two of her home visits. We set out by taxi at 9:00 a.m. and were finished by lunchtime. Hisako apologized straightaway for having to stop just a few blocks from her temple to make a payment at a flower shop for an order for a recent funeral she performed. She was wearing lay clothes, and carried only a small bag. I asked her about her appearance. "In fact, I ought not to go out like this," she replied, tugging at her blazer. "But sometimes on my way home I have to go shopping, and it's just strange to wear the robes all around. The collar and the robe are in here," she explained, pointing to her bag. Not wanting to attribute her embarrassment to being female, she went on to insist, "Even men sometimes are embarrassed to wear their robes all over town."[14]

After a thirty-minute drive in the taxi, we arrived at a strip of shiny new homes one short block back from a busy street in the southern suburbs of Kyoto. We entered a two-story house with only a verbal door-knock ("*Konnichiwa!*"), and Hisako invited me to put on a pair of slippers as we made our way to the back of the ground floor. When we reached a closed door at the end of the hallway, she called out again loudly (the woman we were visiting was older and a bit hard of hearing), knocked, and then opened the bedroom door. We entered a large bedroom crammed full with a Buddhist altar, a bed, a piano, and a small heated coffee table. The woman appeared to live self-sufficiently on the first floor of her son's recently built home, with a door to the adjoining kitchen and a bathroom down the hall. In preparation for our coming, she had set up a low-to-the-ground swivel chair for me by the coffee table, where she had laid out a liturgy book and an extra set of beads. She had arranged a chair for herself by the bed, and one for Hisako in front of the altar. She had readied the candles and the incense for Hisako's service at the altar too.

Now Hisako took out her half-robe, collar, and liturgy book and pre-pared them as she chatted with the parishioner. She took three or four incense sticks, broke them in half, lit one side with the candle, and inserted them into the sand-filled dish on the woman's altar. She began intoning the *Smaller Pure Land Sutra* (*Amidakyō*) after clearing her throat several times (later she told me she was actually quite nervous to perform in front of someone other than her parishioners).

When Hisako was about halfway done with the service, the woman got up and went into the kitchen, so that I was left alone listening to the sutra reading. She clanged around in the kitchen a bit and brought out Hisako's tea in a covered cup on a lacquered tray. She arranged it just so on the coffee table, and then went back in to retrieve one for me.

Finally, the woman settled back down into her chair with a loud sigh. It was clear that the ritual performance was not what she had been looking forward to about this visit. At last Hisako finished and turned away from the altar with a few parting *nembutsu*. Not a moment passed before the woman began excitedly, "Well (*ano ne*)…this is a strange thing to talk about, but N-san's health is failing." "Oh really? I thought she was doing fine," Hisako responded as she took off her robe and collar and began to pack them away again. "Don't tell anybody, because it hasn't gotten out yet, but…," and so began the woman's discourse on her friend's failing health. As she listened, Hisako set to work on the tray of money that had been laid out on the coffee table, conducting an efficient exchange of money, receipts, and an unopened honorarium envelope, slipping the latter into her zippered pouch.[15] She then expertly de-lidded her teacup, raised it slightly, saying "*itadakimasu*" (I humbly accept), and drank a few quick sips before replacing the lid. She was appreciative without being leisurely, and accessible without being unprofes-sional. After about ten minutes, Hisako skillfully drew the conversation to a close and led me out of the woman's room. The taxi was waiting outside to take us to our next home visit.

The cab took us back up north to a parishioner's home on the seventh floor of an apartment building somewhat closer to the temple. Hisako used the intercom to call the woman to buzz us in, and while we rode the elevator, she warned me for the third time that day about this women's garrulity, a warning that turned out to be justified. The parishioner's face and manner were youthful and animated, but when she talked the clicking of her dentures betrayed her age. She was accompanied by another woman, whom I took to be her daughter-in-law. The Buddhist altar in her spacious apartment had its own room and was well appointed with fresh flowers and fruit and a pounded rice cake (*mochi*).

Once Hisako finished the brief service there was not even a moment of silence before the woman began talking, without pause or apology, about a series of mundane topics: acquaintances who were sick, what the doctor had told her about her blood pressure medication, what she had seen on TV the other day about an American who had looked a bit like me. She seemed not to draw breath and continued talking while she went into the other room to fetch a tray holding a receipt book, some cash, and another closed honorarium (*orei*) envelope. She was quite excitable, and at one point became so animated that tears came to her eyes, which Hisako had also warned me was apt to happen. Undeterred by her own display of emotion, she wiped the tears away and continued on to another subject. Hisako nodded and responded politely while she wrote out the receipt for the cash and then accepted the *orei* envelope, raising it in the air and nodding her head, saying, "*itadakimasu.*" We were served tea again by the daughter-in-law, and again Hisako drank a few appreciative sips without lingering.

When Hisako finally found a break in the conversation she quickly rose to her feet, adopting a hurried pace as she darted down the hallway to the door; she had her shoes on before I could even follow her out of the room. The two old ladies followed us down the outdoor corridor and all the way to the elevator, waving and bowing, everyone thanking each other over and over. We nodded and waved and bowed even as the glass elevator door closed, until we descended and the parishioners were finally out of sight.

Pastoral Aspects of *Otsukimairi*: A Woman's Work

Hisako's day of visiting two elderly female parishioners' homes was fairly typical of a priest's daily schedule. Many of the parishioners who request the *otsukimairi* every month are retired, elderly, and very often widowed. The *otsukimairi* becomes a very important opportunity to engage in pastoral ministry with these kinds of parishioners, a role to which it is frequently reported that female priests are especially well suited.

Hisako has explained to me that she feels relatively comfortable in her role as a listener on these visits: "You know, it's different talking to a woman than talking to a man. A woman you can say anything to, right? There are things you wouldn't say to a man, but if it's a woman they can relax and talk about various things. So, when I go to a house, sometimes I leave after ten minutes of talking, but there are times that I stay for an hour and a half! Even though I have somewhere to be next, I can't just say 'goodbye,' right?"

When I accompanied Hisako on her home visits, I observed that her parishioners were visibly excited to share their personal news with her as soon as she wrapped up her sutra performance and put down her beads. For some of these parishioners, she is a rare visitor of any kind, but she is also an authority figure in their religious community, so news is eagerly shared to bring her up to date on the status of other community members. If she wasn't deliberate in her schedule Hisako's loquacious parishioners were liable to detain her indefinitely, and her acute concern with time and with tactfully ending her visits was very clear on the day I spent with her.

Hisako's experience echoes that of every single female priest (whether *bōmori* or acting *jūshoku*) that I have interviewed, and the opinion of nearly every male *jūshoku* as well. I was often told that parishioners are less likely to open up their hearts when they are served by the *jūshoku*, whom they presume has somewhere important to be and will not be able to spend all day with them. The *bōmori*, in contrast, is not burdened with the aura of being "important" (*erai*) and thus is more likely to be confided in. To the extent that the *otsukimairi* serves a social or pastoral function, a woman's gender may serve her well in performing the work of a temple priest.

Nakatsugi: *A Stopgap Successor*

On the other hand, Hisako finds that being female is a limitation to her being perceived as a suitable permanent priest. Although she has been *jūshoku* of her temple for some forty years, her parishioners are still delighted when her son replaces her on ritual visits: "Well, in Japan there are some things that are still feudal. For example, every day I work, and here I am at this age.... But when it comes down to it, when my son performs an *otsukimairi* in my place, or helps with a funeral, in fact they are happy. They think, oh good, a man has come with her, and they're happy. I think after all, there are advantages to being a man. No matter how hard I try, in that sense... [*trails off*]." Such a response from her parishioners indicates that they prefer the ritual to be performed by a male priest, as Hisako articulates here. But it also points to the relatively provisional nature of their acceptance of her as *jūshoku*, even though she has performed the role solely since 1970 and in effect ever since she received the *kyōshi* degree at the age of twenty-three.

Despite her legal status as the temple's *jūshoku*, one could argue that Hisako is still viewed as an "intermediate successor" (in Japanese, *tsunagime* or *nakatsugi*). This was the capacity in which the Shin Buddhist sects first recognized female priests: initially, the position of *daimu jūshoku*, or "proxy resident priest," was the only one women were permitted to hold even after obtaining the *kyōshi* degree, the same degree held by male *jūshoku*. In the Honganji-ha, the sect to which Hisako's temple belongs, this bureaucratic restriction was lifted directly after the war when the new sectarian constitution went into effect: women holding the *kyōshi* degree were permitted to register officially as their temple's *jūshoku*.

In the Ōtani-ha, however, this change was much longer in coming. The qualification of women's leadership of the temple inherent in the title "proxy resident priest" remained in place until the 1990s when, after an outcry by *bōmori* feminist groups and the convening of a special advisory committee to the administrative chief of the Ōtani-ha, a series of revisions were issued that removed the restriction. The first round of changes allowed women to become full-fledged *jūshoku* only in the absence of a suitable male successor. Finally, in 1996, this condition was removed so that women could become *jūshoku* regardless of whether or not there was a male successor.[16] My informant Naoko Nagai, whom we met in chapter 1, had been effectively running her temple for two decades as the proxy *jūshoku* by the time these changes in the official regulations took place. When she heard about the change in policy, she called up her local Ōtani-ha administrative official, hoping to become the first female to register as a *jūshoku* in her sect. To her dismay, the official pointed out that, as her son was already ordained, in his twenties, and expecting to succeed, there was "no need" for her to go to the trouble of registering as *jūshoku*.

This attitude probably helps to account for the fact that only around 1 percent of *jūshoku* in the Ōtani-ha are female even today. With one last example, I will highlight the difficulties that arise when the conditional recognition granted to women as priests within the family inheritance system reaches its limits. Kamata Hiroko, born as one of two girls in a temple family in Shikoku, writes of her mixed experience as a member of that 1 percent of *jūshoku* who are female. Her essay was published in *Aiau*, the publication of Higashi Honganji's Office for Women's Affairs.[17] When it became legally possible for women to become *jūshoku*, Kamata underwent training and applied to the sect to take over family's temple herself, as there were no male children. Her somewhat somber story, which I translate at length below, illustrates that, despite her legal standing, there is little room in her parishioners' imaginations for a complete reversal from traditional gender roles in the temple. In other words, although female *jūshoku* are now formally recognized, a scenario in which a woman serves as *jūshoku* and her husband serves as *bōmori* is still unthinkable. The following excerpt is from Kamata's essay, titled "What's It Like to be a Female *Jūshoku*?" (*Josei jūshoku tte dō yo?*).

> When I was a child, my mother wanted to dress me in boys' clothing. In the pictures of me in old albums, I am always wearing green or blue pants, and next to me there is a Peter Pan tricycle. Apparently, when I was inside of her, my mom had prepared the boy's name "Masaru" as she waited for the day she would give birth to me.
>
> Three generations before, my great-grandparents had not been blessed with children, so they adopted my grandfather, who was the fourth son of a private doctor. My grandmother then married into the family, and then my mother and my aunt were born.

I imagine the expectations for my mother, as the eldest daughter, were great....The kinder her parishioners were to her, the more the thought "if only I had been a boy..." would eat away at her. When it came time for her to marry, she believed that she could make it up to the parishioners and the temple by giving birth to a [male] successor, so that even after getting me as her second daughter, she could not rid herself of this thought and this boyish fashion was projected onto me as a toddler....

When I began my duties [as *jūshoku*], not a few parishioners expressed some resistance upon first seeing a "female" *jūshoku*. At this point, a parishioner once refused me, explaining, "I don't want to hear a woman's sutra chanting." But as our encounters began to accumulate I got some understanding, I received voices of support as well, and now I think I am fairly well known.

I hear that there are conversations like "Our temple has a female *jūshoku*"...in which "female *jūshoku*" is used as a title for me. I have also had a chance to speak about my thoughts on the radio, where I was introduced as a "female *jūshoku*." This is probably a kind of special treatment because I am a woman.

Even so, I have gradually been able to do the things I wanted to do, and I think that we [my parishioners and I] have grown accustomed to each other, but even now I hear one thing that is troubling. That is the comment "Aren't you getting married?" Sometimes these words imply that my husband would be the *jūshoku,* or that I should get busy producing a successor, but also sometimes there is the sense that my husband could work outside the house and I could be *jūshoku.*

No one ever says that my husband should be the *bōmori.*

Perhaps this implies that in the case of a husband and wife, it is difficult for the wife to take the lead. From a commonsense perspective, working as a *jūshoku* in a woman's body is nothing more than a temporary measure, rather than being some kind of dream that's come true. In the end, my choice is whether to run the temple alone or to retire: people simply can't imagine the scenario of a husband-and-wife team continuing to perform the rituals.

So, though I may save face by obstinately declaring that I'm going to be their *jūshoku* by remaining unmarried, I realize that absolutely nothing has changed from the times and ways of thinking from which my mother suffered.

Ah, so it comes back to me, I think.

For the sake of whom, and for what, am I living? When I am alone in the main hall performing the morning service, one verse from the *Amidakyō* [The Smaller Pure Land Sutra] comes into my head: "The blue ones radiating blue light, the yellow a yellow light, the red a red light, and the white a white light."[18]

These words by which the Buddha asked for the dignity of each and every person will be the theme of my faith from here on out as well, I think.[19]

The resistance that Kamata feels to her acting as a resident priest comes from several parties: her mother, who, disappointed in herself for not being born a boy, had hoped to provide a male successor; the local sect administrators, who saw her gender as an inconvenience that did not fit more neatly into the fields of their bureaucratic forms; the radio host who saw her as a gender-bending object of fascination; and finally her own parishioners, even those who had gradually grown used to her but still could not imagine a female *jūshoku* married to a male *bōmori*.

We can see from Kamata's experience that the central bureaucratic institution may play a part in legally defining who can inhabit roles of authority at the temple, but that part is a peripheral one. Practical necessity and personal relationships with parishioners are much stronger influences over succession strategies in the examples I have examined in this chapter. Dorinne Kondo's 1990 study of artisan families showed that the stem-family or *ie* in Japan is somewhat bureaucratic in the sense that it is comprised of "positions" rather than individuals, positions that are to be filled with the primary goal of preserving the *ie*. Gender is certainly one of the factors considered in the process of succession, but ultimately a utilitarian concern with preserving the continuity of the *ie* prevails. The stakes of temple succession are actually broader than just a single-family line: the parishioners are also stakeholders, and their expectations often guide the succession process. Still, the stake felt most acutely by temple wives who guard the temple by becoming its *jūshoku* is likely their obligation to care for and protect their own family members.

The characters that comprise the term *bōmori* literally mean "temple protector." In chapter 2, I described the strong pull that many *bōmori* feel to stay at home in the temple to provide a hospitable presence for the laity, particularly when their husbands are out. In this chapter, another dimension of the duty of temple wives to protect the temple has come to the fore: in her husband's absence, a *bōmori* may often be called on to take over his priestly duties until another male priest becomes available. This may be only temporary, like covering a weekday visit to a parishioner's home altar, or may last for a whole generation, as in the case of wartime temple wives who took over the operation of the temple after their husbands had died.

My examination of the ritual activities of wives who have made moves to take their husband's place in front of the Buddhist altar reveals the gender-related implications of a Shin Buddhist clerical definition that rests primarily on familial relationships. It is a woman's position in the family that empowers her—as the sole adult body in the temple—to act as a priest, whether or not she has obtained official ordination. When wartime exigencies forced both the Honganji-ha and the Ōtani-ha to expand sacerdotal privileges to females, it was on women's obligations as wives and daughters that their authority and responsibility to act as priests was founded.

This chapter also adds nuance to our understanding of women's power and authority in the context of family temples. In the introduction to the 1974 volume *Women, Culture and Society,* Michelle Rosaldo wrote that "Women gain power and a sense of value when they are able to transcend domestic limits, either by entering the men's world or by creating a society unto themselves" (p. 41). Rosaldo's implicit reliance here on the dichotomy of private/public and inside/outside in assessing women's status masks a more fluid and complex dynamic. Reflecting on my informant Hisako's experience as a female *jūshoku* reveals that, in addition to playing a more visible part in rituals and leaving the house to perform monthly home visits, performing the "man's work" of a priest actually takes her regularly into the domestic sphere of her widowed parishioners. The intimacy—on Hisako's part, a measured intimacy—that she cultivates with her parishioners on these visits is what allows her to serve successfully as the center of her temple's community.

Some still might be tempted to read these women's actions as being indicative of an unarticulated feminist project. However, the informants treated in this chapter were not (consciously, at least) motivated by a desire for "empowerment" in a liberal feminist sense; nor were they seeking to increase their status at the temple (except in the case of Keiko Mochizuki, the public feminist interviewed in the sect's academic journal). Rather, they consistently described themselves as acting out of a desire to protect their home and family. In their performances as ritual specialists, like the other more obviously domestic activities I have highlighted in this book, it is difficult to deny the centrality of interpersonal relationships and family obligations.

Nevertheless, the de facto clerical glass ceiling in the form of parishioner expectations can be a source of vague disappointment, acute frustration, or even humiliation for temple women who seek to perform rituals. Many of my informants were dismayed by the double standards that their parishioners held for temple leadership and ritual performance. Keiko Mochizuki and many other less prominent feminists in the Jōdo Shinshū are quick to express their wish that the man and the woman in the temple clerical partnership could be truly interchangeable. The next chapter focuses on those cases in which women's choices were more explicitly driven by a desire for autonomy (*shutaisei*) and freedom (*jiyū*) during and after the Ōtani-ha feminist movement.

Equality and Freedom in the Ōtani-ha

I used to carry around the ideal image of a *bōmori*. I thought, "a *bōmori* has to be like this," so I would do the cleaning and making tea for the parishioners, and I never stopped smiling, even if it was a manufactured smile. There was a time when I was frantically trying to play the part of a *bōmori*. But for these last ten years, I have not been like that—you could say I have become much more free (*kekkō jiyū to iu ka*).

—Mochizuki Keiko, Ōtani-ha bōmori leader

THIS CHAPTER TRACES TEMPLE WIVES' NEGOTIATION OF Buddhist notions of karmic contingency and social obligation with the modern ideal of the self-determining individual in both the domestic and political realms. *Bōmori* are situated within a complex web of relationships and obligations, which we can imagine as concentrically related social institutions: family, congregation, sect, and society. Those who embrace a Pure Land Buddhist worldview may understand their debt to social institutions and teachers as being subsumed within their debt to the Buddha.[1] Premodern Pure Land Buddhist teachings hitched social obligations to religious burdens quite explicitly; in both senses, women were at a distinct disadvantage compared to men. As the Higashi Honganji sermonizer Tokuryū (1772–1858) explained, "Because of the Five Obstacles and Three Obediences (*goshō sanshō*), it is said that a woman's body is more deeply sinful than that of a man.... Her envy and jealousy are unceasing. The root of this is that her body is not free, and this is a result of past karma" (1891, p. 3). Although the notion of women's special karmic and social disadvantage no longer holds currency in the public discourse of the Shin Buddhist sects, the negotiation of liberal values like gender equality and individual self-determination with Buddhist explanations of karmic contingency continues to be a complicated affair in both public and private venues.

Because the public consideration—both doctrinal and political—of concepts like autonomy (*shutaisei*), individual awakening (*ko no jikaku*), and freedom of choice (*jiyū sentaku*) has been so rich in the twentieth-century Ōtani-ha, my discussion in this chapter concentrates on examples from that denomination. I begin by surveying the prescriptive accounts of the female condition propounded by Jōdo Shinshū priests up until the middle of the twentieth century. The cumulative picture is somewhat bleak, with an emphasis on the gender-specific social and karmic limits that women face. In the 1980s, feminist *bōmori* leaders in the Ōtani-ha began to push back against some of those limits by pressuring the sect to recognize women's autonomy as Buddhist practitioners by removing outdated restrictions on their ordination. Like second-wave American feminists, Ōtani-ha feminists espoused a dialectic relationship between the personal (for example, domestic relationships and individual women's instantiation of the role of *bōmori*) and the political (social activism and institutional reform). These two spheres—the personal and the political—largely correlate to the two modalities in which I have been tracking the activities and experiences of *bōmori* throughout this book, that is, the domestic and the public. We will find that in the case of translating liberal reforms into everyday practice the relationship between these two spheres is not one of mutual isolation but rather of complex interplay.

Here a note about the problem of religious women's agency is in order. Generally speaking, religious practitioners do not understand the self to be autonomous and self-determining. Nonetheless, scholarship on women in religion has tended to assume that women's agency can be expressed only through "acts that challenge social norms and not those that uphold them" (Mahmood 2005, p. 5). The problem with this approach is that it presumes the desire for a certain type of freedom must be universal among human beings—and that freedom tends to be defined by Western liberal thought. Recent postcolonial scholarship has pointed out that reading the lives of Asian women through the lens of Western scholars' own liberal feminist sensibilities implies "that nuns' lives 'need' intervention and assistance of various forms that can come only through access to Western ideas and resources, be they financial, educational, or otherwise" (Salgado 2013, p. 75). In her work on female renunciants in Sri Lanka, Nirmala Salgado highlights modes of self-realization that bear little resemblance to the types of status and power that might win approval from Western feminists, whom she points out are often preoccupied by whether women have been able "transcend" domestic roles and move into the public sphere of men. Salgado's informants articulate an understanding of the self that clearly does not align with what Veena Das calls "the fetishized autonomous subject of liberal political discourse" (Das and Addlakha 2001, p. 529); instead, they seek to overcome attachment to their individual selves through the disciplined cultivation of morality (*sila*).[2]

With such warnings in mind, scholars in recent years have begun to look beyond the somewhat limited definitions of "agency" and "freedom" that have previously been employed in feminist scholarship. Dorothy Ko (2005), Wendi Adamek (2009), and Lori Meeks (2010), for instance, have begun to carve out a middle path in talking about women's agency in premodern East Asian contexts in ways that avoid the trap of classifying women *either* as oppressed victims *or* unwitting feminists. As I explored in chapters 4 and 5, the desires of temple wives are complicated and diverse: my informants variously expressed desires to be free from the tyranny of their mothers-in-law, to fulfill their social roles successfully, and to entrust themselves to the saving power of Amida's vow, among other things. The nature and range of women's desires are thus much more complicated than would be permitted by the rather narrow sense of agency prescribed by "the goals of progressive politics," whose definition of freedom and autonomy has "led to the incarceration of the notion of agency within the trope of resistance against oppressive and dominating operations of power" (Mahmood 2005, p. 34). In this chapter, therefore, I want to avoid confining women's agency within a simplistically dualistic framework. The negotiation of individual desires in everyday life, as everyone knows, is no simple matter.

The individual *bōmori* I profile in this chapter is Sachiko Hino, an Osaka temple wife who resented and rebelled against her assigned role of temple wife for some time before finally becoming reconciled to it. Born in 1949 in the Ōtani-ha temple in which she still lives, Sachiko's postwar education was infused with liberal democratic values, and she attended a sectarian-affiliated university in nearby Kyoto.[3] Throughout her adolescence, she attempted to escape from what she saw as her bondage to the temple as an only child responsible for ensuring the temple's succession. As an active member of her local *bōmori* association, she has a keen awareness of feminist critiques of her Buddhist institution, and has come to hold the equality of gender roles at the temple as an ideal, equating it to an issue of human rights. However, she still struggles with her own timidity in transgressing gender norms, along with her anxieties about not living up to the ideal of a good "temple person."

Sachiko's story is a striking example of the difficulty of putting the liberal ideal of gender equality into practice in the dense web of interpersonal relationships within which the *bōmori* lives and operates. She claims to have "given up" on enacting gender equality at her temple, although her relationship with her husband has evolved to include more mutual understanding and more recognition of the importance of her social work outside of the temple. The attitudes of her temple's parishioners have proven more difficult to revolutionize, however, so she tends to live her life among her parishioners in a more conservative, restrained key. Nonetheless, she continues to maintain close relationships with them, and is even asked to perform funerals for some families. On the other hand, she lives a "second life" outside of the temple, traveling all over Japan, and even abroad, to do work related to liberal social causes.

Limits to Women's Freedom in the Jōdo Shinshū

In the Pure Land and especially the Shin Buddhist tradition, the human condition is thought to be defined by the possession of a body of accumulated karma (*shukugyō no mi*); it is precisely the contingency and powerlessness of this condition that must be accepted by unenlightened beings in order to receive the salvation offered by Amida. Shinran (1173–1263), the founder of the Jōdo Shinshū, described two aspects of the "entrusting mind" of one who has attained faith:

> One is to believe deeply and decidedly that you are a foolish being of karmic evil caught in birth-and-death (*samsara*), ever sinking and ever wandering in transmigration from innumerable kalpas in the past, with never a condition that would lead to emancipation. The second is to believe deeply and decidedly that Amida Buddha's Forty-Eight Vows [in the *Larger Pure Land Sutra*] grasp sentient beings, and that allowing yourself to be carried by the power of the Vow without any doubt or apprehension, you will attain birth [in the Pure Land] (Hirota 1997, 1:85).

Embracing one's helplessness as a "foolish being" (*bonbu*) is a necessary stage in surrendering to the saving grace of Amida's forty-eight vows. In modern Jōdo Shinshū Ōtani-ha theology, influenced by Kiyozawa Manshi (1863–1903), a practitioner can only recognize his or her helplessness through the practice of introspection (*naikan*). Kiyozawa was inspired by the Greek philosopher and slave Epictetus, in particular the distinction he drew between that which one could control (for example, one's mind) and that which one could not (for example, wealth, fame, social position, and death; Yasutomi 2003). Given this doctrinal emphasis on the humble, deluded nature of human beings, whose realization of their own limitations was an essential step in their salvation, the tension that remained in propagation to female followers was whether women's karmic disadvantage was *more* acute than that of men, and whether the acceptance of their subservient position to men in family and society was a necessary component of their cultivation of humility and attainment of faith.

In Japanese Buddhism, women's social and spiritual limitations were for centuries cinched together with the tidy set phrase the Five Obstacles and Three Obediences (*goshō sanshō* or *sanjū*). This phrase, which appears in many medieval, early modern, and even modern Buddhist sermons for women, links the notion that those born into female bodies are obstructed from becoming buddhas (along with four other states of samsaric existence) to the fact of their social subjugation. Specifically, in addition to—or perhaps because of—suffering from these five karmic obstacles, women must be obedient to three men corresponding to three different stages of their lives: their fathers in childhood, their husbands in adulthood, and their sons in old age.

Because of their unique karmic impairments and social disadvantages, women have been the audience for a gender-specific body of teachings within Pure Land Buddhism known as *nyonin kyōka* or *kyōke* (religious propagation for women). Tokuryū, the nineteenth-century proselytizer for Higashi Honganji I quoted at the beginning of this chapter, leaned heavily on the linkage of the karmic and social limits to women's existence. He explained in his sermon to *bōmori* that women were especially in need of Amida's compassion in order to attain salvation:

> As she has the [Five] Obstacles, during the time in which she is wandering lost, she will never have a body that is free and happy in its karmic fruition. Further, she cannot attain the body of a Buddha. This is also preached in the Lotus Sutra.[4] Thus it is often said that even though [men and women] may appear to have the same physical measurements, if one gathered the ignorance of the men of all the three thousand worlds, it would be the same as the karmic obstructions of a single woman. (Tokuryū 1891, p. 3)

Though Tokuryū himself died before the Meiji restoration in 1868, his and other similar sermons in this genre were reprinted with little to no alteration in modern educational materials for Buddhist women. The notion of women's possessing a particular karmic disadvantage thus remained a commonplace in Buddhist propagation for women until after World War II (Starling 2013).

Of course, male Shin Buddhist teachers were obviously aware of the first wave of Japanese feminism that took place in the first few decades of the twentieth century. An unattributed article in the Jōdo Shinshū women's journal *Katei*, produced by the publishing house Kōkōdō from 1901 to 1905, was entitled "My Theory of Equal Rights for the Sexes" (*Gojin no danjo dōken-ron*). The authors, presumably members of the editorial staff of the journal, address the idea of equal rights by redirecting the conversation to one concerning the radical interconnectedness—and therefore equality—of everything in existence (from an ultimate perspective) and the need to "acquiesce" in the face of the humbling reality of interdependence:

Of course I affirm equal rights for men and women. But [with the
following conditions] do I affirm them. If one argues for rights,
then they are the same rights for all the myriad things, not just
individual men and women. The brothers and sisters who argue for
equal rights for men and women of the world want for them to be
recognized from this standpoint. From my standpoint, women are
necessarily opposed to men, and it is necessary for them to com-
pete with men over things. In other words, women as women have
their own duties. Thus, the fact that women obey men is certainly
not something to be run away from. Fundamentally, whether one
is a man or woman, I believe that acquiescence (*fukujū*) is a beautiful virtue. I could not exist for one day without acquiescence.

In the broadest sense, I can say that I am obedient to everything in the world.[5]

The Ōtani-ha's "Spiritualism" (Seishinshugi) movement that grew
out of Kiyozawa Manshi's teachings viewed acquiescence as the only proper
response to human beings' karmic contingency.[6] Offering what they referred
to as "the vital point in the resolution of the women's problem," the writers
working out of Kiyozawa's Kōkōdō publishing house were quick to relativ-
ize the significance of gender differences in light of karmic interdependence
(Fukushima 2006, p. 30). They inevitably returned to the basic soteriological
framework of the Spiritualism movement, which required the humble examination of one's limits, whether they be physical, social, or spiritual. Historian
Fukushima Eiju has noted with regard to the messages contained in the journal *Katei* that, despite the authors' professed concern with taking a spiritual
(rather than social or political) stance on gender issues, "it is hard to avoid
the impression that the real emphasis of their argument is on explaining the
necessity of women's obedience to men" (2006, p. 33).

The discourse on these interlocking limits on women's freedom—
that of karmic contingency and social subordination—continued through
much of the twentieth century. In the 1950s, Kaneko Daiei (1881–1976), an
important Ōtani-ha theologian and professor at Ōtani University, affirmed
the hierarchical relationship between the sexes in a sermon titled "*Bōmori
ni nozomu*" (Hopes for *bōmori*).[7] Kaneko uses the example of the complementary but hierarchical relationship between husband (*jūshoku*) and
wife (*bōmori*) to illustrate the religious virtue of obedience or acquiescence
(*fukujū*). He begins by addressing the concept of the Three Obligations:

I may be thought old-fashioned, but I believe that the proper practice is for the husband to be the head, and the wife to follow.... The
saying, "when young, follow your parents, when married, fol-

low your husband, when old, follow your child" does not [only describe] feminine virtue. It can also be seen as, when you are a young boy, being brought up by your mother, as a husband to be helped by your wife, and as an old man to be nourished by your children, and in this way it also points to the weakness of men. I have given much thought to this "virtue of following." (1976, p. 34)

Kaneko intimates that the "three obediences" or "obligations" usually attributed to women can in fact be universalized so that men, too, might cultivate a sense of their own weakness and dependency. But he soon returns to the idea that women are of necessity socially submissive to their husbands in the context of the Shin temple partnership:

> In the temple, the *jūshoku* is the central pillar, and the *bōmori* is the support. The problem arises when the pillar is insufficient.... Thus, it may be that the *bōmori* is more brilliant than the *jūshoku,* or that the *jūshoku* only reluctantly became so because of the inheritance system. In such cases too—in fact, precisely in such cases—the supporting *bōmori* must obey the leading *jūshoku.* Just because the *jūshoku* is insufficient, the *bōmori* must not use it as an excuse to disobey. That's because it doesn't contribute to their united effort. Inasmuch as the temple is a place for the harmonious co-performance of the *jūshoku* and the *bōmori,* the *bōmori* must follow the *jūshoku.* (1976, pp. 35–36)

As he interweaves the religious virtue of "acquiescence" with his description of complementary social relationships, Kaneko evokes the imagery of the house (*ie*) to demonstrate the gender-specific mode of acquiescence that is required of temple wives inasmuch as domestic partnerships exhibit the hierarchical mode of complementarity that women are the "supporting beam" to men's "main pillar." In a common trope, the spatial imagery of the house is used to prescribe appropriately complementary gender roles.[8] Kaneko's is certainly an idealized vision of the gender contract, but his sermon resonated enough to be redistributed in the educational materials given to *jūshoku* in training in the Ōtani-ha until the 1990s.

A slightly later tract in the same tradition reflects an increasing awareness that female listeners might not readily accept teachings such as the Five Obstacles and Three Obediences in any kind of literal sense. Takamatsu Shin'ei, an Ōtani-ha priest who held a PhD in Shin Buddhist studies from Otani University and was an administrator and professor at Iida Women's Junior College, published a collection of sermons he had preached to an audience of women as a book entitled *Okāsan no Shinshūgaku* (Shin Buddhist studies for mothers), first published in 1975 and reprinted in 1980. Takamatsu begins the book by acknowledging how difficult it might be for women to learn from Buddhist texts like the *Lotus Sutra,* which contains the notorious Devadatta chapter in which Sariputra points out that women's bodies are impure and carry the Five Obstructions. This sutra, so well known in Japan, is frequently pointed to by Pure Land proselytizers as a locus classicus for the concept of the Five Obstacles (despite the fact that the very drama of this scene derives from the fact that Sariputra, despite his low opinion of female bodies, is shown up by a young girl). Takamatsu's pedagogical interest here seems to be in discouraging a selective reading of the Buddhist sutras simply because they may contain messages that are difficult to hear or values that are out of line with contemporary sensibilities. He tells his audience: "When broaching a sutra like this, immediately someone will object: 'This is an androcentric expression that looks down on women. There's no way I can believe such an absurd thing.' But we cannot understand the teachings if we take them in that way" (1980, p. 3).

Takamatsu refers his readers to the Chinese Pure Land patriarch Shandao's (613–681) hermeneutical approach of treating the sutras like mirrors for the self. He warns that one should not become preoccupied with whether the sutra's messages are good or bad for women; that would be like fretting over whether a mirror itself was pretty or ugly, smudged or clear, rather than one's face. He admonishes:

> When staring into your own handheld mirror, you aren't investigating the quality of the mirror. Is your hair askew? Is your makeup smudged? Is there anything on your face? It doesn't matter about the mirror, because it's as if you yourself are lying atop a cutting board. That is precisely your interaction with the mirror.
>
> Asking whether there is a hell or a Pure Land, or saying that the teaching that women cannot be saved is an example of the chauvinism of the time, someone who makes these kinds of criticisms is doing no more than debating the quality of the mirror. When studying Buddhism, the one who must act—who must do *something*—is not Buddhism, it's you yourself!
>
> Keeping this way of studying in mind, let's return again to the words of the *Lotus Sutra.* [Sariputra says things like], "Woman, your body is full of impurities." Without getting angry and thinking, "Hey, my body is clean!" let's instead take these words and have a try at applying them to our selves. (1980, p. 5)

Takamatsu goes on to describe a daily life in which the young mother cannot win: her child's teacher scolds her for not teaching her child manners well enough at home, and she is accused of being a bad mother no matter what she does. This, he implies, is the experience to which the sutra's language about being "unclean" and disrespected by others must refer. The Five Obstructions are similarly applied to the contemporary features of a woman's social existence—this time, a woman who struggles to have it all:

> The sutra talks about the Five Obstructions borne by women. Let's try to calmly apply these to ourselves. We might not have understood it when we were just following the logic on the surface, but isn't it giving expression to a deep world of feelings? When you were a girl, you thought you would live a pure, upright, beautiful life. And yet, when you became a housewife (*katei no shufu*) and a mother, doubtless you felt the reality that you couldn't have all these things. (p. 6)

He goes on to list many things over which a woman might feel powerless in her present domestic life, the various double-binds in which she finds herself: for instance, she might want to try and work outside of the home like a man does, but then her children will be neglected and she will be criticized as a mother. He then reminds his readers: "When we look at it this way, in the very sutra that appeared at first glance to contain an argument that was derisive toward women, an image of the inescapable reality of your life as a housewife and a mother has come to the surface" (Takamatsu 1980, p. 7).

Giving male authors like Takamatsu the benefit of the doubt, we could observe that in its conscious intention at least, this kind of propagation did not *pre*scribe women's submissiveness, but rather *de*scribed it. If indeed one achieves a mature faith in the modern Ōtani-ha by turning inward and reflecting on one's own experiences—especially those of hardship, difficulty, and powerlessness—then that process is certain to be informed by one's gender. When we reflect on what each of the male authors has to say about a woman's particular experience of being a foolish person (*bonbu*) or wicked person (*akunin*), the basic message is that a woman's experience of the world is different from that of a man, and thus she has her own hardships to suffer. As female *bonbu*, women must acknowledge and acquiesce to a particularly female form of contingency.

Giving voice to the gender norms of the times in which they were living, the quoted male authors affirmed that this contingency included being subservient to men in their social and domestic life. Those writing later in the twentieth century were less likely to emphasize women's special karmic obstructions as literal barriers to spiritual progress and instead were more likely to describe them as metaphors for the types of suffering that they would likely experience in this lifetime. Still, the twentieth-century male propagators of Shin Buddhist doctrine primarily seemed to view karmic contingency and gendered social roles as being interlocking limits to women's freedom.

Pushing Back: Ōtani-ha Feminism

Messages about women's karmic inferiority, their unique forms of suffering, their submissiveness to men, and the inevitability of their receiving critiques on their parenting might have been easier for women to "apply to themselves" (as Takamatsu had suggested) if they had been propounded by female preachers. However, there were no female resident priests or female teachers at the Ōtani-ha's training facilities until the very end of the twentieth century. Feminists in the Ōtani-ha took note of this and in the 1980s began to raise the issue in various public forums. They primarily took aim at what they viewed as material and institutional barriers to *bōmori*'s self-realization as religious practitioners.

The door to many of the feminists' arguments was opened by the Ōtani-ha's postwar reform movement, founded on the ideas put forth by Kiyozawa Manshi and other theologians in his Seishinkai group. The Dōbōkai Movement was officially launched in the Ōtani-ha in 1962, on the occasion of Shinran's seven-hundredth memorial celebration. Propounded by successive chief administrators beginning with Kurube Shin'yū, the movement emphasized the religious equality of Shin Buddhist practitioners and sought to strengthen lay participation in the sect. The movement's rhetoric built upon the personal, interiorized religiosity described by Kiyozawa and his students Soga Ryōjin (1875–1971) and Kaneko Daiei (Mizushima 2007, pp. 16–31). Among its earliest slogans was "From a religion of the family to one of individual awakening" (*ie no shūkyō kara kojin no jikaku e*). With the use of such language, the leaders of the Ōtani-ha sought to valorize a model of religious affiliation based on individual awakening (*ko no jikaku*), which was to replace the empty and unreflective family system of temple affiliation.[9] Throughout the 1960s and 1970s the administration sought greater democratization while struggling to obtain concessions from Higashi Honganji's abbot, who traced his birthright claim to authority through a blood lineage to Shinran himself. Finally, in 1981, the Ōtani-ha adopted a new constitution whose preface summarized the principles of the Dōbōkai Movement, including its lofty egalitarian rhetoric.[10] Thus, the movement and its religious and democratic claims had become institutionalized through this new legal framework.

Starting in the mid-1980s, feminist leaders in the sect began to lodge complaints against the Jōdo Shinshū Otani-ha about institutionalized sexual discrimination. They claimed that, despite the reform movements that had sought to democratize the institution, women were still not recognized as equals and were not adequately enfranchised in the sect's governing bodies. Their criticisms raised fundamental questions about how women—specifically female religious professionals—should be affiliated with the Jōdo Shinshū, a tradition without celibate nuns. Their petitions gave rise to the "temple wife problem" (*bōmori mondai*), a lively public debate that lasted for several decades.[11]

Throughout the 1980s and 1990s, leaders of national and regional temple wife associations (*bōmori kai*) wrote numerous essays and articles for the sect's journals and general Buddhist publications. They also submitted petitions to Higashi Honganji insisting that the sect recognize women's "autonomous participation in the sect" (*shutaiteki sankaku*) and promote their "autonomous religious activities" (*shutaiteki katsudō*). From among these politically active *bōmori*, several women anticipated the need to act independently of the sect-sponsored associations, so they formed an independent group called the Women's Group to Consider Discrimination against Women in the Shinshū Ōtani-ha (Shinshū Ōtani-ha ni Okeru Josei Sabetsu o Kangaeru Onnatachi no Kai; hereafter Onnatachi no Kai). The group submitted the following petition to the Ōtani-ha administration on December 8, 1986:

PETITION

We have gathered for these two days from all over the country in order to deeply consider the condition of women in our sect....

Our sect revolves around the Dōbōkai Movement. In the process of promoting this revival of a religious organization founded on faith, there was a conflict with those parties, such as the Ōtani family, who had old-fashioned attitudes about the sect, and it is well known that we are still feeling reverberations from that. Now, at the end of the fifteen-year conflict, we believe it is precisely the time to make an appeal regarding the real conditions of women.

In the new sect constitution, which was proudly promulgated at the end of the conflict as "a constitution of a government of fellow companions (*dōbō*), open to 100,000 sentient beings," the women's problem (*josei mondai*) receives not a single mention. This fact unexpectedly discloses the [true] character of this conflict.

Even the French Revolution, which was putatively the flagbearer of freedom, equality, and philanthropy, in fact only defined males as citizens. This is the background of modern Europe, but here now, some 200 years later, the Shinshū Otani-ha is repeating this mistake of democracy's past, and making a horrible spectacle.

Our *nembutsu* religious organization, which supposedly raises issues that go beyond democracy, expresses its arrogance despite lagging 200 years behind democracy. This is truly an organization causing its own collapse, destroying its own teachings. However, considering that the organization has social responsibility for its million followers, it is not an overstatement to say that the sect wields great significance and influence over the actual culture of Japan. That is why we make these recommendations....

We would like for it to be realized that our religious organization is haunted broadly and deeply with a sense that male and female lives (*inochi*) are weighted differently.

With their respective lives unequally valued in this way, it is not possible for men and women to meet each other as fellow companions in faith. We are convinced that in fact this was always the case, even while the life of Shinran and critiques made by outcastes (*hisabetsu buraku*) were being discussed. We therefore make the following petition.

1. Open the way for women as well as men to equally become temple priests!
2. Equality for women and men in their treatment within the administration, for instance as training staff and attendants at the Dōbō Hall!
3. Completely revise the election system!
4. Remove the disparity in age requirements for boys and girls to receive ordination!
5. Eliminate discriminatory structures such as temple and clerical rankings! (Obata 2016, p. 120)

To the extent that they sought to decenter or de-monopolize power in the Ōtani-ha institution, the feminists' project was a political one, guided by the liberal feminist ideal of gender equity and respect for the individual autonomy of women as well as men. By allying themselves with groups that were advocating social justice for *burakumin* (outcastes), the feminists ultimately won reforms from the sect.[12] Among these changes were provisions for women to be able to become certified resident priests and for girls to be permitted to take ordination at nine years old, just as boys could. Still, a tension remained between what we might call institutional or judicial policy and the lived experience of temple wives.

For instance, if it were possible for women to become *jūshoku*, would their husbands then be called *bōmori?* This seemed counterintuitive, and the Ōtani-ha convened deliberative committees in 1994, 1999, and 2008 to advise the administration on what definition and status the role of *bōmori* should be given in the Ōtani-ha's bylaws for individual temples (*jiin kyōkai jōrei*). For nearly ten years, the sect debated the "*bōmori* problem," attempting to come to official terms with the position of the temple wife that squared both with the reality of family-run temples and with the modern Shin Buddhist ideal of practitioners who were affiliated through individual faith rather than family association, which was now seen as old-fashioned and "feudal" (*hōkenteki*).

Obata Junko, who was a founding member of the Onnatachi no Kai and a member of several of these deliberative committees, pointed out that to define a *bōmori* as a wife from the top down would only normalize and harden the sense of her being the domestic help (*naijo no kō*) for the *jūshoku*. She also emphasized that individual choice should be involved in undertaking a religious profession. She once told me that the sect was outdated in its thinking on this matter: "Religion and marriage are different. It is feudalistic to assume that a wife will just automatically adopt the faith of her husband, that she won't want to keep her own faith." In a 2004 article, Obata espoused a definition of *bōmori* that (1) was not limited to a spousal relationship with the *jūshoku*, (2) required some basic qualifications (such as *tokudo* or the lay confirmation ceremony called *kikyōshiki*) and was freely chosen, and (3) that was recognized as a profession (*shokumu*; Obata 2004, p. 49).

Keiko Mochizuki was a member of the 1994 deliberative committee and one of the first two females elected to the Shūgikai, the Ōtani-ha's clerical governing body—an accomplishment that itself attested to the effectiveness of the feminist movement. Mochizuki's position during the debate was that the relationship of modern-day temple wives and temple priests should be modeled on the relationship of Shinran and his wife, Eshinni. Mochizuki wanted to preserve the long-standing married clerical partnership of the Jōdo Shinshū, and in the meantime to work on concrete ways to make that partnership more equal. In a 2006 interview, she proposed heightening the status of *bōmori* by requiring temple wives to be certified religious specialists, thus encouraging equality in the division of labor at the temple:

> My understanding is that the *dōjō bōzu* [congregational priest] is the male religious specialist, and the *dōjō bōmori* is the female religious specialist. So, I have said at the *bōmori* association meetings that *bōmori* should study more and take the *kyōshi* [religious instructor] certification. That's because I want the *bōmori*, as a religious specialist, and as someone who runs the Shinshū temple together with the *jūshoku*, to take that responsibility. (2006, p. 131)

Mochizuki's idea that the role of *bōmori* was originally and essentially a female one was not ultimately adopted by the sect. Defining the *bōmori* as a wife and mother, though reflective of the lived reality at temples across Japan, threatened to make their official status contingent upon that of their husbands, thereby threatening women's autonomous participation in the religious organization (Obata 2004; Kawahashi 2012, pp. 120–121). It did not work, in modern times, as a judicial principle by which the Buddhist institution could govern its members.

In the spirit of equal opportunity for the sexes, the 2008 deliberative committee decided to leave the position of both *jūshoku* and *bōmori* open to either men or women ("'Bōmori no ichizuke ni kan suru iinkai' tōshin," 2008). Regardless of the deletion of gender-specific language in the bureaucratic rules, however, Mochizuki's espousal of the *bōmori* as a specifically female religious specialist continues to reflect the reality at most temples. As she notes in the same interview, in the earliest case of a female *jūshoku*'s husband having taken on the title of *bōmori,* temple parishioners told him that it seemed "unmanly," and he ultimately surrendered the title. In the view of many *bōmori,* because of the intimacy that exists between the temple family and their parishioners, while gender-specific wording might be deleted from the sect's bylaws, gender could never be removed from their personal relationships with the laity.

Mochizuki herself has had trouble putting her ideal of a gender-equal clerical partnership into practice at her home temple. After describing herself and her husband as "equal partners" in running the temple, with both of them holding the same ordination credentials, she noted that she continues to have problems making the temple's gardener see them as interchangeable: "Our gardener will only come by to tend to the garden if I am there. If the *jūshoku* [her husband] is there by himself, I have him take care of the three o'clock snack [and afternoon tea]. But this old man says that he could not bear to be served tea by the *jūshoku*" (Mochizuki 2006, p. 131).

Women like Mochizuki remain undiscouraged by such encounters, insisting that through their example they will be able to change the culture, one parishioner at a time. These public feminists in the Ōtani-ha largely embrace the notion, popular among second-wave American feminists in the 1960s, that "the personal is political."

In 1991 the Ōtani-ha constitution was amended to allow for the registering of women as full rather than just proxy *jūshoku* in the event that there was no male successor. The restriction that women must be twenty years old before receiving basic ordination was removed so that girls as well as boys could become ordained at nine years old. In addition, an Office for Women's Affairs (Josei Shitsu) was added to the Ōtani-ha's administrative offices at Higashi Honganji in 1996 to continue to address issues of sexism and other forms of discrimination. It was initially staffed with three men and five women, and it continues to hold yearly women's conferences (*josei kaigi*) in Kyoto, where gender and other discrimination issues are publicly discussed.[13]

The feminist generation of *bōmori* association leaders who were active in the 1980s are now in their sixties and seventies, and have handed over the leadership of the national *bōmori* association to the next generation of mid-career temple wives. The current *bōmori* association officers, these feminists note, seem much more passive and traditional. In one conversation, Obata Junko commented to me: "the *bōmori* association leaders now are so concerned with being good wives and staying in the background that they are unlikely to make a fuss. They always choose male teachers to speak at their workshops. In my day we made sure to have female teachers, because we thought that was important."

In the course of my twenty-seven months of fieldwork I interviewed sixty temple wives, some leaders in local or national temple-wife networks, and others who were more isolated in their home temples. The vast majority of these women were unlikely to attend events such as the annual women's conference hosted by the Office of Women's Affairs, if they were even aware of them. One *bōmori,* currently an officer in the national League of Bōmori Associations, even confided that she found the women who run the conference somewhat sharp (*surudoi*) and a bit scary (*kowai*). The pendulum of mainstream *bōmori* attitudes may have swung back toward the more apolitical.

Religion in the Public and Private Spheres: Sachiko's Story

The resonance of "Ōtani-ha feminism" with the majority of *bōmori* is comparable to the resonance of the broader second-wave Japanese feminist movement (known as "women's lib" [*ūman ribu*]) with secular Japanese housewives: in many ways feminist gains remain relatively marginal to most women's lives.[14] Anthropologist Amy Borovoy cites Kawano Kiyomi, the founder of "feminist therapy" in Japan, who divides contemporary Japanese women into three groups: "(1) 'traditional women,' who live day by day without considering broader issues of social change; (2) 'career women,' who are very few but who manage to find 'a new kind of self'; and (3) 'those in between,' who refuse the traditional role of women and for whom feminism is appealing, even though they cannot quite identify themselves with it" (Borovoy 2001, p. 89). We could probably classify many *bōmori* in the Ōtani-ha within these three groups as well. My informant Sachiko Hino spent her forties and fifties striving to be in the second group, but in her middle age has settled, with some amount of disappointment, into the third group.

Sachiko was born in an urban Osaka temple in 1949 and had no siblings. Women who are born into a temple and remain there for their whole lives by marrying a priest in order to take over are known as "temple princesses" (*tera no ojōsan*).[15] The consensus among those in the temple world is that princesses enjoy something of an advantage over women who marry into the temple from another household because they are already familiar

Table 2 Timeline of Temple Wives in the Modern Shinshū Ōtani-ha (Higashi Honganji) Organization

1925	Bōmori Regulations are established
1928	Bōmori Association is formed
1942	Women permitted to take the religious instructor exam (*kyōshi kentei*)
	Women who have passed religious instructor exam permitted to take basic ordination (*tokudo*), become "proxy resident priests" (*daimu jūshoku*)
1950	National Bōmori Association (Zenkoku Bōmorikai) formed
1958	League of Bōmori Associations (Bōmorikai Renmei) formed
1959	Regional *Bōmori* associations established in 27 districts (*kyōku*)
1960	Basic ordination (*tokudo*) recommended for *bōmori*
1962	Dōbōkai Movement begins
1967	Regulations for Temples and Churches (Jiin Kyōkai Jōrei) revised to institute a *bōmori* registration
1982	League of Bōmori Associations submits a petition demanding:
	Female *jūshoku*; women's participation in the national and local legislative bodies; men's and women's ordination at the same age; elimination of the temple and priestly ranking system
1984	Identical petition submitted by each district's Bōmori Association
1990	League of Bōmori Associations submits petition, demanding:
	Female *jūshoku*; men's and women's ordination at the same age; elimination of the temple and priestly ranking system; *bōmori* investiture ceremony and basic educational system
1991	Regulations for Temples and Churches amended:
	Female *jūshoku* permitted if there is no male successor; temple and clerical ranking system eliminated
1992	As a result of above revision to Regulations for Temples and Churches:
	First female *jūshoku* is installed
	Lower age limits for female ordination removed
	Bōmori clerical-collar system established
1994	*Bōmori* inauguration ceremony (*bōmori shūninshiki*) established
	League of Bōmori Associations submits petition, demanding:
	Training course for *bōmori*; *bōmori* participation in sectarian governance;
	Deliberative committee on "women's activities in the sect" convened, members from League of Bōmori Associations appointed
1996	League of Bōmori Associations submits petition, demanding:
	Bōmori participation in sectarian governance; plan for expediting the process for *bōmori* to receive religious instructor (*kyōshi*) certification
	Regulations for Temples and Churches amended:

	Gender specification removed from definition of *jūshoku;* conditions on female *jūshoku* removed; Office of Women's Affairs (Josei Shitsu) established
1998	National gathering of one hundred *bōmori*
1999	League of Bōmori Associations submits petition, demanding:
	Continuation of *bōmori* system; establishing *bōmori* as a "professional position" at the temple; defining *bōmori* as "a spouse, family member, or parishioner who has undergone the lay ordination ceremony (*kikyōshiki*)"; application to be a *bōmori* to be submitted by the individual, the *jushoku,* or the parishioner representative; *bōmori* participation in sectarian governance
	First Young Bōmori Conference held
	Deliberative committee to consider *bōmori* regulations convened; four members of League of Bōmori Associations appointed; directives for deliberations listed as: "temples should be run as places for listening to the dharma, open to all followers," and "the religious organization should be made by both men and women"
2001	League of Bōmori Associations submits petition, demanding:
	that the sect consider a *bōmori* elected representative to the Sect's Congress (Shūgikai) and voting rights
2003	League of Bōmori Associations submits petition, demanding:
	that the sect appoint a committee to consider the election system in order to promote women's and *bōmori* participation in the Shūgikai and introduce provisions in every district in which the sect suggests a quota for female candidates
	First two female members of the Sangikai (lay legislative body)
2005	First two female members of the Shūgikai (clerical legislative body)
2007	Deliberative committee to consider the status of *bōmori* convened; four members of the League of Bōmori Associations appointed
2008	Regulations for Temples and Churches amended as follows:
	Article 20.1 (Definition) The term "*bōmori*" designates the spouse of the *jūshoku.* Article 20.3 When the *jūshoku* does not have a spouse, when necessary, another member of the temple family who is at least twenty years old may be designated the *bōmori*.
	Article 22.1 (Duty) As someone who has received basic ordination (*tokudo*) in order to spread the teachings to temple members along with the *jūshoku*, the *bōmori* must faithfully listen to the teachings, eagerly engage with temple members, and work hard for the flourishing of the temple.

Sources: Shinshū Ōtani-ha Bōmorikai Renmei 2008 and Obata 2016.

with the parishioners and the temple's ritual practices and they do not have to weather a potentially tempestuous relationship with their mothers-in-law. The fact that they grew up in the temple, however, does not mean they possess any great love for it: many women grow resentful of their limited options and the pressure placed on them to meet, marry, and bear the children of a priest, regardless of their personal desires. Sachiko is one such resistant *bōmori*.

From an early age, Sachiko bore the weight of two rather burdensome expectations stemming from her residence in the temple. As a child, she found the temple restrictive mainly because of the expectations of perfect behavior that she felt people had for temple residents. It is in her nature, she explained, to be conscious of the gaze of others. As she entered adolescence, her discomfort with such expectations grew and was compounded by a second expectation: as the only child of the temple, Sachiko was expected to provide the temple's successor by marrying a priest. She heard this message constantly from both her father and her parishioners, who would say things like, "You must find us a good son-in-law, right?" But she resisted this expectation, resenting the fact that she was not free to choose her own partner. By the time I met Sachiko, she had benefited from two decades of active involvement in some rather liberal groups in the Shinshū world, starting with her local *bōmori* association, which was known for making pointed feminist critiques of the Shinshū's family inheritance system since the early 1990s. Thus, as she looks back now on her father's disregard of her wishes, she tends to frame it in terms of human rights: "So that I wouldn't fall in love and leave home, my father would not let me take calls from my male friends. He also forced me to quit [a club at university] because of its strong political connotations.... Even as my father was participating in the sect's Dōbōkai Movement and working on the problem of discrimination against *burakumin,* he was violating the human rights of his own daughter."[16]

For a while in her early twenties Sachiko plotted to escape her destiny by eloping with her college boyfriend, who was from a lay family. She worked at a part-time job and began to save money, all the while asking around among her male temple friends if there was someone willing to inherit her temple. In a stroke of bad timing, however, her father fell ill and claimed that he was no longer able to run the temple. At this point in the telling of her story, Sachiko usually shook her head, suggesting that this was at least partly a ruse on her father's part in order to force her to give up her life outside of the temple. At any rate, with no successor in line, her obligation had come due prematurely, and she broke up with her boyfriend and set about finding a temple son to marry. After a few arranged dates, she settled on her current husband. "On first impression, he wasn't really my type, but our core values were very similar. What's more, it wasn't unpleasant to be with him, so I decided to marry him. I suppose the primary factor was that he wanted to do the temple work."

At twenty-three, then, Sachiko's destiny was sealed, and she sank into a bog of resentment about the temple world and the men who ran it, who she felt had no regard for her own desires. When she gave birth to two sons in succession, she could barely mask her resentment at her parishioners' delight that she had provided a successor to the temple. "There," she thought, "my obligation is done." When her children started school, she used her free time to become involved in non-temple activities that made her happy, such as social work and cooking classes. She began volunteering as a public reader. As she describes it, her involvement at the temple at that time was the bare minimum—cleaning up and setting out the cushions when her husband performed a service and making sure tea was available for parishioners who came to visit.

The women around her who cheerily led the local *bōmori* association events only accentuated Sachiko's own feelings of disaffection toward the temple, and she stubbornly avoided associating with them if she could. "I used to hate those women," she confided in me once. "They were like superwomen, and so happy about being *bōmori*. It was always, 'I'm grateful for this, I'm grateful for that.' They made me feel even worse, and I always tried to avoid them." Finally, however, the much dreaded rotating post as an officer in her local association landed on her, and she had no choice but to become involved. She wrote the following about how this experience affected her as a *bōmori* and a human being:

> Becoming an officer of the *bōmori* association was the beginning of a major change for me. I did so quite reluctantly, but I subsequently encountered a different kind of Shinshū teaching than the "sermon of gratitude" that I had previously heard at my temple's services. Fortunately, the main members of both my neighborhood and the district committees were so-called liberal people. Of the lecturers at the workshops that I attended, very few were teachers from the sect's universities or *jūshoku* of temples, as I recall.

Due to her distaste for what she had perceived as a male-dominated and hypocritical temple tradition, which she associated with her father, husband, and other men who sought to control her or disregard her interests, the fact that her local *bōmori* association featured "liberal" people, women leaders, and lecturers from other walks of life made it easier for Sachiko to feel at home among them. At the *bōmori* association meetings Sachiko attended, instead of the standard dharma talks by a male priest about the importance of gratitude, individuals from the world outside of the Shinshū circle would present lectures on issues of human rights and discrimination. These presentations moved her. Those speakers who were Shin Buddhists would often give more personal accounts of the significance of the Shin teachings to them and would encourage temple wives to use their position to bring those teachings out into the world. Sachiko recounted a particularly stirring message of this kind:

> [One teacher's] words have remained in my heart: "The fish-monger's wife can tell you the about the name and preparation of fish, and the green grocer's wife can tell you about the name and cooking of vegetables. What about the temple wife? Are you going to just get by with, 'I'll ask the *jūshoku*'?" Indeed, for all this time I had been saying, "I hate the temple!" without actually knowing anything about it. So I made up my mind, and sought out a place to study.

As a disenchanted forty-year-old temple daughter-turned-*bōmori,* Sachiko's obligatory involvement in her local *bōmori* association enabled her to find friends, mentors, and teachers, as well as embrace a new concept of herself as having a special opportunity—indeed, responsibility—to engage with society as a temple person. Her pivotal moment of realization rested upon her recognition of both the responsibility and the possibility that were inherent in her position (*tachiba*) at the temple.

Sachiko followed the teacher's exhortation to do more than just leave the religious duties to her husband: she began to pursue her own education in the Shinshū teachings. She took basic ordination and then completed a three-year course, during which she attended classes once a week in order to finally receive the religious instructor (*kyōshi*) certification at the age of forty. Sachiko recalls that one of the women she met through her *bōmori* association activities at that time had bragged that she and her husband were perfect equals at the temple, sharing both the ritual and the domestic work. So, now that she possessed the same priestly credentials as her husband, after her two sons had left home for college Sachiko attempted to divide the ritual duties equally with him. She took over the monthly visits that were within walking or biking distance of the temple and assisted him at funerals and memorial services for parishioner families with whom she was especially close. However, she was immediately discouraged by her parishioners' negative reactions to her visiting them in place of her husband.

Despite her early efforts to win over her parishioners and forge a path for female priests by her own example—the kinds of actions urged by Ōtani-ha feminist leaders like Obata Junko and Mochizuki Keiko—Sachiko has now, in her own words, "given up." "I just got tired of it," she finally explained to me after we had known each other for almost two years. This was not the first version of her story of getting ordination—which had emphasized the pride she had felt in receiving both levels of priestly credentials as a crowning stage in her journey of embracing her identity as a temple person—nor was it the version she would tell in front of her husband or son. "It's a lot of work. And I have other ways to be involved in the temple now, and social activities that I enjoy. These are just easier and more natural for me. These are really my life's work now." I could tell from her tone that she wished she had a more heroic story to tell me for my research; indeed, she had told me in the past that she deeply admires the feminist leaders of the *bōmori* networks. But the fact was that Sachiko is the kind of person who is sensitive to the expectations and reactions of others; now that her sons were adults and were again living in the temple, it seemed the easiest thing to leave the ritual work to them.

Outside her temple, however, Sachiko has used her position as a *bōmori* to become involved in a number of social causes, such as advocating for awareness about AIDS, and befriending recovered leprosy patients, who have long been the subjects of forced quarantine and other forms of marginalization in Japan. Along with other priests and *bōmori* from the Osaka area, Sachiko frequently visits several state-run leprosaria, which were established throughout Japan and its colonies beginning in the 1930s, and where many elderly leprosy patients still reside. There, she helps carry out Buddhist services and roundtable discussions with residents. Some of her closest friendships are with the other Jōdo Shinshū priests and *bōmori* who accompany her on these day trips. A yearly visit to a leprosy colony in Taiwan also provides Sachiko with a regular opportunity to travel abroad without her husband that is rare among Japanese housewives. Indeed, she confided to me once that on such trips she looked forward as much to the nights of drinking with her friends and sampling the local delicacies as to the satisfaction of the social work.

Although Sachiko was able to find a place among a more liberal contingent of the Shinshū world, when she is at home at the temple she still struggles with the pressures that weigh on her as a temple wife. I once asked her what remained difficult for her about living in a temple, despite the strides she has made in embracing her role. She explained that it was hard to have to be always at the ready to host parishioners and play the public role of the *bōmori* even when she was at home. Without pausing, she went on:

> We cannot leave the temple unattended. It's one of the really hard things about the temple.
>
> Like when I have made a plan, and then later the *jūshoku* has to add something at the last minute, and [I have to cancel my plan]. For instance, yesterday there was a presentation on leprosy at [a local university], and I had made a promise to help out with the event. But then the *jūshoku* scheduled a memorial service [at the temple] in the morning.... That's something I can't get out of—at

the very least, I'd have to prepare a little tea in advance, and perhaps then I could leave a bit early. But anyway, here is my own
work [raising awareness about leprosy], and it gets cancelled out
by this place. [*The word she uses is* koko *or "here," but she gestures toward her husband in the next room, who is napping in
between home visits.*] It's hard to make my own plans. It's hard to
get out of the temple.

Sachiko's feeling of being bound to the temple as if by ball and chain
is sharpened by her competing desire to leave it so she can engage in the activities she has come to see as her own personal "life's work" (for which she uses
the English-derived phrase, *laifu wāku*). Specifically, her leadership roles in
organizations that promote awareness of leprosy and *burakumin* discrimination are activities that she became involved with through her local temple-wife
community. Her sense of vocation with regard to these causes is intimately
related to her Shin faith, which she often notes requires respect for life (*inochi*) in all its forms. However, her husband deems her outside activities to be
extracurricular: they do not supersede her primary obligation to stay at the
temple while he conducts the ritual duties.

Finally, when Sachiko is at home in the temple, she still suffers from
a sense of being monitored and having to switch into professional mode—to
act like a good temple wife—whenever her parishioners drop by. The reader
will recall from chapter 2 the importance of casual hospitality in building connections between the laity, the temple, and by extension Amida. As Sachiko
explains, she does not mind and even enjoys this aspect of her role, and yet it
wears on her:

Of course, I want people to come to the temple, but…[*heaves a
sigh and shrinks into her chair*] to be honest I get tired! If it's a
friend, or someone like you, I don't have to watch myself, but if
it's a parishioner, I have to be on guard (*migamaeru*). It's probably no bother for people who are always put together, but for
me…[*smiles and gestures self-deprecatingly at herself*]. I really
am happy when people come, if only I was prepared. I like people,
so talking to people is a lot of fun for me too. If I can just get ready,
then I really do want them to come. But the preparation…[*sighs
and laughs*]. And the cleaning! I don't like cleaning.

Sachiko has come to enjoy the human connections that are part of her role as
bōmori but feels a responsibility to be professional—in her words, "on guard"
or "prepared"—when her parishioners arrive unannounced, which can happen at any time. This constant demand tends to tire her out, given her sen-

sitive tendencies. One dimension of this professionalism that infiltrates her private life is the requirement to constantly keep the temple clean. Most temples are large and sprawling compared to the average Japanese home. It is expected that the temple wife will keep everything tidy, hospitable, and in a state ready to receive visitors.

Nearly twenty years after her "awakening" to the significance of her position as a temple wife, Sachiko is currently serving another term as a *bōmori* association officer. She continues to invite speakers for the group's workshops who are not necessarily from the temple world but whose life and actions nonetheless embody Shinran's teachings in a broader sense. "People always tell me our events don't seem very temple-like,"[17] she admitted, "but Shinran's teachings also live outside the temple." This approach to engaging the Buddhist teachings with liberal social causes permits Sachiko the room to breathe that she was lacking in her early adulthood.

In many ways, Sachiko's adulthood has been shaped by Japanese feminism, in particular the Ōtani-ha feminist movement. In her rebellious adolescence she resisted the expectations placed on her by her father and her parishioners, hoping to have the freedom to determine her own future career and husband. But the choices she made as she settled into adulthood reflect a more duty-driven ethical orientation than a belief in the primacy of asserting her individual will. Nonetheless, the self-realization she achieved in her forties and fifties resulted from her encounter with liberal social causes and feminist friends who inspired her. When questioned by me, an American woman and scholar, about her life path, she sometimes intimated that certain of her choices—like her "giving up" on being an equal partner with her husband and a ritual performer at her temple—were somehow a compromise of her feminist principles. She seemed rather disappointed that she was not able to put the ideal of true gender equality into practice in her own marriage and role as temple wife. In Sachiko's life story we read a poignant account of her personal decisions, which were made primarily out of duty and a consideration of others' reactions, even though they sometimes seemed inadequate or cowardly in the face of her lofty political ideals.

Sachiko's resolution of this tension between her restrictive domestic roles as a *bōmori* and her attraction to liberal activist causes—by which she brings her Shin Buddhist faith into the world—has required her to compartmentalize her religious life into two spheres. When she is at home in the temple performing the role of *bōmori,* she tries to adhere to a relatively conservative gender role by keeping a tidy house and being a warm, available host and sympathetic listener to her parishioners. She does this because she cares about her parishioners and about what they think; she has also found that the task of liberalizing their view of gender roles day in and day out through her own example of embodying gender equality is simply too exhausting for her.

On the other hand, when she boards the train for one of her monthly visits to a leprosy village in Okayama Prefecture two hours away, she settles into her second life among liberal, well-educated religious professionals in the temple world. In turn, she brings the knowledge and confidence she gains from these exhilarating public activities to her role as her local *bōmori* association president, challenging her neighborhood temple-wife colleagues to become educated about and active in social causes ranging from pacifism to sexual violence to advocating for the blind, the outcaste, or those afflicted with leprosy and AIDS.

Sachiko is not alone in experiencing a dissonance between her negotiation of gender roles on a personal, domestic level and her public advocacy for equality and human rights for women and other marginalized groups in Japan. One of the lessons learned from the Ōtani-ha feminist movement is that the institution of the Japanese family was in some ways more difficult to change than the national Jōdo Shinshū Ōtani-ha organization, from which temple-wife leaders successfully won a number of reforms.[18] Indeed, it was at the point at which the highly individualized and family-specific roles of *bōmori* were finally wrangled into the judicial language of the sect with the intention of giving the position greater "status" (*i'chi*) that the momentum of the Ōtani-ha feminist movement began to dissipate.

In temple families, the scales weighing individual desires against social obligations tend to tip in favor of the continuity of the stem-family (*ie*) and the temple community it supports. Although neoliberal values have grown more salient in Japanese society at large and have begun to affect family structures (Alexy 2011b), the obligation to protect the temple across generations and not to disappoint parishioners still weighs heavily on those were born in or married into a temple. As many of my informants were eager to point out, this also means that gender roles in the temple world tend to lag a few decades behind the changes that are seen in the broader Japanese society.

Nonetheless, in this age of individualism, we might ask why more women do not resist the confining forces of the temple—for instance, by refusing their duties and identities as temple wives, or, even more radically, by divorcing their husbands. Careful observation of the actual conditions of the wives of Buddhist temples reveals that there may simply be more to be gained by their becoming reconciled. Anthropologists have observed a variety of compelling reasons for why more Japanese women do not divorce their husbands. For instance, several observations made by Amy Borovoy in her study of women who had sought out "feminist therapy" (2001) and those who attended an Alanon group (2005) are as applicable to temple wives as they are to secular wives. Borovoy found that her informants, despite facing major challenges in their marital relationships, rarely brought up the possibility of divorce. One typical informant instead "focused on the ways her home life was connected to other opportunities for her, including employment, recreation, and solidarity among neighbors. The same system that precluded the possibility of pursuing a career or leaving her husband for fear of appearances allowed her the opportunity to cultivate a community and to support herself through the home. From this perspective, she had little incentive to leave her marriage" (2001, p. 109). For *bōmori,* the social capital associated with their being temple residents is considerable. In the case of my informant Sachiko, it was through embracing her position as a temple wife and the doors it opened into political and religious involvement that she found her life's work and a sense of fulfillment.

On the other hand, there are a large number of women who, even after marrying a priest and moving into a temple, remain protective of their freedom of belief, their privacy, and their free time. Many are willing to perform just the minimum duties required for their husband's work to go well and the temple to stay viable. Some refuse the role completely, or are refused by their parishioners and in-laws. These women face severe isolation, however. Their de facto identity as a temple person is likely to dominate their relationships outside of the temple, and so if they completely reject the duties commonly ascribed to the wife of a temple priest, they will have a difficult time building social networks. It is much more likely that the temple world will in some way come to color their social involvement and to define their position in relation to their world.

The relationship between individual agency and the social structures in which individuals are embedded is the subject of ongoing debate among social theorists (Archer 2005; Ortner 2006; Biehl, Good, and Kleinman 2007; Noland 2009). What has become clear is that the ideal of individual autonomy so important to liberal politics is more precisely understood as a "procedural principle" than an "ontological or substantive feature of the self" (Mahmood 2005, p. 11). In other words, it is not meant to describe the actual condition of human selves; it merely sets the parameters for individuals acting in public society. Feminists who sought institutional reform in the Ōtani-ha to provide equal opportunities for women's individual awakening understood freedom— in the sense of freedom to choose the religious vocation of being a *bōmori* rather than having it chosen *for* them by virtue of their marriage—primarily in this political sense. The content of that individual awakening (*ko no jikaku*), on the other hand, could well be the realization of one's helplessness and dependency on Amida's compassion and Buddhist teachers.

In some cases, *bōmori* do engage in a willful cultivation of docility, as when they embrace the view that their experiences of suffering and contingency at the temple are actually manifestations of Amida's compassion. In chapter 4, I noted how young temple wives were encouraged to construe their difficulties in adjusting to temple life and their experience of hardship based on their structural position in the family as young daughters-in-law in light of Shin Buddhist doctrine. In the face of such difficulties, some women who attended the sect's conference might ultimately accept a Shin Buddhist account of their karmic contingency as foolish beings (*bonbu*) who lack the capacity to effect their own salvation.

I have tried in this chapter to spotlight other types of desires and agendas that are pursued by temple wives, particularly in the Ōtani-ha, where feminist pushback against a long tradition of androcentric institutions and doctrinal messages has been public and emphatic. My informant Sachiko thrives among her liberal friends outside of the temple and is tirelessly involved in social causes throughout Japan. Once she received her priestly credentials at the age of forty, she attained political and institutional status equal to her husband's. However, in the exhausting negotiation of everyday life, she ultimately resigned herself to many of the limits of her position as a domestic religious professional and is relatively content to adopt a conservative persona when interacting with her parishioners. Individual women in the Ōtani-ha, as we might expect, can change their minds, act in contradiction to their professed beliefs, and simultaneously hold different and even competing senses of freedom as ideals.

Conclusion

IN THIS BOOK, I HAVE USED THE back rather than the front stage as the focal point of my study of contemporary Jōdo Shinshū. Recall the equinox ritual at the Nagais' temple with which this book began. In typical studies of Buddhism, the scholar might try to understand the significance of the rite by keeping her or his eyes trained on the inner altar or the main hall. What is visible from this perspective? A male priest dons ritual garb and conducts a liturgy that involves the recitation of canonical texts. From a textual perspective, this conceivably completes the circuit of Buddhist meaning making: the individual in robes is one of the religious professionals described in the monastic codes, and the words he intones are from the sutras we study in the academy. In other words, ritual and other material forms of Buddhism are considered interesting and relevant only insofar as they correlate with textual sources.

Yet, if we are willing to widen our focus, we will soon see the entrance of the priest's mother, who either wears or leaves off her clerical robes depending on the role she is playing. We notice the energetic bounding of two young girls in and out through the sliding door and the hive of feminized activity that is taking place in the kitchen simultaneously with the ceremony. These observations should lead us to look for another possible center of this event, one that is not elevated onto a ritual stage or any other conventionally sacred—in the sense of singularized or cordoned-off—space. The evidence presented in this book suggests that sacred space does not contain religion, but rather that religion is performed in different ways in different spaces.[1]

I suggest that domesticity—which often coincides with feminized space and feminized labor but is not necessarily spatially demarcated—is one of the less noticeable yet crucial modes in which religion is performed. Domestic religion involves relations of intimacy, vulnerability, and informality. It takes place in venues where behavior is governed by unarticulated, tacit rules rather than legal codes or scripts. This is clearly true in the case of temple wives and the manner in which they facilitate connections to Buddhism. They come to experience an affinity with the tradition through these daily acts, sometimes after years of domestic service. Like Elizabeth Perez' study of the importance of cooking and casual conversation in Black Atlantic religions in the Southern United States, this book "answers the need to look beyond valorized genres of ritual action to see the centrality of micropractices in fashioning sacred selves, spaces, and societies."[2] By widening my ethnographic lens beyond formal liturgy and published texts, I have highlighted the importance of these intimate, unstaged, and unscripted activities that create and transmit the Shin Buddhist tradition.

Personal relationships are one aspect of Buddhism that have received short shrift in scholarship, yet it is hard to deny their significance in the religion of temple wives. In an essay in which she urges a renewed scholarly focus on relationships in the study of religion, Constance Furey could just as well be talking specifically about the domestic religion of *bōmori:*

> What makes religious relationships—relationships construed in relation to divine as well as human beings—especially intriguing is the particular nuance and intensity of the way they combine the extraordinary and the ordinary, the normative and the transcendent. Studies focused on personal relationships can expose the complexity of how body, society, and subjectivity interact through an intimate, relational process of internalization, transformation, and rejection. (Furey 2012, p. 25)

It is through such relationships with other members of the temple family, parishioners, and the Buddha that temple wives quietly impact the shape of Buddhism as practiced in Japan today. Though most *bōmori* hesitate to bring up Buddhist doctrine directly in their conversations with parishioners, we should not discount the significance of their relationships with the laity. These friendships are in fact the intimate stuff of which religious communities are made.

Because doctrine is such an important category for scholars of Buddhism (some would even say it constitutes the essence of Buddhism), we must also assess what temple wives' activities can tell us about it. An ethnographic study such as this one, I argue, shows how doctrine plays out in a domestic key in addition to the more formal (for instance, liturgical and scholarly) ones with which we are more familiar. Despite my informants' hesitance to claim authority in the Buddhist teachings, it turns out that their intimate relationships, far from being irrelevant to the doctrinal dimension of Buddhism, are in fact constitutive of it. A focus on intimacy, domesticity, and vulnerability is indispensable if we are to understand how doctrinal ideas are lived—if indeed they are lived—by Buddhists. Following the lead of Veena Das' study of "domestic modalities" among African American communities, my study endeavors to take seriously those "fugitive sentiments...and expressions about life, offered in the course of everyday conversations rather than as didactic explanations."[3] While scholarly attention is often preoccupied with didactic explanations and ritual performances—religion's more public register—it is the fugitive sentiments and spontaneous expressions—the domestic register—that bring home the existential reality of Buddhist doctrinal notions for many practitioners.

The temple wives examined in this book employed Buddhist doctrinal repertoires in a number of contexts and for a number of reasons.[4] The ideas espoused by Buddhist teachers and texts that were available to these women included theories of the self as interconnected rather than atomistic, as helpless or limited in its capacities, and as replete with afflictions. Several of my informants came to see their individual selves as being integrated into a holistic universe where one's material conditions and interpersonal encounters were subsumed within the all-encompassing agency and compassion of Amida. Shin Buddhist doctrine also includes theories of a salvation achieved by acquiescing to one's lack of control over one's living conditions and learning to entrust one's life to the power of the Buddha. These images were among the tools women used to give meaning and structure to their difficult experiences. In their autobiographical narratives, many of my informants articulated their life paths as having been directed by fortuitous, fateful human connections, whether with their husbands or a religious teacher. These encounters were seen, not as chance, but as manifestations of their karmic conditions and of Amida's compassion.

Glossary

akunin	悪人	*gejin*	外陣
Amidakyō	阿弥陀経	*goen*	御縁
atotsugi	跡継ぎ	*goshō sanshō*	五障三従
betsuin	別院	*henjō nanshi*	変成男子
bōmori	坊守	*hondō*	本堂
bonbu	凡夫	Honganji-ha	本願寺派
bonnō	煩悩	*hō-onkō*	報恩講
bōzu	坊主		
buppan	仏飯	Jiin Kyōkai Jōrei	寺院教会条例
buppō	仏法	*jiriki*	自力
burakumin	部落民	*jizoku*	寺族
butsudan	仏壇	Jōdo Shinshū	浄土真宗
button hōsha	仏恩報謝	*jūshoku*	住職
daimu jūshoku	代務住職	Kakushinni	覚信尼
danjo byōdō	男女平等	*katei*	家庭
danjo kyōdō	男女共同	*kikyōshiki*	帰郷式
Dōbōkai Undō	同朋会運動	Kiyozawa Manshi	清沢満之
dōjō	道場	Kōkōdō	浩々洞
		ko no jikaku	個の自覚
Eshinni	恵信尼	*kuri*	庫裏
		kurō	苦労
fujinkai	婦人会	Kyōgyōshinshō	教行信証
fujin kyōka	婦人教化	*kyōka*	教化
fukujū	服従	*kyōku*	教区
fuku jūshoku	副住職	*kyōshi*	教師
fukyō	布教	*kyōshi shikaku*	教師資格
fuse	布施		

monbō	問法	Shinran	親鸞
monto	門徒	*shokuzen no kotoba*	食前の言葉
naijin	内陣	*shōmyō*	声明
naijo no kō	内助の功	*Shōshinge*	正信偈
naikan	内観	*shufu*	主婦
nembutsu	念仏	*shukke*	出家
nisō	尼僧	*shukuen*	宿縁
nyonin ōjō	女人往生	*shukugō*	宿業
		shutaisei	主体性
obon	お盆	*so*	組
Ofumi (Gobunshō)	御文 (御文章)	Sōboku	僧僕
ohigan	お彼岸	*sōdai*	総代
Ōtani-ha	大谷派		
otoki	お斎	*tamatama*	偶々
otsukimairi	お月参り	*tariki*	他力
		tokudo	得度
renku	連区	Tokuryū	徳龍
Rennyo	蓮如		
ryōsai kenbo	良妻賢母	*waka bōmori*	若坊守
		zaike	在家
Seishinshugi	精神主義	*zenbōmori*	前坊守
shinjin	信心		

Notes

ACKNOWLEDGMENTS

Epigraph. The words to this Jōdo Shinshū hymn are taken from Shinran's Shōzōmatsu wasan 59. The English translation here is from Denis Hirota et al., trans., *The Collected Works of Shinran* (Kyoto: Jōdo Shinshū Hongwanji-ha, 1997), 1: 412.

INTRODUCTION

1   Rennyo (1415–1499), often referred to as the second founder of the Jōdo Shinshū, the Buddhist tradition to which this temple belongs, penned a large number of letters to followers of this tradition, many of which were later collected into the *Gobunshō* (also called *Ofumi*), which became a popular liturgical text in Jōdo Shinshū rituals.

2   Although the Nagais, and the other temple families described in this book, are affiliated with the Jōdo Shinshū, their lives resemble temple life in any of the major Buddhist schools in Japan. Roughly 90 percent of Buddhist temples in Japan are parish temples (*dankadera*), as opposed to training monasteries or administrative temples (Covell 2005).

3   Though the blurring of boundaries in reality also occurs for men as well, my argument here is that focusing on women's activities effectively *forces* us to attend to this fact; if we watched what the men were doing, we might be content to begin our observation with the emergence of the priest onto the ritual stage and stop paying attention after he receded, as that marks the end of the formal liturgy.

4   In the study of early Buddhism, one of the only female-authored texts available to scholars has been the *Therīgāthā,* a collection of verses by enlightened women contained within the Pali Canon. These seventy-three verses have been the exclusive subject of a large number of articles and books—for instance, Miller 1984, Lang 1986, Murcott 1991, Blackstone 1998, Wright 1999, and Appleton 2011.

5   See, for instance, Yoshida 2002, Moerman 2005, and Abe 2015.

6   For example, Kasahara 1975, Oguri 1987, Taira 1992.

7   Such studies are not limited to Japan, of course. Miriam Levering (1992), Beata Grant (1995, 2008), and Wendi Adamek (2009) are notable examples of scholars of Chinese Buddhism who do attempt to discern female interpretations of androcentric doctrines, symbols, and institutions based on transmission records, hagiographies, and dedicatory inscriptions.

8   Asad goes on to note that "the paradox inadequately appreciated here is that the self to be liberated from external control must be subjected to the control of a liberating self already and always free, aware, and in control of its own desires"

(2003, p. 73). Such a notion of individual autonomy quite clearly does not reso-
nate with Buddhist understandings of the nature of the self.

9   Examples of anthropological studies that take this perspective include Spiro
1970 and Gombrich 1971.

10   Kawahashi has more recently argued that the married clerical partnership of the
Jōdo Shinshū is pervaded with its own form of inequality— namely, its entanglement in the gender ideology of the complementary division of labor between
husband and wife (2012, pp. 119–128). Her scholarship has highlighted women's
strategies for reconstructing a gender-equal Buddhism (2003), and she also supports such efforts materially through her work with the Tokai/Kanto Buddhist
Women's Network, which has published several books on Buddhism and gender
issues (Josei to Bukkyō Tōkai Kantō Nettowāku 1999, 2004)

11   Shinran drew upon a text called the *Mappō tomyōki,* attributed to the founder of
the Tendai school, to draw conclusions about the diminished faculties of practitioners during the latter age of the dharma (Rhodes 1980; Marra 1988; Dobbins
2002). For an overview of Indian and Chinese Buddhist theories of cosmic and
dharmic decline, see Nattier 1991.

12   See Starling 2012 and 2013 for studies of normative portrayals of Shin Buddhist
wives in the Tokugawa and Meiji periods. Richard Jaffe has summarized the
defense of clerical marriage made by several scholar-priests of the Edo period
(2001, pp. 36–57).

13   Since the 1960s, certain anthropologists have also formulated similar ground-
level conceptions of religion-as-lived, particularly in the study of Buddhism; see,
for instance, Leach 1968. I thank Nicolas Sihlé for this reference.

14   See Rogers and Rogers 1991, especially pp. 289–315, for an analysis of Rennyo's
contribution to the extension of Shin piety from just the *nembutsu* uttered in
gratitude to more worldly actions (such as fulfilling social obligations) undertaken in a spirit of gratitude.

15   See Starling 2012. I also discuss these sermons as they relate to home economics
at the temple in chapter 2.

16   A few other scholars have previously used the term "domestic religion" to draw
attention to the home as a private sphere of religious activity in contrast to public
venues like temples or monasteries. Perhaps most notably, Jonathan Z. Smith
discusses domestic religion in ancient Judaism as one of three spatial categories
in his typology of religion as existing "here, there and anywhere." Domestic religion corresponds to the "here," in contrast to the "there" of public temples and
the "anywhere" of traveling religionists (2004, p. 325). In the context of Smith's
focus on Mediterranean late antiquity, domestic religion refers to rituals that
take place inside of homes rather than in public temples. According to Smith,
these domestic rituals' scope of concern is limited to the extended family. "The
domestic realm," he writes, "because it is not situated in separated sacred space,
invites ambiguity as to significance" (2004, p. 325). The majority of the temple
wives I studied would instantly recognize some truth in Smith's statement: their
lives are lived astride the two realms of the private and public, which scholars
imagine to be worlds apart. And yet, for temple wives in the Jōdo Shinshū, the
scope of concern of their domestic activities is much wider than just their own
family line. Their work supports an entire community of parishioners and, by
some prescriptive accounts, is crucial for the livelihood of the entire Buddhist
sect (Starling 2013). My analysis of Japanese Buddhism as seen through the
lens of domesticity is an attempt to set aside the temptingly tidy—but ultimately
misleading—distinction between matters of domestic and public concern.

17   Amy Borovoy writes: "Through a series of interventions into home life, the Japanese state promoted the image of domestic work as public service, and fur-
thermore, as 'rational,' modern work that is intimately linked to productivity in

commercial sectors" (Borovoy 2001, p. 97, citing Garon 1997). Sharon Nolte and Sally Ann Hastings have shown that the vocation of professional housewife as it was crafted in official discourse during the Meiji effectively cast wives as "public figures, veritable officers of the state in its microcosm, the home" (1991, p. 157). As Borovoy points out, "the state's solicitation of women's work in national agendas of modernization and productivity…undercut the distinction between the 'private' world of the home and the 'public' world of political and market relations; it also undercut the equation of paid work with productive work." The result, she writes, is that in Japan "the 'domestic' is no longer coterminous with the 'private'" (Borovoy 2001, p. 94).

18   To date, anthropological studies of gender in Japan have made no attempt to understand how such gender roles might apply to religious contexts—for instance, Kondo 1990, Hendry 1993, Long 1996, Allison 1996, Goldstein-Gidoni 1997 and 2012, Holloway 2010, and Ronald and Alexy 2011. In the world of scholarship on Buddhism in Japan, studies predominantly focus on women as nuns, casting them as celibate resistors of the conventional gender roles that accompany familial obligations. Two important exceptions are Noriko Kawahashi's scholarship on temple wives in the Sōtō Zen School (1995) and Simone Heidegger's work on gender discrimination in the Jōdo Shinshū (2006, 2010).

CHAPTER ONE: A FAMILY OF CLERICS

Epigraph. Personal interview, July 18, 2009, Kyoto.

1   Though my own focus is on the Jōdo Shinshū, a tradition that has historically rejected monastic forms of practice, the reality of inherited parish temples across Japan and the continued trend of lay affiliation with Buddhist temples according to the *ie* or family line suggest that family is central to the continuance of all the Buddhist sects. See, for instance, Starling 2015.

2   He later noted that the sect has since revised its template for these temple bylaws, deleting "first son" in an effort to encourage gender parity, so that it now reads: "At Muryōji, someone in the Nagai family will be the successor of the temple." Any individual temple can amend its bylaws to reflect its preferred successor, but it requires the agreement of the entire board of trustees (*sekinin yakuin*), which includes parishioners and temple family members, and requires a great deal of paperwork. Very few temples opt to do this.

3   See Heidegger 2010 and chapter 6 of this book for an explanation of the critiques raised by feminists in the Ōtani-ha about gender discrimination and the response of the sectarian administration in reforming their policies.

4   The *Amidakyō*, referred to in English as the *Smaller Pure Land Sutra*, is a Pure Land text, possibly of Indian origin, that is one of three canonical sutras in the Pure Land traditions. It is perhaps the most frequently recited canonical text in Jōdo Shinshū liturgies. The *Shōshinge*, as noted previously, is a section of Shinran's longer opus, the *Kyōgōyshinshō*, that is often studied and used in liturgy.

5   *Bōmori* are not alone among Japanese women in abandoning their chosen professions upon marrying, of course—indeed, the desire to freely choose one's profession and continue to work at it after marriage is one of the major causes for resistance to marriage among young Japanese women (Holloway 2010; Nakano 2011).

CHAPTER TWO: STAYING AT HOME AS BUDDHIST PROPAGATION

1   By "reproductive labor," I refer to unpaid and often invisible work that is nonetheless necessary to sustain the family and the temple community. This concept

is of course inspired by the insights into gendered labor developed by Marxist feminists (Weeks 2011).

2   Fukushima (2006, p. 35), citing "Shōshakai no sekinin," in *Katei*, vol. 2, no.12. *Katei* was published by Seishinkai, a group led by Kiyozawa Manshi (1863–1903), doctrinal reformer of the Jōdo Shinshū Otani-ha.

3   Susan Orpett Long (1996, p. 165) cites a study of 1,300 families conducted in Kobe by the Hyogo Institute for the Study of Family Issues.

4   See, for instance, Cook 2013 and Alexy 2011b. Lunsing's sociological study in the 1990s of "people who fail to fit Japanese common-sense constructions of either female or male gender" also suggests that there is a much more room for ambiguity and strategic shifting of roles and identities than is allowed for by binary, ideal-type models of Japanese gender norms (2015, p. 13).

5   Post on mixi.co.jp, under the topic "Working outside the temple," May 17, 2009.

6   Depending on their geographic location, temples may have a full-fledged cemetery on the grounds where parishioners may come to visit their ancestral plot. Some temples have more compact reliquaries somewhere in the temple building. Others do not host graves in any form.

7   "Dai kyūkai shūsei kihon chōsa chūkan hōkoku," *Shūhō* 521 (July 2010): 72.

8   "Dai kyūkai shūsei kihon chōsa chūkan hōkoku," *Shūhō* 521 (July 2010): 44.

9   Helen Hardacre found a similar gender preference among laypeople belonging to the new religious group Kurozumikyō. The Shinto-derived church has both male and female ministers, but female ministers are far more in demand for their effectiveness in listening to and helping parishioners resolve personal problems. Hardacre attributes this discrepancy to "general cultural expectations that hold that women are more sensitive to emotional nuance and the details of personal situations and thus are more desirable as counselors" (1986, p. 121).

10   Further, 9 percent of *bōmori* reported serving on a civic, youth, or social welfare committee, and another 2.9 percent reported performing a role at a rehabilitation or elderly care facility (*Shūhō* 521 [July 2010]: 41).

11   "Zadankai: Kyōdan, jiin no genjō to tenbō: Mizuko kuyō o megutte, tera ni kurasu josei no shiten kara," *Kyōka kenkyū* 113 (April 20, 1995): 62.

12   In Shinshū temples, the basic ritual calendar consists of the late autumn or early winter *hō-onkō*, the spring and autumn *higan-e*, and the *obon-e* in August. In many temples, the *eitaikyō* ceremony in the late spring provides a seasonal counterbalance to the *hō-onkō* in the fall, and some temples host a formal or informal gathering of laity during the New Year's Season, known as *shūseikai*. The precise timing of these may vary by temple or region, and according to sect or temple there may be additional ritual events, or some of these may be omitted. See Shinshū Shinjiten Hensankai (1983, pp. 537–539).

13   For an explanation of the historical origin of the *hō-onkō*, see Blum (2000, pp. 200–201).

CHAPTER THREE: HOME ECONOMICS

Epigraph. Sōboku, *Bōmori saisoku no hōgo* (Dewa: Saitō Riemon, 1775).

1   While the "Protestant bias" in Buddhist studies, which tended to privilege texts over material forms, was long ago exposed by Gregory Schopen (1991), the tendency to interpret the meaning of Buddhist "practice" only insofar as it accords with what the texts describe (or prescribe) has proven a hard scholarly habit to break. See Walters 1999, Sharf 2001, Bielefeldt 2005, Rambelli 2007, and Clarke 2014.

2   To cite but one example, Monica Lindberg Falk has shown that, by performing the role of being recipients of donations and therefore "fields of merit," the oth-

erwise ambiguous lay-nuns in Thailand were able to establish themselves, in some local contexts, as Buddhist monastics (Falk 2007).

3   Justin McDaniel has recently offered up the study of liturgy as a fruitful means of understanding the value of a given Buddhist text beyond just its "semantic meaning or its place in a canon" (2011, p. 140). In other words, even discursive forms of Buddhism are not always important because of their semantic meaning alone.

4   Some temple families have begun to outsource this labor, hiring cleaners or a team of college students by the hour. I asked Akira about this, and he responded that his temple was fortunate to have plenty of able-bodied parishioners who were happy to volunteer to spend a day helping with this rather tedious task.

5   McDaniel writes of amulet sales at Thai Buddhist monasteries: "the wonderings, reflections, and visualizations that take place while looking at an image or walking around a monastery"—here, a family temple—"generate questions that can be posed to texts or help individuals develop new beliefs. The conversations that take place over the trading of amulets"—here, the polishing of the altar's decorations—"can be seen as emerging doctrine" (2011, p. 208).

6   See Jaffe 2001 for a detailed discussion of critiques and defenses of Shin clerical marriage in the Edo period.

7   This quotation is from Tokuryū's Bōmori kyōkai kikigaki (pp. 3–4), but he also preached sermons to temple priests with a similar message (Kashiwahara and Fujii, pp. 35–103).

8   It is fairly common for the male child of a temple family to receive ordination at the earliest opportunity—age nine (in the Ōtani-ha) or fifteen (in the Honganji-ha). Temple daughters, having somewhat more volition in the matter, frequently choose to become ordained when they are a bit older and have considered that their futures may lie in the temple, much as Noriko's daughters have done. The requirements for ordination and the history of ordination for women in the Jōdo Shinshū are discussed in more detail in chapter 5.

9   The image problem of the contemporary Japanese priesthood has been aptly surveyed by scholars (Covell 2005; Borup 2008; Rowe 2011; Nelson 2013). As I have discussed elsewhere, while the traditionally monastic schools of Buddhism like Zen and Tendai are haunted by the "renunciant ideal" with which their current status as married clerics compares unfavorably, priests in the Jōdo Shinshū are less susceptible to this particular critique, as a married priesthood has been a custom of their tradition since the time of the founder, Shinran (Starling 2015). In this chapter, I leave the issue of clerical marriage aside in order to focus on the economic dimension of Temple Buddhism's authenticity problem.

10   The scene from Itami Jūzō's 1984 film "The Funeral" (Osōshiki) in which a Tokyo couple tries in vain to ascertain how much they should pay a priest to perform the wife's father's funeral accurately portrays the perspective of modern urban laypeople trying to puzzle their way through a ritual custom and a Buddhist tradition with which they have lost touch.

11   My informant explained that the rice would be left there until after noon, at which time it was acceptable for the temple family to eat it themselves.

12   One of the more famous typologies of exchanges in "primitive societies" was put forth by Marshal Sahlins (1996 [1978]). Arjun Appadurai's edited volume *The Social Life of Things: Commodities in Cultural Perspective* contained a number of studies that sought to distinguish, for instance, "political economies" from "moral economies" (Appadurai 1986). A recent collection of articles on "the Buddhist gift" published in *Religion Compass* put a new spin on the large body of scholarship that already exists on this topic. In his introduction, anthropologist Nicolas Sihlé urged scholars to distinguish "gifts" from contexts in which there is remuneration (which in Buddhism is nearly always) and to employ the

term "transfers" rather than "exchanges" (Sihlé 2015). I have tried to take his advice here.

13 This is one of the observations we can make by also viewing exchanges in the aggregate, rather than individually, as Sihlé (2015) points out. The gift community seen here is perhaps similar to that observed by Michael Ames in the Sri Lankan Buddhist contexts, in which cumulative gift exchanges involved both lay and clerical practitioners in a Buddhist moral community (Ames 1966, p. 32).

CHAPTER FOUR: SOCIAL NETWORKS AND SOCIAL OBLIGATIONS IN THE DISCIPLINING OF *BŌMORI*

Epigraph. Personal interview, October 12, 2009, Higashi Honganji.

1 A survey taken in 2008 by the Honganji-ha indicated that 33.7 percent of current *bōmori* came from non-temple backgrounds ("Dai kyūkai shūsei kihon chōsa chūkan hōkoku," *Shūhō* 521 [2010]: 26). In the more recent iteration of the same survey, this one conducted in 2015, the proportion of *bōmori* who were non-temple born had grown to almost a half. About one-third were born in a Buddhist temple other than the one they married into, primarily of the same Shinshū sect, but with smaller numbers of women coming from another sect within Shinshū, and even fewer from another school of Buddhism altogether ("Dai jūkai shūsei kihon chōsa chūkan hōkoku," *Shūhō* 581 [2016]: 51).

2 It also conforms to the pattern identified by Saba Mahmood among participants in the Egyptian mosque movement, who follow ritual conventions as a way of cultivating a virtuous subjectivity—a mode of embodied ethical practice that Mahmood summarizes as "exteriority as a means to interiority" (2005, p. 134).

3 This area, because of political conflicts between the Shinshū and the region's ruling clans during the Edo period (1603–1868), had experienced a persecution of Shin Buddhism, resulting in the movement's going into hiding. This episode is now referred to as *kakure nembutsu*, the hidden *nembutsu* practice. The branch office where Kayoko's husband worked for two years hosts an archive and museum of artifacts from the period, such as parasols into which hidden compartments had been stitched to hide the Shinshū scriptures. Later, when the Meiji restoration took place and the regional lords fell from power, the ban on Shin Buddhism was lifted and the underground *nembutsu* congregations came out of hiding, as a stream of ministers were sent from Kyoto to fill the clerical vacuum and build temples to accommodate these dedicated followers. For a book-length study of Shin groups that continue to practice in secrecy even today, see Chilson 2014.

4 Roughly 8 percent of temples in the Honganji-ha run either day-care or nursery school (*yōchien*) facilities. See "Dai kyūkai shūsei kihon chōsa chūkan hōkoku," *Shūhō* 521 (2010): 13.

5 In rural areas or in the case of family-owned businesses, multiple generations often still live under one roof. Many scholars have noted that, while the nuclear family is propounded as the ideal in official policy, economic fluctuations since the 1970s have caused living situations to fragment into increasingly diverse configurations such as singles, childless couples, and married couples living separately. See, for instance, Ronald and Alexy 2011, p. 9.

6 Post on mixi.jp, under the topic "Life at the Temple," May 9, 2009.

7 Rennyo's Letters (*Gobunshō*), translated in Rogers and Rogers 1991, p. 160.

8 Local all-women's confraternities, known as *nyonin-kō* or *ama-kō*, have existed in the Jōdo Shinshū as early as the fifteenth century. Beginning in the 1830s, the abbot of Nishi Honganji ordered the formation of local chapters of a Shin Buddhist women's association it called Saishōkō (Chiba 2002, p. 61).

9 Aside from the administrative duties of these meetings, the pressure of playing

host to a group of professional hostesses can be quite burdensome and require days of preparation, according to many of the women I have interviewed.

10   The Ōtani-ha dates the beginning of its National League of Bōmori Associations to November 23, 1958. It is now a registered organization of the sect, overseen by the Organizations Section at Higashi Honganji. The leaders of the national organization serve three-year terms and are chosen from among the officers of each regional block and district. The four chief officers meet for business several times a year at Higashi Honganji, and all of the members gather once a year for a national conference in Kyoto ("'Josei no shūmon katsudō ni kan suru iinkai' tōshin," *Shinshū*, May 1996, p. 41). This national organization enabled *bōmori* to assert collective agency within the sect, for instance, during the Ōtani-ha feminist movement, which I discuss in chapter 6.

11   This emphasis on introspection (*naikan*), examining one's own experience of suffering and hardship in order to embrace the other-power of Amida, reflects the continued influence in the Ōtani-ha of the Meiji period theologian Fukuzawa Manshi's approach to self-cultivation (Yasutomi 2003; Mizushima 2007).

CHAPTER FIVE: WIVES IN FRONT OF THE ALTAR

Epigraphs. First, *Kyōkai ichiran* 752 (June 25, 1929): 2; second, personal interview, November 23, 2009, Kyoto.

1   See Starling (2012). Meiji and Taisho institutional discourse on temple wives struck a balance between idealizing them as a unique model of female Buddhist clerics while also casting them as paradigmatic good wives and wise mothers (Starling 2013).

2   A "sōryo" is anyone who has attained tokudo or basic ordination. Numbers for the Honganji-ha are from the sect's 2008 internal survey, a report of which I received from Nishi Honganji's Kikan Movement Department (Kikan Undō Suishin Honbu). For the Ōtani-ha, I refer to the sect's 2009 survey results contained in the Shūmon gense no hōkoku (Higashi Honganji 2009).

3   "Dai jūkai chūsei kihon chōsa chūkan hōkoku" (2016, p. 43) and Higashi Honganji (2009).

4   "Dai jūkai chūsei kihon chōsa chūkan hōkoku" (2016, p. 43).

5   Japan's Equal Employment Opportunity Act (Danjo koyō kikai kintō hō) went into effect in April 1986. For more on the feminist movement in Japan, see Buckley (1997) and Mackie (2003). The impact of this movement on women's status in the Jōdo Shinshū is discussed in more detail in chapter 6 of this book and in Heidegger (2010).

6   Roughly one-third of *jūshoku* in the Honganji-ha also work at another job outside of the temple ("Dai jūkai chūsei kihon chōsa chūkan hōkoku" 2016, p. 75).

7   The pricing of monthly home visits is an inexact affair: unlike fees for temple membership, regular collections for temple repairs, and other fixed contributions, the amount given for the *otsukimairi* and other rituals is left up to the temple member. For regular monthly visits, contributions may range from one thousand yen (about ten dollars) to seven thousand yen (about seventy dollars). If a parishioner is unsure how much to give, they can either call the temple and ask for a suggested amount or consult with a lay leader who is familiar with the customary price. In this way, the establishment of norms for temple donations, like other aspects of ritual practice, is extremely localized.

8   These informants were among the founding members of the group Shinshū Ōtani-ha ni Okeru Josei Sabetsu o Kangaeru Onnatachi no Kai (Women's Group to Consider Discrimination against Women in the Shinshū Ōtani-ha), and are now also active members of the Tōkai/Kantō Josei to Bukkyō Nettowāku. See chapter 6 for a description of the activities of these two groups.

9   Kakushinni in effect established the first temple in the Jōdo Shinshū, the Otani memorial chapel for her father. See Dobbins (2002, p. 80; 2004, p. 82).

10 Certainly, the language of mobilization and the conflation of one's debt to Amida with their duty to their country had entered the lexicon of the Honganji-ha by the 1930s. See Starling (2013, p. 294) for an example of a speech given by the wife of the abbot of Nishi Honganji—in a sense the "first lady" of the sect—enjoining her fellow temple wives to simultaneously fulfill their duty to the Buddha, the sect, and the state by guarding the temple.

11 I was unable to conduct any interviews in person with temple wives who had taken over their temples during wartime (the surviving number is quickly decreasing), but I collected several stories of mothers and mothers-in-law and received written answers to a questionnaire from two women who lived in Ishikawa Prefecture. The letter I cite here was obtained by the Ōtani-ha's Osaka district office and was included in an exhibit on gender equality at Higashi Honganji in 2011.

12 The letter, written in 1942, was part of an exhibit in February 2011 at Higashi Honganji with the theme "A Gender-Equal Organization" (Danjo kyōdō sangaku kyōdan).

13 This was the official definition of the role of bōmori, first codified by the sect in 1925. The regulations for bōmori read: "The bōmori shall, with good deportment, gravity and austerity, perform the duties of the wife of the religious household. . . . For the sake of her own practice and the teaching of others she shall provide domestic help for the jūshoku" ("Bōmori kitei," Shinshū 87 [1925]: p. 1).

14 The sight of male priests dressed in robes buzzing around the streets of Kyoto on their mopeds is fairly common; a priest standing in line at the grocery store in clerical garb is less so, however. In the majority of cases, a priest's wife would be the one to do the shopping and similar errands, so there would be no need for him to enter such secular locations still dressed in his religious garb.

15 Hisako explained later that the temple asks for a set amount (one thousand yen per head within the household) every month for upkeep and improvements on the temple (ijihi). She collects this on her otsukimairi visit and gives them a receipt; she also collects another envelope, an honorarium for the visit itself, which the parishioners give at their own discretion.

16 Elsewhere, I explore the public debates and institutional changes surrounding the introduction of gender equality into the legal language of the Ōtani-ha (Starling 2017).

17 See chapter 5 for an explanation of the origins and activities of the Ōtani-ha's Office for Women's Affairs.

18 Translation of the Smaller Pure Land Sutra from Inagaki (1995, p. 354).

19 Kamata Hiroko, "'Josei' jūshoku tte dō yo?!" Menzu Aiau, no. 4 (2009): 14.

CHAPTER SIX: EQUALITY AND FREEDOM IN THE ŌTANI-HA

Epigraph. "Hontō no dōbō kyōdan o negatte: Bōmori mondai e no torikumi," Kyōka kenkyū 135 (May 2006): 128.

1   Scholarship on the relationship between the "Buddhist Dharma" and "Worldly Law," particularly within the Jōdo Shinshū, is plentiful. At the 2016 American Academy of Religion Annual Meeting, for instance, the International Association of Shin Buddhist Studies convened a panel on this theme.

2   This insight about religious practitioners' disciplined cultivation of their own contingency recalls Michael Lambek's observation that "one might say that what religion is not is freedom" (2012; italics in original).

3   On the "democratization of social consciousness" in Japan as a result of the GHQ-dictated postwar educational ethos, see, for instance, Kikkawa and Todoroki 1998.

4   The *Lotus Sutra* is one of the most influential Buddhist texts in East Asia. Chapter 12, known as the "Devadatta Chapter," contains the famous episode wherein a daughter of the king of the *naga*s is told by the Buddha's disciple Sariptura: "A woman's body is filthy, it is not a dharma receptacle.... Also, a woman's body even then has five obstacles" (Hurvitz 2009, p. 184). Although the *naga* girl goes on to defy Sariputra's expectations and become a buddha extremely rapidly, her incredible spiritual achievement despite being a woman relies on the power of the *Lotus Sutra* and is usually not the focus of Jōdo Shinshū interpreters.

5   "Gojin no danjo dōkenron," *Katei* 1 (2): 3.

6   This notion of obedience (*fukujū*) is articulated by Kiyozawa himself to the general audience of the journal *Seishinkai* in articles such as "Jiyū to fukujū no soren" (The complementarity of freedom and obedience; *Seishinkai*, no. 3) and "Manbutsu ittai" (The oneness of the 10,000 things; *Seishinkai*, no. 2). See Blum and Rhodes (2011) for English translations of several of Kiyozawa's works.

7   The sermon was included in a collection of lectures for temple priests called *Jūshoku michi*, which was distributed by Higashi Honganji to *jūshoku* in training for many years (Kaneko 1976).

8   As Allison Alexy reminds us, "houses are structural in two senses—as the literal structures in which family lives unfold, and as a key set of social norms that structure family relationships and expectations" (2011a, p. 237). Though the focus of my own study is on female gender roles, the house looms large (and heavy) in constructions of masculinity as well. See Hidaka 2011 on the prevalence of *daikokubashira* (pillar of the house) ideology in contemporary Japan.

9   "Dōbōkai no keisei sokushin (dai nana jū kai shūgikai shūmu sōchō ensetsu)," in Shinshū dōbōkai undō gakushū shiryō, pp. 12–17 (originally published in *Shinshū*, July 1962, pp. 2–7).

10   "Shinshū dōbōkai undō wa, junsui naru shinkō undō de aru," in Shinshū dōbōkai undō gakushū shiryō 2003, p. 3 (originally published in the December 1962 issue of *Shinshū*).

11   Many of the developments I discuss in this section regarding gender discrimination-related reform can be found in Simone Heidegger's book (2006, in German) and her English chapter (2010).

12   In 1987, a temple wife from Takayama publicly questioned the Ōtani-ha's chief administrator, Kurube Shinyū, one of the founders of the Dōbōkai Movement, about the rules that prevented women from becoming full-fledged *jūshoku*. He responded with a slew of ill-considered remarks about the proper role of women as being to stay at home to support their husbands. These remarks, in addition to discriminatory comments about *burakumin*, prompted an extended denunciation campaign to be waged by the Buraku Liberation League lasting from 1987 until 1989. At a 1988 meeting, the league declared that not recognizing female *jūshoku* was an act of discrimination by the Ōtani-ha. In response, the administration promised that the reality of female *jūshoku* would be implemented within five years. See Heidegger 2010; Ukō 1999; "'Josei no shūmon katsudō ni kan suru iinkai' tōshin" (1996, pp. 39–40).

13   Now housed in the Office for the Promotion of Liberation Movements (Kaihō Undō Suishin Honbo), the Women's Affairs staff also contribute to the publication of booklets and magazines on gender issues.

14   For book-length studies of Japanese feminist movements, see Buckley 1997, Mackie 2003, and Dales 2009.

15   The Honganji-ha's 2015 survey found that 12.7 percent of current *bōmori* are temple daughters who stayed in their home temples and married a priest who took over as the *jūshoku* ("Dai jūkai shūsei kihon chōsa," 2016, p. 53). The Ōtani-ha does not currently collect data on *bōmori*, but the situation is roughly comparable.

16   Detailed accounts of the Shinshū's historical relationship to the *burakumin* can be found in Amstutz 2010 and Main 2010.

17   The phrase she uses is *"otera no nioi ga shinai"*—literally, "don't smell like the temple."

18   Here I allude to a similar observation Amy Borovoy has made about the broader Japan feminist movement: "The overwhelming lesson of Japanese feminism appears to be that legally dictated equality can only scratch at the surface of long-standing social practice and cultural values" (2001, p. 201).

CONCLUSION

1   Scholars in recent decades have already done the heavy lifting to expose the reasons for our scholarship's persistent pull toward the past and more sacralized forms of religion—a pull perfectly captured by the title of Mircea Eliade's well-known 1959 work, *The Sacred and the Profane*. Although Eliade's "sui generis" definition of religion has fallen out of vogue (McCutcheon 1997), his evocative title is consonant with a prestigious tradition of scholarship on religion spanning from Emile Durkheim (1912) to Ann Taves (2009), a tradition that divides human activity into two spheres—or sometimes plots it along an axis—in which the sacred and the profane are defined in contradistinction to one another. In this view, the quotidian domestic activities that the temple wife oversees would by necessity fall on the opposite side of the divide from properly spiritual endeavors.

2   Perez 2016, p. 11. According to Perez, micropractices refer to "routine and intimate sequences of operations," which, "[d]espite their modest scale and narrow limits,...sustain religious formations by naturalizing the conventions that govern particular communities." Though often unglamorous and rarely celebrated by the religious tradition itself, quotidian practices like cleaning, cooking, and having casual conversations over tea nonetheless work to "organize space, time, and intensities of affect for participants" (Perez 2016, p. 9).

3   Das, Ellen, and Leonard 2008, p. 352. Das and her coauthors open their article with the offhand comment of an informant: in the in the midst of chatting with the researchers about something mundane, the young man introduced a profound observation: "Life is just so fragile. You never know. There's so much [*sic*] cracks you can slip in. It's just bad." Das and her coauthors observe how "[t]he statement just flitted by as a rabbit might scoot across a landscape drawing an exclamation rather than [representing] a well-articulated thought" (350).

4   Ann Swidler (2001), Robert Campany (2003), and Justin McDaniel (2011) have demonstrated the usefulness of thinking of religion (and culture) in terms of repertoires of resources rather than as holistic, coherent systems.

Works Cited

Abé, Ryūichi. 2015. "Revisiting the Dragon Princess: Her Role in Medieval Engi Stories and Their Implications in Reading the Lotus Sutra." *Japanese Journal of Religious Studies* 42 (1): 27–70.

Adamek, Wendi Leigh. 2009. "A Niche of Their Own: The Power of Convention in Two Inscriptions for Medieval Chinese Buddhist Nuns." *History of Religions* 49 (1): 1–26.

Alexy, Allison. 2011a. "The Door My Wife Closed: Houses, Families, and Divorce in Contemporary Japan." In *Home and Family in Japan: Continuity and Transformation,* edited by Richard Ronald and Allison Alexy, pp. 236–253. New York: Routledge.

———. 2011b. "Intimate Dependence and Its Risks in Neoliberal Japan." *Anthropological Quarterly* 84 (1): 895–918.

Allison, Anne. 1996. "Producing Mothers." In *Re-imaging Japanese Women,* edited by Anne E. Imamura, pp. 135–155. Berkeley: University of California Press.

Ambros, Barbara R. 2015. *Women in Japanese Religions.* New York: NYU Press.

Ames, Michael M. 1966. "Ritual Prestations and the Structure of the Sinhalese Pantheon." In *Anthropological Studies in Theravada Buddhism.* Cultural Report Series 13, edited by Manning Nash. New Haven, CT: Yale University Southeast Asia Studies.

Amstutz, Galen. 2010. "Shin Buddhism and Burakumin in the Edo Period." In *The Social Dimension of Shin Buddhism,* edited by Ugo Dessi, pp. 59–110. Boston: Brill.

Appadurai, Arjun. 1986. "Commodities and the Politics of Value." In *The Social Life of Things: Commodities in Cultural Perspective,* edited by Arjun Appadurai. New York: Cambridge University Press.

Appleton, Naomi. 2011. "In the Footsteps of the Buddha? Women and the Bodhisatta Path in Theravāda Buddhism." *Journal of Feminist Studies in Religion* 27 (1): 33–51.

Arai, Paula Kane Robinson. 1999. *Women Living Zen: Japanese Soto Buddhist Nuns.* New York: Oxford University Press.

———. 2011. *Bringing Zen Home: The Healing Heart of Japanese Women's Rituals.* Honolulu: University of Hawai'i Press.

Archer, Margaret S. 2005. "Structure, Culture and Agency." In *The Blackwell Companion to the Sociology of Culture,* edited Mark D. Jacobs and Nancy Weiss Hanrahan, pp. 17–34. Hoboken, NJ: Blackwell Publishing.

Asad, Talal. 1993. *Genealogies of Religion: Discipline and Reasons of Power in Islam and Christianity.* Baltimore: Johns Hopkins University Press.

———. 1997. "Remarks on the Anthropology of the Body." In *Religion and the Body,* edited by Sarah Coakley, pp. 42–52. New York: Cambridge University Press.

———. 2003. *Formations of the Secular: Christianity, Islam, Modernity.* Stanford, CA: Stanford University Press.

Bartholomeusz, Tessa J. 1994. *Women under the Bō Tree: Buddhist Nuns in Sri Lanka.* Cambridge Studies in Religious Traditions 5. New York: Cambridge University Press.

Biehl, João Guilherme, Byron Good, and Arthur Kleinman. 2007. *Subjectivity: Ethnographic Investigations.* Ethnographic Studies in Subjectivity 7. Berkeley: University of California Press.

Bielefeldt, Carl. 1998. "Practice." In *Critical Terms for the Study of Buddhism,* edited by Donald S. Lopez, Jr., pp. 229–244. Chicago: University of Chicago Press, 2005.

Blackstone, Kathryn R. 1998. *Women in the Footsteps of the Buddha: Struggle for Liberation in the Therīgāthā.* Richmond: Curzon Press.

Blair, Heather. 2016. "Ladylike Religion: Ritual and Agency in the Life of an Eleventh-Century Japanese Noblewoman." *History of Religions* 56 (1): 1–22.

Blum, Mark L. 2000. "Stand by Your Founder: Honganji's Struggle with Funeral Orthodoxy." *Japanese Journal of Religious Studies* 27 (3/4): 179–212.

Blum, Mark, and Robert Rhodes, eds. 2011. *Cultivating Spirituality: A Modern Shin Buddhist Anthology.* Albany: SUNY Press.

"Bōmori ga bōmori to yobareru yō ni." 1977. *Shūhō* 34:16.

"Bōmori kitei." 1925. *Shinshū* 87 (September): 1.

"'Bōmori no ichizuke ni kan suru iinkai' tōshin." 2008. *Shinshū* (May): 27–33.

"'Bōmori no kitei ni kan suru iinkai' tōshin." 2000. *Shinshū* (July): 84–91.

Boret, Sebastian Penmellen. 2014. *Japanese Tree Burial: Ecology, Kinship and the Culture of Death.* New York: Routledge.

Borovoy, Amy B. 2001. "Not 'A Doll's House': Public Uses of Domesticity in Japan." *US–Japan Women's Journal* 20–21 (January): 83–124.

———. 2005. *The Too-Good Wife: Alcohol, Codependency, and the Politics of Nurturance in Postwar Japan.* Ethnographic Studies in Subjectivity 6. Berkeley: University of California Press.

Borup, Jørn. 2008. *Japanese Rinzai Zen Buddhism: Myōshinji, a Living Religion.* Leiden: Brill.

Bourdieu, Pierre. 1977. *Outline of a Theory of Practice.* Translated by Richard Nice. Cambridge Studies in Social Anthropology 16. New York: Cambridge University Press.

———. 1990. *The Logic of Practice.* Translated by Richard Nice. Stanford, CA: Stanford University Press.

Buckley, Sandra. 1997. *Broken Silence: Voices of Japanese Feminism.* Berkeley: University of California Press.

"Bukkyō katei no keizaihō." 1903. *Katei* 3 (10): 5.

Campany, Robert F. 2003. "On the Very Idea of Religions (in the Modern West and in Early Medieval China)." *History of Religions* 42 (4): 287–319.

Cheal, David. 1996. "Moral Economy." In *The Gift: An Interdisciplinary Perspective,* edited by Aafke E. Komter, pp. 81–94. Amsterdam: Amsterdam University Press.

Cheng, Wei-Yi. 2007. *Buddhist Nuns in Taiwan and Sri Lanka: A Critique of the Feminist Perspective.* New York: Routledge.

Chiba Jōryū. 2002. *Shinshū to josei.* Chiba Jōryū Chosakushū 5. Kyoto: Hozokan.

Chilson, Clark. 2014. *Secrecy's Power: Covert Shin Buddhists in Japan and Contradictions of Concealment.* Honolulu: Hawai'i University Press.

Clarke, Shayne. 2014. *Family Matters in Indian Buddhist Monasticisms.* Honolulu: University of Hawai'i Press.

Cogan, Gina. 2014. *The Princess Nun: Bunchi, Buddhist Reform, and Gender in Early Edo Japan.* Cambridge, MA: Harvard University Asia Center.

Cook, Emma E. 2013. "Expectations of Failure: Maturity and Masculinity for Freeters in Contemporary Japan." *Social Science Japan Journal* 16 (1): 29–43.

Covell, Stephen G. 2005. *Japanese Temple Buddhism: Worldliness in a Religion of Renunciation*. Honolulu: University of Hawai'i Press.

"Dai jūkai shūsei kihon chōsa chūkan hōkoku." 2016. *Shūhō* (581): 34–85.

"Dai kyūkai shūsei kihon chōsa chūkan hōkoku." 2010. *Shūhō* (521): Supplement.

Dales, Laura. 2011. *Feminist Movements in Contemporary Japan*. New York: Routledge.

Das, Veena, and Renu Addlakha. 2001 "Disability and Domestic Citizenship: Voice, Gender, and the Making of the Subject." *Public Culture* 13 (3): 511–531.

Das, Veena, Johnathan M. Ellen, and Lori Leonard. 2008. "On the Modalities of the Domestic." *The Journal of Architecture, Design, and Domestic Space* 5 (3): 349–371.

Dobbins, James C. 2002. *Jōdo Shinshū: Shin Buddhism in Medieval Japan*. Honolulu: University of Hawai'i Press.

Donaldson, Laura E., and Pui-lan Kwok. 2002. *Postcolonialism, Feminism, and Religious Discourse*. New York: Routledge.

Durkheim, Emile. 1947. *The Elementary Forms of Religious Experience*. Glencoe, IL: Free Press.

Dutton, Anne. 2002. "Temple Divorce in Tokugawa Japan: A Survey of Documentation on Tokeiji and Mantokuji." In *Engendering Faith: Women and Buddhism in Premodern Japan*, edited by Barbara Ruch, pp. 209–245. Ann Arbor: Center for Japanese Studies, University of Michigan.

Eliade, Mircea. 1959. *The Sacred and the Profane*. London: Harcourt Brace Jovanovich.

Endō Hajime. 2000. *Bukkyō to jendā: Shinshū no seiritsu to "bōmori" no yakuwari."* Tokyo: Akirashi Shoten.

Falk, Monica Lindberg. 2007. *Making Fields of Merit: Buddhist Female Ascetics and Gendered Orders in Thailand*. Seattle: University of Washington Press.

Faure, Bernard. 2003. *The Power of Denial: Buddhism, Purity and Gender*. Princeton, NJ: Princeton University Press.

Fitzgerald, Timothy. 1997. "A Critique of 'Religion' as a Cross-Cultural Category." *Method & Theory in the Study of Religion* 9 (2): 91–110.

———. 2003. *The Ideology of Religious Studies*. New York: Oxford University Press.

Fukushima Eiju. 2006. "'Seishin shugi' no josei kyōkaron—*Katei* ni miru 'Bukkyō katei,' 'josei kyūsai,' 'sensōkan.'" *Kyōka kenkyū* 135: 35.

Furey, Constance M. 2012. "Body, Society, and Subjectivity in Religious Studies." *Journal of the American Academy of Religion* 80 (1): 7–33.

Giddens, Anthony. 1984. *The Constitution of Society: Outline of the Theory of Structuration*. Cambridge: Polity Press.

Gojin no danjo dōkenron. 1901. *Katei* 1 (2): 3.

Goldstein-Gidoni, Ofra. 1997. *Packaged Japaneseness: Weddings, Business, and Brides*. Honolulu: University of Hawai'i Press.

———. 2012. *Housewives of Japan: An Ethnography of Real Lives and Consumerized Domesticity*. New York: Palgrave Macmillan.

Gombrich, Richard F. 1971. *Precept and Practice: Traditional Buddhism in the Rural Highlands of Ceylon*. Oxford: Clarendon Press.

Gómez, Luis O., trans. 1996. *Land of Bliss: The Paradise of the Buddha of Measureless Light: Sanskrit and Chinese Versions of the Sukhavativyuha Sutras*. Honolulu: University of Hawai'i Press.

Grant, Beata. 1995. "Patterns of Female Religious Experience in Qing Dynasty Popular Literature." *Journal of Chinese Religions* 23 (1): 29–58.

———. 2008. *Eminent Nuns: Women Chan Masters of Seventeenth-Century China*. Hawaii: University of Hawai'i Press.

Gross, Rita M. 1993. *Buddhism after Patriarchy: A Feminist History, Analysis, and Reconstruction of Buddhism*. Albany: State University of New York Press.

Gutschow, Kim. 2004. *Being a Buddhist Nun: The Struggle for Enlightenment in the Himalayas*. Cambridge, MA: Harvard University Press.

Harrison, Paul. 1998. "Women in the Pure Land: Some Reflections on The Textual Sources." *Journal of Indian Philosophy* 26 (6): 553–72.

Hasegawa Michiko. 2009. "Fushigina go-en de tera de funtō chū desu." *Honganji shinpō* (December 20): 7.

Heidegger, Simone. 2006. *Buddhismus, Geschlechterverhaltnis und Diskriminierung: Die gegenwartige Diskussion im Shin-Buddhismus Japans*. Studies in Modern Asian Religions, edited by Michael Pye and Monica Schrimpf. Berlin: LIT Verlag.

——. 2010. "Shin Buddhism and Gender: The Discourse on Gender Discrimination and Related Reforms." In *The Social Dimension of Shin Buddhism*, edited by Ugo Dessi, pp. 165–208. Boston: Brill.

Hendry, Joy. 1993. *Wrapping Culture: Politeness, Presentation, and Power in Japan and Other Societies*. Oxford: Clarendon Press.

Hidaka, Tomoko. 2011. "Masculinity and the Family System: The Ideology of the 'Salaryman' across Three Generations." In *Home and Family in Japan: Continuity and Transformation*, edited by Richard Ronald and Allison Alexy, pp. 112–130. New York: Routledge.

Higashi Honganji. 2009. *Shūmon gense no hōkoku*. Report.

Hirota, Dennis, et al., trans. 1997. *The Collected Works of Shinran*. 2 vols. Kyoto: Jōdo Shinshū Hongwanji-ha.

Holloway, Susan D. 2010. *Women and Family in Contemporary Japan*. Cambridge: Cambridge University Press.

Hurvitz, Leon, trans. 2009. *Scripture of the Lotus Blossom of the Fine Dharma: The Lotus Sutra*. New York: Columbia University Press.

Inagaki, Hisao. 1995. *The Three Pure Land Sutras: A Study and Translation from Chinese*. Kyoto: Nagata Bunshodo.

Itami Jūzō. 2009. *Osōshiki*. Itami Productions. Film.

Jaffe, Richard M. 2001. *Neither Monk Nor Layman: Clerical Marriage in Modern Japanese Buddhism*. Princeton, NJ: Princeton University Press.

"'Josei no shūmon katsudō ni kan suru iinkai' tōshin." 1996. *Shinshū* (May): 28–41.

Josei to Bukkyō Tōkai Kantō Nettowāku, ed. 1999. *Bukkyō to jendā: Onnatachi no nyosei gamon*. Osaka: Toki Shobō.

——. 2004. *Gendā ikōruna Bukkyō o mezashite*. Osaka: Toki Shobō.

Kamata Hiroko. 2009. "'Josei' jūshoku tte dō yo?!" *Menzu Aiau* 4:14.

Kaneko Daiei. 1976. *Jūshoku michi*. Kyoto: Higashi Honganji Shuppanbu.

Kasahara Kazuo. 1975. *Nyonin ōjō shisō no keifu*. Tokyo: Yoshikawa Kōbunkan.

Kashiwahara Yūsen and Fujii Manabu, eds. 1995. *Kinsei Bukkyō no shisō*. Nihon shisō taikei (special edition). Tokyo: Iwanami Shoten.

Katsuura Noriko. 1989 "Amasogikō: Kamigata kara mita ama no sonzai ketai." In *Ama to Amadera*, edited by Nishiguchi Junko and Ōsumi Kazuo, pp. 11–42. Shirīzu Josei to Bukkyō, 1. Tokyo: Heibonsha.

——. 1995. *Onna no shinjin: tsuma ga shukke shita jidai*. Tokyo: Heibonsha.

Kawahashi, Noriko. 1995. "*Jizoku* (Priests' Wives) in Soto Zen Buddhism: An Ambiguous Category." *Japanese Journal of Religious Studies* 22 (1–2): 161–83.

——. 2003. "Feminist Buddhism as Praxis: Woman in Traditional Buddhism." *Japanese Journal of Religious Studies* 30 (3/4): 291–313.

——. 2012. *Saitai Bukkyō no minzokushi: Jendā shukyogaku kara no apurōchi*. Tokyo: Jinbun Shoin.

Kikkawa, Toru, and Makoto Todoroki. 1998. "School Education and Democratization of Social Consciousness in Postwar Japan." *International Journal of Sociology* 28 (1): 92–108.

Ko, Dorothy. 1994. *Teachers of the Inner Chambers: Women and Culture in Seventeenth-Century China*. Stanford, CA: Stanford University Press.

———. 2005. *Cinderella's Sisters: A Revisionist History of Footbinding.* Berkeley: University of California Press.

Kondo, Dorinne K. 1990. *Crafting Selves: Power, Gender, and Discourses of Identity in a Japanese Workplace.* Chicago: University of Chicago Press.

Kyōkai ichiran, vol. 752 (June 25, 1929), p. 2.

Lambek, Michael. 2012. "Is Religion Free?" *The Imminent Frame.* http://blogs.ssrc .org/tif/2012/06/19/is-religion-free/ (accessed May 15, 2017).

Lang, Karen C. 1986. "Lord Death's Snare: Gender-Related Imagery in the Therīgāthā and the Therīgāthā." *Journal of Feminist Studies in Religion* 2 (2): 63–79.

Leach, Edmund Ronald, ed. 1968. *Dialectic in Practical Religion.* Cambridge Papers in Social Anthropology 5. London: Cambridge University Press.

Levering, Miriam L. 1992. "Lin-Chi (Rinzai) Ch'an and Gender: The Rhetoric of Equality and the Rhetoric of Heroism." In *Buddhism, Sexuality, and Gender,* edited by José Ignacio Cabezon, pp. 137–156. Albany: State University of New York Press.

Long, Susan Orpett. 1996. "Nurturing and Femininity: The Ideal of Caregiving in Postwar Japan." In *Re-imaging Japanese Women,* edited Anne E. Imamura, pp. 156–176. Berkeley: University of California Press.

Lopez, Donald S., ed. 1995. *Curators of the Buddha: The Study of Buddhism under Colonialism.* Chicago: University of Chicago Press.

Lunsing, Wim. 2015. *Beyond Common Sense: Sexuality and Gender in Contemporary Japan.* London: Routledge.

Mackie, Vera. 2003. *Feminism in Modern Japan: Citizenship, Embodiment, and Sexuality.* Cambridge: Cambridge University Press.

Mahmood, Saba. 2005. *Politics of Piety: The Islamic Revival and the Feminist Subject.* Princeton, NJ: Princeton University Press.

Main, Jessica L. 2010. "To Lament the Self: The Ethical Ideology of Takeuchi Ryō'on (1891–1968) and the Ōtani-ha Movement against Buraku Discrimination." In *The Social Dimension of Shin Buddhism,* edited by Ugo Dessi, pp. 137–163. Boston: Brill.

Marra, Michele. 1988. "The Development of *Mappō* Thought in Japan (II)." *Japanese Journal of Religious Studies* 15 (4): 287–305.

Massey, Doreen B. 1994. *Space, Place, and Gender.* Minneapolis: University of Minnesota Press.

McCutcheon, Russell T. 1997. *Manufacturing Religion: The Discourse on Sui Generis Religion and the Politics of Nostalgia.* Oxford: Oxford University Press.

McDaniel, Justin T. 2011. *The Lovelorn Ghost and the Magical Monk: Practicing Buddhism in Modern Thailand.* New York: Columbia University Press.

Meeks, Lori. 2010. *Hokkeji and the Reemergence of Female Monastic Orders in Premodern Japan.* Honolulu: University of Hawai'i Press.

Miller, Barbara Stoler. 1984. "The Therīgāthā: Women's Songs of Early Buddhism." *Journal of South Asian Literature* 19 (2): 129–135.

Miyake, Yoshiko. 1991. "Doubling Expectations: Motherhood and Women's Factory Work under State Management in Japan in the 1930s and 1940s." In *Recreating Japanese Women, 1600–1945,* edited by Gail Lee Bernstein, pp. 267–295. Berkeley: University of California Press.

Mizushima Ken'ichi. 2007. *Ōtaniha naru shūkyōteki seishin.* Kyoto: Shinshū Ōtaniha Shūmusho Shuppanbu.

Mochizuki Keiko. 2006. "Intabyū: Hontō no dōbō kyōdan o negatte: Bōmori mondai e no torikumi." *Kyōka kenkyū* 135 (May): 127–137.

Moerman, D. Max. 2005. *Localizing Paradise: Kumano Pilgrimage and the Religious Landscape of Premodern Japan.* Harvard East Asian Monographs, 235. Cambridge, MA: Harvard University Asia Center.

Moore, Brenna. 2015. "Friendship and the Cultivation of Religious Sensibilities." *Journal of the American Academy of Religion* 83 (2): 437–463.

Morgan, David, ed. 2010. *Religion and Material Culture: A Matter of Belief.* New York: Routledge.

Munro, Moira, and Ruth Madigan. 1999. "Negotiating Space in the Family Home." In *At Home: An Anthropology of Domestic Space,* edited by Irene Cieraad, pp. 107–117. Syracuse, NY: Syracuse University Press.

Murcott, Susan. 1991. *The First Buddhist Women: Translations and Commentaries on the Therigatha.* Berkeley, CA: Parallax Press.

Myerhoff, Barbara. 1978. *Number Our Days: A Triumph of Continuity and Culture among Jewish Old People in an Urban Ghetto.* New York: Simon and Schuster.

Nakano, Lynne Y. 2011. "Working and Waiting for an 'Appropriate Person': How Single Women Support and Resist Family in Japan." In *Home and Family in Japan: Continuity and Transformation,* edited by Richard Ronald and Allison Alexy, pp. 131–151. New York: Routledge.

Nattier, Jan. 1991. *Once upon a Future Time: Studies in a Buddhist Prophecy of Decline.* Freemont, CA: Jain Publishing Company.

Nelson, John K. 2013. *Experimental Buddhism: Innovation and Activism in Contemporary Japan.* Honolulu: University of Hawai'i Press.

Nishiguchi Junko. 1987. *Onna no chikara: Kodai no josei to Bukkyō.* Tōkyō: Heibonsha.

Noland, Carrie. 2009. *Agency and Embodiment: Performing Gestures/Producing Culture.* Cambridge, MA: Harvard University Press.

Nolte, Sharon H., and Sally Ann Hastings. 1991. "The Meiji State's Policy towards Women, 1890–1910." In *Recreating Japanese Women, 1600–1945,* edited by Gail Lee Bernstein, pp. 151–174. Oakland: University of California Press.

Obata Junko. 2004. "Shinshū Ōtaniha ni okeru 'bōmori mondai' ni tsuite: Katte ni sōshūhen." In *Jendā ikōruna Bukkyō o mezashite,* edited by Josei to Bukkyō Tōkai Kantō Nettowāku, 38–54. Osaka: Toki Shobō.

———, ed. 2016. *Shinshū Ōtani-ha ni okeru joseisabetsu wo kangaeru onnatachi no kai hōkokushū,* no. 10. Kyoto: Shinshū Ōtani-ha ni Okeru Josei Sabetsu wo Kangaeru Onnatachi no Kai.

Oguri Junko. 1987. *Nyonin ōjō: Nihonshi ni miru onna no sukui.* Kyoto: Jinbun Shoin.

Orsi, Robert A. 1997. "Everyday Miracles: The Study of Lived Religion." In *Lived Religion in America: Toward a History of Practice,* edited by David D. Hall, pp. 3–21. Princeton, NJ: Princeton University Press.

———. 2005. *Between Heaven and Earth: The Religious Worlds People Make and the Scholars Who Study Them.* Princeton, NJ: Princeton University Press.

Ortner, Sherry B. 2006. *Anthropology and Social Theory: Culture, Power, and the Acting Subject.* Durham, NC: Duke University Press.

"Otera ni umarete." 1977. *Shūhō* 34: 17.

Pérez, Elizabeth. 2016. *Religion in the Kitchen: Cooking, Talking, and the Making of Black Atlantic Traditions.* New York: New York University Press.

Rambelli, Fabio. 2007. *Buddhist Materiality: A Cultural History of Objects in Japanese Buddhism.* Stanford, CA: Stanford University Press.

Reader, Ian. 1991. *Religion in Contemporary Japan.* Honolulu: University of Hawai'i Press.

Reader, Ian, and George Tanabe. 1998. *Practically Religious: Worldly Benefits and the Common Religion of Japan.* Honolulu: University of Hawai'i Press.

Rennyo. 1997. *Goichidaiki kikigaki.* In Shinshū Shōgyō Zensho Hensansho, ed., *Shinshū shōgyō zensho,* vol. 3. Kyoto: Ōyagikōbundō.

Rhodes, Robert. 1980. "Saichō's *Mappō Tōmyōki:* The Candle of Latter Dharma." *The Eastern Buddhist,* n.s. 13 (1): 78–103.

Rogers, Minor L., and Ann T. Rogers. 1991. *Rennyo: The Second Founder of Shin Buddhism.* Berkeley, CA: Asian Humanities Press.

Ronald, Richard. 2011. "Homes and Houses, Senses and Spaces." In *Home and Family in Japan: Continuity and Transformation,* edited by Richard Ronald and Allison Alexy, pp. 174–199. New York: Routledge.

Ronald, Richard, and Allison Alexy. 2011. "Continuity and Change in Japanese Homes and Families." In *Home and Family in Japan: Continuity and Transformation*, edited by Richard Ronald and Allison Alexy, pp. 1–24. New York: Routledge.

Rosaldo, Michelle Zimbalist. 1974. "Woman, Culture, and Society: A Theoretical Overview." In *Woman, Culture and Society*, edited Michelle Zimbalist Rosaldo, pp. 17–42. Stanford, CA: Stanford University Press.

Rowe, Mark. 2011. *Bonds of the Dead: Temples, Burial, and the Transformation of Contemporary Japanese Buddhism*. Chicago: University of Chicago Press.

Ruch, Barbara, gen. ed. 2002. *Engendering Faith: Women and Buddhism in Premodern Japan*. Ann Arbor: University of Michigan Press.

Sahlins, Marshall D. 1996. "On the Sociology of Primitive Exchange." In *The Gift: An Interdisciplinary Perspective*, edited by Aafke E. Komter, pp. 26–38. Amsterdam: Amsterdam University Press.

Salgaldo, Nirmala S. 2013. *Buddhist Nuns and Gendered Practice: In Search of the Female Renunciant*. Oxford: Oxford University Press.

Sand, Jordan. 2003. *House and Home in Modern Japan: Architecture, Domestic Space, and Bourgeois Culture, 1880–1930*. Harvard East Asian Monographs, 223. Cambridge, MA: Harvard University Asia Center.

Sasson, Vanessa R., ed. 2013. *Little Buddhas: Children and Childhoods in Buddhist Texts and Traditions*. New York: Oxford University Press.

Schopen, Gregory. 1991. "Archaeology and Protestant Presuppositions in the Study of Indian Buddhism." *History of Religions* 31 (1): 1–23.

———. 1997. *Bones, Stones, and Buddhist Monks: Collected Papers on the Archaeology, Epigraphy, and Texts of Monastic Buddhism in India*. Honolulu: University of Hawai'i Press.

Sharf, Robert H. 2001. "Prolegomenon to the Study of Japanese Buddhist Icons." In *Living Images: Japanese Buddhist Icons in Context*, edited by Robert H. Sharf and Elizabeth Horton Sharf, pp. 1–18. Stanford, CA: Stanford University Press.

Shimazono, Susumu. 1998. "The Commercialization of the Sacred: The Structural Evolution of Religious Communities in Japan." *Social Science Japan Journal* 1 (2): 181–198.

Shinshū Ōtani-ha Bōmorikai Renmei. 2008. *Kessei goju shunen kinen jigyō*. Kyoto: Shinshū Ōtani-ha Shūmusho.

Shinshū Shinjiten Hensankai, ed. 1983. *Shinshū shinjiten*. Kyoto: Hōzōkan.

Smith, Jonathan Z. 2004. *Relating Religion: Essays in the Study of Religion*. Chicago: University of Chicago Press.

Sōboku. 1775. *Bōmori saisoku no hōgo*. Dewa: Saitō Riemon.

Spiro, Melford E. 1970. *Buddhism and Society: A Great Tradition and Its Burmese Vicissitudes*. Berkeley: University of California Press.

Sponberg, Alan. 1992. "Attitudes toward Women and the Feminine in Early Buddhism." In *Buddhism, Sexuality, and Gender*, edited by José Ignacio Cabezon, pp. 3–36. Albany: State University of New York Press.

Starling, Jessica. 2012. "Domestic Religion in Late Edo Period Sermons for Temple Wives." *The Eastern Buddhist* 43 (1/2): 271–297.

———. 2013. "Neither Nun nor Laywoman: The Good Wives and Wise Mothers of Jōdo Shinshū Temples." *Japanese Journal of Religious Studies* 40 (2): 277–301.

———. 2015. "Family Temples and Religious Learning in Contemporary Japanese Buddhism." *Journal of Global Buddhism* 16: 144–156.

Stone, Jacqueline L. 2006. "Buddhism." In *Nanzan Guide to Japanese Religion*, edited by Paul L. Swanson and Clark Chilson, pp. 38–64. Honolulu: University of Hawai'i Press.

Swidler, Ann. 1986. "Culture in Action: Symbols and Strategies." *American Sociological Review* 51 (April): 273–286.

———. 2001. *Talk of Love: How Culture Matters*. Chicago: University of Chicago Press.

Taira Masayuki. 1992. *Nihon chūsei no shakai to Bukkyō.* 2nd edition. Tokyo: Hanawa Shobō.

Takamatsu Shin'ei. 1980 [1975]. *Okāsan no Shinshūgaku.* Kyoto: Buneidō.

Taves, Ann. 2009. *Religious Experience Reconsidered: A Building-Block Approach to the Study of Religion and Other Special Things.* Princeton, NJ : Princeton University Press.

Tokuryū. 1891. *Bōmori kyōkai kikigaki.* Kyoto: Nishimura Kurōemon.

Trainor, Kevin. 1997. *Relics, Ritual, and Representation in Buddhism: Rematerializing the Sri Lankan Theravāda Tradition.* Cambridge Studies in Religious Traditions, 10. New York: Cambridge University Press.

Ukō Kikuko. 1999. "Otera ni ikiru onna no ibasho to seido: Shinran no tsuma to musume wa nani to miru." In *Bukkyō to jendā,* edited by Josei to Bukkyō Tōkai Kantō Nettowāku, pp. 127–135. Osaka: Toki Shobō.

Unno, Taitetsu, trans. 1996. *Tannisho: A Shin Buddhist Classic.* Honolulu: Buddhist Study Center Press.

Uno, Kathleen S. 1991. "Women and Changes in the Household Division of Labor." *Recreating Japanese Women, 1600–1945,* edited by Gail Lee Bernstein, pp. 24–25. Berkeley: University of California Press.

Walsh, Judith E. 2004. *Domesticity in Colonial India: What Women Learned When Men Gave Them Advice.* Lanham, MD: Rowman & Littlefield Publishers.

Walters, Jonathan S. 1999. "Suttas as History: Four Approaches to the 'Sermon on the Noble Quest' (Ariyapariyesanasutta)." *History of Religions* 38 (3): 247–284.

Watanabe Noriko. 1999. "Josei sōryo no tanjō: Nishi Honganji ni okeru sono rekishi." In *Bukkyō to jendā,* edited by Josei to Bukkyō Tōkai Kantō Nettowāku, pp. 108–126. Osaka: Toki Shobō.

Weeks, Jacquilyn. 2011. "Un-/Re-Productive Maternal Labor: Marxist Feminism and Chapter Fifteen of Marx's Capital." *Rethinking Marxism* 23 (1): 31–40.

Wilson, Liz. 1996. *Charming Cadavers: Horrific Figurations of the Feminine in Buddhist Hagiographic Literature.* Chicago: University of Chicago Press.

Wilson, Liz, ed. 2013. *Family in Buddhism.* Albany: SUNY Press.

Wright, J. C. 1999. "Old Wives' Tales in Therīgāthā: A Review Article." *Bulletin of the School of Oriental and African Studies, University of London* 62 (3): 519–528.

Yamauchi Sayoko. 2006. "Kindai ni okeru Shinshū Ōtani-ha no josei kyōka soshiki." *Kyōka kenkyū* 135 (May): 60–85.

Yasutomi, Shin'ya. 2003. "The Way of Introspection: Kiyozawa Manshi's Methodology." *The Eastern Buddhist,* n.s. 36 (1–2): 102–114.

Yoshida Kazuhiko. 2002. "The Enlightenment of the Dragon King's Daughter in the Lotus Sutra." In *Engendering Faith: Women and Buddhism in Premodern Japan,* edited by Barbara Ruch, pp. 297–324. Ann Arbor: University of Michigan Press.

Yü, Chün-fang. 2001. *Kuan-yin: The Chinese Transformation of Avalokiteśvara.* New York: Columbia University Press.

"Zadankai: Kyōdan, jiin no genjō to tenbō: Mizuko kuyō o megutte, tera ni kurasu josei no shiten kara." 1995. *Kyōka kenkyū* 113 (April): 48–71.

Index

Page numbers in **boldface** refer to tables or photos.

About the Author

Jessica Starling is assistant professor of religious studies and Asian studies at Lewis & Clark College in Portland, Oregon. Her work has appeared in *The Eastern Buddhist, Journal of Japanese Religious Studies,* and *Journal of Global Buddhism.*